Bit Part Players of the Bible

Act 2

Over 80 lesser-known characters on God's stage

Bit Part
Players
of the
Bible

Act 2

Ray Markham

CWR

OTHER BOOKS BY RAY MARKHAM

What Kind of Power is This?
(on the miracles of Jesus) ISBN 978-1-87379-692-4

Pointed and Personal
(on the parables of Jesus) ISBN 978-1-903921-04-3

Greater Expectations
(on the Sermon on the Mount) ISBN 978-1-903921-01-2

These three are published by Autumn House and come with
questions for group study.

The Olympics of Life
(a thought-for-the-day book) ISBN 978-0-902731-48-6

Keep Your Eye on the Ball
(a thought-for-the-day book) ISBN 978-0-902731-58-5

Both these books are published by The Leprosy Mission International.

Bit Part Players of the Bible published by CWR
(Over 100 lesser-known characters on God's stage) ISBN 978-1-85345-445-5

Published 2009 by CWR, Waverley Abbey House, Waverley Lane, Farnham, Surrey
GU9 8EP UK. Registered Charity No. 294387. Registered Limited Company No. 1990308.

See back of book for list of National Distributors.

Concept development, editing, design and production by CWR

Cover image: Istockphoto/Justice Images

Printed in Finland by WS Bookwell

ISBN: 978-1-85345-526-1

Contents

Other bit part players also making an appearance in the following chapters are:

Other bit part players mentioned in the following chapters are:

2. Mary, Joseph
3. Mary, Joseph
17. Manaen, King Agrippa I
30. Stephen
33. Rhoda
36. Gaius, Aristarchus, Alexander
37. Judas Barsabbas, Gaius of Derbe, Clement, Euodia,
     Syntyche, Gaius, Aristarchus, Secundus, Sopater,
     Dionysius, Damaris, Eutychus
38. Titius Justus, Crispus, Chloe, Stephanas, Fortunatus,
     Achaicus, Phoebe, Tertius, Erastus, Quartus, Sosthenes,
     Gallio, Trophimus, Tychicus, Onesiphorus
39. Aristarchus, Luke, Publius
40. Epaphras, Tychicus, Apphia, Archippus
41. Demetrius
42. Tertius, Priscilla, Mary, Junias, Tryphena, Tryphosa, Persis

To all those at Bretton Baptist Church, Peterborough, who have faithfully prayed for me and supported me over the years.

Information about the author

Ray Markham is a graduate of Nottingham University. He is married to Sheila and they have two grown-up sons and four grandchildren. A teacher of Religious Studies for 28 years (and also Head of Year for 10 years), Ray is now a writer. *Bit-Part Players of the Bible – Act 2* is his seventh title.

Ray has always been very keen on sport and currently is a professional cricket scorer, scoring for both the Cambridge University cricket team and for the media in the press box at Test Matches and One Day Internationals.

After many years in church leadership, Ray's preaching and teaching ministry is now being appreciated by an increasing number of churches. He also delivers speaker training courses and is an after-dinner speaker. Ray is an active member of Gideons International and does voluntary work for The Leprosy Mission.

Preface

Many of the characters who appear on the stage of the New Testament do so because they came into contact with either Jesus or the apostles.

This book looks at the impact those occasions had on the lives of these 'bit part players' or examines the part they played in the spread of the gospel. It attempts to present what occurred in an interesting, thorough and thought-provoking way and in a style that is stimulating, engaging and readable.

As 'bit part players' ourselves, there is much we can learn from these characters that will both encourage and challenge us.

A Godly Couple

Zechariah and Elizabeth

(Other bit part player appearing: Mary)
Luke 1:5–25,39–45,56–79

Once-in-a-lifetime

Zechariah the priest was about to experience a once-in-a-lifetime opportunity: to offer incense in the Holy Place. Some priests went through the whole of their ministry without ever having this revered privilege. This was the greatest moment of his life; a moment which would never be repeated, as a priest could not offer incense more than once. By now Zechariah was an old man, who had faithfully served God by carrying out the priestly duties of teaching the Scriptures, directing the worship services and managing the upkeep of the Temple for many years. Perhaps he had even thought that this supreme honour of being chosen to offer incense would never come his way; and then, when the lots had been cast to determine which priest would perform which priestly function that day, the lot had fallen to him (vv.8–9).

As he stood there in the Holy Place, surrounded by the other priests, he felt no doubt the thrill of anticipation, and trembled with excitement at the prospect. He probably couldn't wait to tell his wife, Elizabeth, the news; but he would have to see out the rest of his week of service in the Temple before being able to head for his home in the hill country of Judea. Twice a year, each division of priests served for a week in the Temple. There were twenty-four such groupings made up of approximately one thousand priests, according to King David's directions (1 Chron. 24:3–19). The division to which Zechariah belonged was the eighth of the twenty-four, and bore the name of Abijah, one of the 'leaders of the priests' (Neh. 12:4,7). And this was 'Abijah week'!

Never too old

As the other priests withdrew and left him alone in the Holy Place, little did Zechariah realise what God had in store for him. He had no idea that this hadn't all happened by the chance of casting lots, but rather because God wanted to speak to him. Zechariah thought he was going to remember this day for the rest of his life solely because he had offered incense; in fact, he would remember it for other extremely important reasons too. Little did this elderly man realise that, as old as he was, God had chosen him to play a part in His great plan to bring salvation to the world through His Son Jesus.

Interestingly, there was no retirement age for priests, although there was for Levites, who were workers in the Temple. A priest continued to serve God until he died. In his epistle, Peter describes us as being members of a 'royal priesthood' (1 Pet. 2:9). Is it not true to say then, that since we are all priests of our God, there can be no retirement, early or otherwise, for any of us in our service for God? We can never sit back and say that God has finished with us now, and has nothing more for us to do. There are no slippers or fireside chairs in the kingdom of God! Be encouraged: none of us is ever too old to be used by God! May God help us to continue to be open to Him, and willing to be used by Him.

Aching hearts

Elizabeth would have well understood and shared Zechariah's excitement at the prospect of offering incense. Her father had also been a priest, and both their families were descended from Aaron (Luke 1:5). Elizabeth was the ideal wife for Zechariah because, having grown up in a priestly family, she was fully aware of the demands and responsibilities of the priesthood. She must have been a great support to him at this time when many of the priests and religious leaders lived hypocritical lifestyles, which Jesus would not be slow to point out. Luke records God's glowing reference for Zechariah and Elizabeth: 'Both of them were upright in the sight of God, observing all the Lord's commandments and regulations blamelessly' (v.6). Unlike many of their contemporaries, their obedience was far more than following a set of laws. Their obedience was from the heart and it affected their lifestyle; such that they became known for their personal holiness. They were devoted to God and to each other.

But, although they had obedient hearts, they also had aching hearts. They had no children – and were never likely to have any (v.7). In their Jewish culture, they were considered to be lacking God's blessing. They must have made this lack of children situation a matter of persistent and fervent prayer for many years. Imagine the turmoil of emotions they must have gone through. They would have undoubtedly felt humiliated, not to mention totally bewildered and puzzled; it made no sense that God had not blessed them with children, considering their utter devotion to Him. And yet, in spite of their deep despair and disappointment, they did not become disillusioned, but remained totally devoted to God. Their holy living, dedicated service and wholehearted obedience continued just the same.

What amazing people Zechariah and Elizabeth must have been; and what an example this godly couple are to us! And what a challenge! Do we show such spiritual maturity and devotion to God in every aspect of our lives? Shouldn't we each seek to be an example of what it means to be a godly person? Zechariah and Elizabeth found that obedience to God doesn't guarantee us everything we want. How do we react when things happen or don't happen in our lives that seem so unfair, considering the way we try to serve God? Do we stop believing; do we stop serving? Or, like Zechariah and Elizabeth, do we just carry on believing, serving and obeying out of sheer love for God?

God needed a couple like this: a couple who were devoted to Him; a couple who came from a priestly background, which would enable them to bring up their son in the required manner; a couple who would understand God's calling on their son's life, and the consequences of it – which would seem very strange to most parents, and be hard for them to cope with. Zechariah and Elizabeth met God's requirements in every respect. Their prayers were about to be answered, but not perhaps in the way they'd expected, given that their son would not be a priest, but a prophet; and not just any prophet, but the herald of the coming Messiah!

Angelic encounter
At the altar of incense

The incense was offered twice a day: once before the morning sacrifice and once after the evening sacrifice. It seems most likely that Zechariah was to perform that function in the evening. While the priest was offering incense, the worshippers would wait in the outer court of the Temple. When they saw the smoke ascending from the burning incense, they would pray (v.10). The smoke was symbolic of their prayers rising to God.

Zechariah waited for the signal, and then began to offer the incense. While he was doing so, he would have been in prayer. As he was ministering on behalf of the people, his prayer was probably for the redemption of Israel and the coming of the Messiah, rather than for his own personal needs. Suddenly, he was aware that he was no longer alone! Standing at the side of the altar of incense was 'an angel of the Lord' (v.11).

It is interesting to notice that the angel appeared and spoke to Zechariah in his place of work, while he was occupied in doing his job. This had happened several times in Israel's past: for example, an angel appeared to Moses, who was looking after his sheep, and to Gideon, who was threshing wheat. Jesus would appear to the fishermen as they were mending their nets. And so it is that God often seems to speak to us when we least expect it, when we are caught up with other things, in the routine of the day.

'Don't be afraid'

I wonder how we would react if an angel appeared to us in the middle of our daily tasks? I can certainly identify with Zechariah's reaction: 'he was startled and was gripped with fear' (v.12). The shock of it must have been enormous; and it was just all so unexpected! Added to the fact that the appearance of an angel in Jewish thought was often associated with divine judgment rather than good news, and Zechariah's terror is completely understandable. Not to mention that this was the first time for 400 years that anything like this had happened. God had been silent for all that time, and now Zechariah found himself quaking with fear in the presence of God's messenger. Nor was this any angel; this was none other than the archangel Gabriel whom God had sent, though Zechariah may not have realised that until later in the conversation (v.19).

Aware of Zechariah's terror at his appearance, Gabriel immediately sought to calm his fears by saying, 'Do not be afraid, Zechariah' (v.13), and then proceeded to tell him that his prayer has been heard. The tense of the verb used in the original Greek suggests that Gabriel was referring to a prayer that had been offered on one specific occasion. This indicates that the archangel was referring to the prayer made by Zechariah while offering the incense which, in the light of what Gabriel goes on to say, must have been to do with the coming of the Messiah. And yet, in answering Zechariah's prayer for the nation, God was also going to wonderfully and miraculously answer his prayer for a son, even though he may have actually given up praying for this to happen years ago when it became physically impossible: 'Your wife Elizabeth will bear you a son, and you are to give him the name John' (v.13).

Names were considered to be very significant in those days,

and 'John' means 'Jehovah is gracious'. God by His grace was about to send the Messiah, and John was to play a significant role in His coming, as Gabriel would go on to explain. The name 'Zechariah' means 'Jehovah has remembered'. God had remembered the prayers of Zechariah and his wife, and was about to answer them. 'Elizabeth' means 'God is my oath' or 'promise', and she was being promised a son by God, so she could be sure that it would come to pass.

Once again we are reminded that God answers prayer in His own way and in His own time. Here, He worked in an 'impossible' situation to bring about the fulfilment of prophecies concerning the Messiah. We are also reminded that we often have to wait for answers to our prayers; sometimes until it seems impossible! In my experience, during that waiting time it's hard to stay patient, but should we not determine to keep on believing in the God of the impossible? What happened to Zechariah and Elizabeth shows us that God uses ordinary people to bring about His extraordinary purposes. The question is: Am I willing and available?

Amazing prophecy

Gabriel continued with an amazing prophecy about Zechariah's son (vv.14–17). John was to be set apart for God right from the start; it was God Himself who was giving the boy his name. Not only would he be 'a joy and delight' to his parents, but he would be great in God's sight. Like the Nazarites (Num. 6:1–8), he was to abstain from strong drink and spirits throughout his life, but he would be 'filled with the Holy Spirit even from birth' (Luke 1:15). He would have 'the spirit and power of Elijah' (v.17), the prophet whom the Jews believed would return to prepare the way for the Messiah. They always laid a special place for him at the Passover table – and still do to this day. Jesus Himself identified John as the 'Elijah' who was to come first before the Messiah (Mark 9:12–13). John would prepare the way for the coming of the Messiah as the prophet Isaiah had promised (Isa. 40:1–5) by bringing people to repentance, which would be marked by baptism, and re-educating them about the Messiah who was to come. This would culminate in John the Baptist's great statement from the river Jordan: 'Look, the Lamb of God, who takes away the sin of the world!' (John 1:29).

Reality kicks in

Whatever joy and jubilation Zechariah might have felt at Gabriel's announcement that he and Elizabeth were to have a son may have evaporated by the time the archangel had concluded his prophecy. Reality had kicked in. 'How can I be sure of this?' he asked Gabriel. 'I am an old man and my wife is well on in years' (v.18). Like all of us, if we're honest, when faced with God's promise of something supernatural happening in our situation, Zechariah's eyes became firmly fixed back on the natural. The human perspective took over. No way could he and Elizabeth have a child at their age. He needed some sign to reassure him.

It's at this point that I sense Gabriel began to stiffen and bristle with indignation that his words had not been believed. He was definitely not impressed with Zechariah's declaration of unbelief, and I can imagine a sharpening in his tone of voice. 'I am Gabriel,' he bristled. 'I stand in the presence of God, and I have been sent to speak to you and to tell you this good news. And now you will be silent and not able to speak until the day this happens, because you did not believe my words, which will come true at their proper time' (vv.19–20).

Zechariah got his 'sign' all right – and a very personal one it was too: being struck dumb for nine months, and possibly also deaf (v.62)! At first sight, this may seem a bit unfair; but there are many occasions in the Bible where God deals drastically with unbelief, because it is the antithesis of faith; and similarly with disobedience, because it can thwart what He wants to do. It's a sobering thought that we can be stumbling blocks to God's purposes, even if we are as 'upright' (v.6) as Zechariah. It's easy to criticise Zechariah, but I wonder how many times we have deserved to be struck dumb for speaking words of unbelief rather than words of faith?

The aftermath

Meanwhile, the people were waiting in the outer court for Zechariah to emerge and pronounce the blessing upon them, as was the custom (Num. 6:24–26). Usually, it didn't take long for the priest to offer the incense and to appear, so it's not surprising that they began to wonder 'why he stayed so long in the temple' (Luke 1:21). They must have been stunned when he finally appeared, and couldn't speak a word to them (v.22). They put it down to the fact that he must have seen a vision.

Despite his handicap, Zechariah completed his week of service in the Temple, and then returned home. What Elizabeth's reaction was when she found out that her husband couldn't speak a word, we can only imagine! He couldn't even say, 'Guess what happened to me at work the other day, dear!' Zechariah had no choice but to write it all down – I wonder how many writing tablets that took! – punctuated, no doubt by impatient questions from his wife, which she may also have had to write down. I wonder how long it took before Elizabeth understood everything that had occurred?

We can only imagine her joy when she found that she was pregnant (v.24). '"The Lord has done this for me," she said. "In these days he has shown his favour and taken away my disgrace among the people"' (v.25). It seems that Elizabeth had suffered much reproach from those around her, who considered childlessness to be a punishment from God. Like Elizabeth, we too can be misunderstood because people don't see the whole picture – but God does, which is why He is the only one in a position to judge (Matt. 7:1).

The visit of Mary

For reasons that are not clear, Elizabeth spent the first five months of her pregnancy 'in seclusion' (v.24). But when she was six months pregnant, she had a visit from her young relative, Mary (vv.39–40), and a beautiful, poignant and joyful exchange ensued. Before Mary had the chance to tell Elizabeth her news, Elizabeth was 'filled with the Holy Spirit' (v.41) and pronounced blessings on Mary and the child she was to bear (v.42) – and she wasn't afraid who heard her either! What God had revealed to her about Mary's child was well worth shouting and rejoicing about! This baby was the promised Messiah, and Elizabeth saw herself as favoured to have a visit from 'the mother of [her] Lord' (v.43). Even the baby in Elizabeth's own womb was getting in on the act and joining in the rejoicing (v.44)! Indeed, this could have been the moment when the promise given by Gabriel that John would be filled with the Spirit from birth (v.15) was fulfilled. Elizabeth also made a special point of referring to Mary's faith (v.45), which was in stark contrast to the lack of faith shown by Zechariah, and maybe by Elizabeth herself when her husband first told her.

Elizabeth displayed such a wonderfully humble attitude. She was truly thrilled that Mary had come all that way from Nazareth in the north down to Judea in the south of the country just to visit her. Rather than being jealous of her much younger relative, whose child would be greater than her own, she was instead full of joy and blessings for Mary and her baby. In my experience, this is a good model to follow. Rejoicing with people in their success, and praying that God would continue to use them, is a good way of dealing with any jealousy there might be. To allow jealousy to fester unchecked is a recipe for disaster.

Mary responded with a wonderful song of praise to God (vv.46–55). The joy of the two mothers was unconfined as they embraced each other and fellowshipped together for the next three months. Elizabeth must have been delighted that Mary was there with her to help her during the latter stages of her pregnancy, which she must have found difficult to cope with, given her age. Whether Mary was with Elizabeth or not when John was actually born is unclear (v.56), but it would be nice to think that she was.

'His name is John'

Eight days after the birth, the family and friends of the happy couple gathered together for the circumcision ceremony of the baby boy. The occasion began in an atmosphere of great rejoicing, but this turned to consternation when Elizabeth announced that the child was to be called John (v.60). Everyone had assumed that he would be named after his father, and they refused to accept what Elizabeth had said (vv.59–61). They turned to the dumb Zechariah 'to find out what he would like to name the child' (v.62).

Zechariah indicated that he wanted a writing tablet. Then, no doubt trembling with emotion as his encounter with Gabriel at the altar of incense nine months ago flashed through his mind, Zechariah wrote the words, 'His name is John' (v.63). Everyone present was amazed at this, and the writing tablet was probably passed around from one to the other as they began to realise that Zechariah and Elizabeth were absolutely serious about the child's name being John.

But, even more astonishingly, as soon as Zechariah had finished writing those words, 'his mouth was opened and his tongue was loosed, and he began to speak, praising God' (v.64). He had certainly learned his lesson about obedience! Elizabeth must have been thrilled to hear her husband's voice again after all this time, and to hear him praising God in front of the people, in spite of all he had been through. Presumably Zechariah went on to give them all a full account of what had happened to him, as 'The neighbours were all filled with awe, and throughout the hill country of Judea people were talking about all these things. Everyone who heard this wondered about it, asking, "What then is this child going to be?"' (vv.65–66). Baby John became the talk of the town!

Prophetic song

As Zechariah was praising God, he 'was filled with the Holy Spirit and prophesied' (v.67). His prophetic song of praise, given under the anointing and inspiration of the Spirit, has become known as 'The Benedictus' – after the first words in the Latin translation of this song. When the Holy Spirit comes upon us, who knows what will happen?! The question is: Are we open to the moving of the Spirit?

It is not within the scope of this book to give a detailed analysis of Zechariah's song, but it is interesting to note that it falls into four sections.

The first (vv.68–70) contains an expression of thanksgiving for the Messiah, who is on His way and will bring salvation from the guilt and power of sin. This is so certain to happen that it is spoken of as if it has already taken place.

The second section (vv.71–75) focuses on the great salvation the Messiah will bring as an act of deliverance, an act of mercy and an act of fulfilment of God's covenant.

The third section speaks of John's specific role in the coming of the Messiah (v.76–77): how he would 'prepare the way for him' by giving the people 'the knowledge of salvation through the forgiveness of their sins'. To do this, John would use the humiliating ritual of baptism as the symbol of repentance and forgiveness, although that is not mentioned here. How particularly thrilled Zechariah must have been as he sang this part of the prophecy, no doubt with his baby son in his arms and tears in his eyes, beginning with the words, 'And you, my child, will be called a prophet of the Most High', realising that his son was to be the first prophet for 400 years, and that John was the messenger of whom the prophet Malachi had spoken (Mal. 3:1). Little did he know the heavy price his son would have to pay for his faithfulness to God (Mark 6:14–29).

The final section focuses on the wonder of this salvation that the Messiah brings (vv.78–79): how it is only possible because of God's 'tender mercy' towards each one of us; how it is like light shining into the darkness; how it brings us peace with God. Should we not rejoice continually at the wonder of our salvation and thank God for it daily?

Just as God needed a godly couple like Zechariah and Elizabeth to play a 'bit part' in His plan of salvation, does He not also need us to play our 'bit part' in the furtherance of His kingdom? Few of us are likely to be involved in something as dramatic as what happened to Zechariah and Elizabeth; but who knows what we can accomplish for God, as we lay our lives not on the altar of incense, but on the altar of sacrifice?

Chapter 2

The Ignorant and the Wise

The shepherds and the Magi

(Other bit part player appearing: Herod the Great)

The shepherds (Luke 2:8–20)

Treatment

In the fields outside the town of Bethlehem, a group of shepherds were 'keeping watch over their flocks' in the cold and dark of the night (v.8). Shepherds as a whole had an unsavoury reputation in the community. They were regarded as outcasts, mainly because they were unable to keep the Jewish ceremonial laws due to the nature of their work and were therefore deemed to be 'unclean'. They were also considered to be unreliable and untrustworthy, and were not allowed to give evidence in court. They were treated as a despised underclass of society; but God was about to give them special treatment.

I try to picture the scene, and imagine this group of shepherds wrapped up against the cold, some of them checking up on the sheep, while others took a break, eating and drinking, talking and laughing. And then, suddenly, what has to be one of the greatest conversation-stoppers of all time occurred: 'An angel of the Lord appeared to them, and the glory of the Lord shone around them, and they were terrified' (v.9). Even these hard-bitten shepherds were scared out of their wits by this glorious, supernatural phenomenon. I imagine them being rooted to the spot, their mouths wide open in amazement, their eyes staring upwards in disbelief, wondering what fearful judgment was about to be inflicted upon them.

'Good news of great joy'

But the angel put their minds at rest straight away, telling the shepherds that there was nothing to be afraid of. He was not bringing them bad news at all – in fact, quite the opposite: 'Do not be afraid. I bring you good news of great joy that will be for all the people' (v.10). The shepherds must have wondered what this 'good news of great joy' could possibly be and been staggered to realise that, whatever it was, it included even them. In fact, it was even more staggering than they realised because this 'good news' was for the Gentiles as well as for the Jews.

The angel went on to tell them what the 'good news' was: 'Today in the town of David a Saviour has been born to you; he is Christ the Lord' (v.11). Could it be true, they must have wondered in amazement, that the Messiah (for whose coming all Jews had been looking for centuries) had been born in their local town of Bethlehem? Were they, despised, uneducated, ignorant shepherds, really the first to hear about it?

This Messiah had come to be both the 'Good Shepherd' (John 10) and the 'Lamb of God' (John 1:29), so it seems appropriate that news of His coming should first be given to lowly shepherds outside Bethlehem, whose sheep would more than likely finish up as sacrifices in the Temple. The fact that it was a group of shepherds to whom God chose to reveal the coming of His Son our Saviour also serves to remind us of His grace: He comes to all of us, no matter who we are. Isn't it wonderful to know that no one is too lowly or disreputable to be outside His saving grace; that He comes to us as we are? It was not to the rich and powerful that the message of the 'good news' of 'a Saviour' was announced: it was to the poor and powerless, because God knew that their hearts were open and that they would believe. Are we humble enough to do the same? Are our hearts open to God?

Sign and singing

The angel went on to tell the shepherds how they could know they had found the baby of whom he spoke: 'You will find a baby wrapped in cloths and lying in a manger' (v.12). Babies were commonly wrapped in strips of cloth, but to find one lying in a manger, an eating trough for animals, was unheard of. This was to be the proof that they had indeed found the baby the angel had spoken of and a sign that the message they had heard from his lips was true.

But there was more to astonish these already stunned shepherds! 'Suddenly, a great company of the heavenly host appeared with the angel, praising God and saying, "Glory to God in the highest, and on earth peace to men on whom his favour rests"' (vv.13–14). What a fantastic sight and sound that must have been! We can only imagine the brightness of the glory and the sweetness of the heavenly harmonies sung by that angelic choir.

And the words they sang were extremely significant. Firstly, they indicated that the purpose of the plan of salvation was to bring glory to God's name. Secondly, that God's peace was for those 'on whom his favour rests', namely on those who believe. Unlike the *Pax Romana* that the Roman world was experiencing, this peace from God was spiritual and heavenly, not material and worldly, and it could only be experienced through having faith (Rom. 5:1) in 'Christ' the 'Saviour'. God's peace was not guaranteed for all; it is only for those who put their trust in Him, even though they have done nothing to deserve such grace.

'Amazed'

Once the angels had disappeared, the amazed shepherds must have discussed among themselves what they had seen, just to make sure they hadn't imagined it all. They came to the conclusion that there was only one thing to be done: 'Let's go to Bethlehem and see this thing that has happened, which the Lord has told us about' (v.15). They wanted to find out if it was true and to see the baby born to be the Messiah for themselves. So 'they hurried off' into Bethlehem (v.16), seemingly without getting anybody to keep an eye on the sheep while they were gone. Was this the first 'Christmas rush'?!

Everyone in Bethlehem would have been sleeping peacefully, blissfully unaware of what had been happening above the fields outside the town. I imagine that the people of Bethlehem were not best pleased when this bunch of rowdy, excited shepherds arrived in the town in the early hours of the morning in their quest to find this baby, waking everybody up in the process! It seems that the disgruntled citizens of Bethlehem must have come out onto the streets to find out what was going on, because, having 'found Mary and Joseph and the baby, who was lying in the manger' (v.16), the shepherds proceeded to 'spread the word concerning what had been told them about this child, and all who heard it were amazed at what the shepherds said to them' (vv.17–18).

The townsfolk would indeed have been amazed at the events the shepherds described – that angels had spoken and sung to them. But the fact that shepherds had the reputation of being down-to-earth men, who were not given to flights of fancy, would have persuaded the people that they were telling the truth. Perhaps they wondered why it was shepherds who had been chosen to experience this supernatural phenomenon – and not them. They would certainly have been amazed at the content of the message: that the long-promised Messiah, their Saviour, had been born. Little did they realise that this Messiah had not come to save them from the Romans through military conquest, as they were hoping; but rather He had come to save them from their sins through His sacrificial death on a cross.

Confirmation and witness

I wonder what Mary and Joseph thought when this assortment of scruffy-looking, noisy shepherds appeared at the stable, excitedly babbling on about angels appearing to them who had told them that they would find their newborn Saviour, the Christ, lying in a manger. No wonder 'Mary treasured up all these things and pondered them in her heart' (v.19). What the shepherds said must have brought back into her mind the words of the angel Gabriel when he had told her about the baby she was to bear (Luke 1:31–37). Perhaps Mary recalled that Gabriel hadn't mentioned anything about a stable or a manger – or even Bethlehem for that matter; but the testimony of the shepherds would surely have confirmed to her that this was all part of God's plan. In my experience, God often confirms to us through sources outside ourselves (including other people) that what He has told us to do is indeed part of His plan for our lives.

It seems to me that the shepherds set a good example for us to follow. They believed by faith the message brought by the angel; they obeyed, and found the baby for themselves; they became witnesses of what they had experienced; they praised God for all that had happened (2:20). Having believed the gospel and experienced Jesus for ourselves, are our lives characterised by witness and praise?

I'm sure none of those shepherds ever forgot that night of angelic visitation they had experienced in the fields outside Bethlehem. And isn't it brilliant and extraordinary, not to say ironic, that God used shepherds, who were not allowed be witnesses in court, to be His witnesses to the birth of His Son?!

The Magi (Matthew 2:1-12)
A star in their eyes

It seems that the Magi were a group of astrologers who probably lived in Babylon, or maybe Persia. Astrology was the wisdom of the day and was big business. Astrologers were known as 'wise men' because it was believed that they could foretell the future through studying the stars and their movements in the sky. No self-respecting king or ruler would make a decision without consulting his astrologers. They were treated like royalty and they dressed like kings.

Imagine their excitement, then, when a magnificent new star appeared in the sky. In astrological circles, such an event portended the birth of a new king; a star this size would have indicated a very powerful ruler indeed. So what was this star? Some say it was a supernova, or even a comet. Others say that it was a conjunction of the planets Jupiter and Saturn: which is interesting because, in astrological circles, Jupiter was regarded as a royal star and Saturn was supposed to protect Israel. Of course, it is quite possible that God created a special star to announce the arrival of His Son. Whatever the case, there can be no doubt that God was orchestrating these celestial proceedings.

The question on the minds of the Magi would have been: 'In which country has this king been born?' Somehow, they came to the conclusion that He had been born in Palestine. Although it is possible that God revealed this directly to them, it seems more likely that they would have worked this out by looking at their charts of the heavens. As they did so, they would have seen that this star had appeared in the part of the sky which represented Palestine. This would have meant to them that this new king had been born to the Jews, and was therefore to be found in Jerusalem, the capital city. It would explain why they set off for Jerusalem (v.1), not Bethlehem, to pay homage to this magnificent new king.

I believe that God speaks to us in ways we can understand. He spoke to the shepherds through an angel, but to the astrologers through a star. Jesus spoke to the people of His day through their experiences of life, such as farming, vineyards, sheep and servants. It seems to me that He speaks to us through our experiences in life too, as well as through His Word. The question is: Are we listening? And, like the shepherds and the Magi, do we respond positively to what God is saying?

Arrival

During their long and arduous journey through unfriendly terrain, struggling no doubt with extremes of heat and cold, did the Magi ever pause to wonder if what they were doing was foolishness, and whether it was worth all the effort and inconvenience? If they did, then clearly they overcame such thoughts and travelled on, inspired by the purpose of their journey, until they could finally see Jerusalem in the distance. It must have been with a great sense of excitement that they approached the city, where they were certain they would find this newborn king of the Jews.

We don't know how many Magi there were. Traditionally, it has been thought that there were three, based on the number of gifts they brought, but it seems more likely that there was a larger number of them. They must have been quite a sight to behold as they came into the city. I imagine them wearing their regal robes, riding well-laden camels, and surrounded by a retinue of servants. Their arrival would certainly have made quite an impact on the citizens of Jerusalem, who would have wondered not only who these people were but what they were doing coming to their city.

No doubt a crowd gathered around them as they dismounted, bombarding them with questions. But it was the question which the Magi asked them that threw the city into complete confusion: 'Where is the one who has been born king of the Jews? We saw his star in the east and have come to worship him' (v.2). Nobody knew the answer; indeed, nobody knew what on earth they were talking about! I imagine the people in the crowd turning to one another in bewilderment, trying to find out if anybody had heard anything about the birth of a king. The whole place must have been in uproar as the news of the arrival of these strangers and the question they were asking spread through the city like wildfire. And it wouldn't have been long before reports of what was happening reached the ears of the king, Herod the Great.

'Disturbed'

To describe Herod as being 'disturbed' (v.3) when he heard the news is probably a massive understatement. Herod was 'disturbed' in more ways than one: indeed, he was totally paranoid about any threat to his throne and spared no one, not even members of his own family, if he had the slightest grounds for believing that they were plotting against him. So talk of a new king being born would have been like a red rag to a bull. As far as Herod was concerned, this king must be found and eliminated without delay.

The next thing the Magi knew, they were being summoned to Herod's palace. They must have been aware of Herod's reputation and wondered what sort of reception they would get. But it seems that Herod was pleasantness itself as he spoke with them privately. He seemed particularly interested in finding out from them 'the exact time the star had appeared' (v.7).

The Magi must have been taken completely by surprise at what Herod said next. Herod must have told them that no king had been born in Jerusalem, so they were to go to Bethlehem (a place they had probably never heard of) which lay a few miles to the south of the capital. I imagine Herod calling for a map and showing them how to get there. The Magi must have looked at one another in puzzlement, wondering why Herod seemed so sure that this king had been born in Bethlehem. Little did they know that they were being used by Herod to do his dirty work: to find out if this king was, in fact, the promised Jewish Messiah, whose prophesied birthplace was Bethlehem – a fact that Herod had ascertained from the chief priests and teachers of the law (vv.4–6). It seems Herod had come to the conclusion that the king the Magi were seeking had to be this Messiah (also known as the 'king of the Jews') – a very real threat to his throne. I imagine Herod oozing charm as he said to the Magi, 'Go and make a careful search for the child. As soon as you find him, report to me, so that I too may go and worship him' (v.8).

The 'child' in the 'house'

Were the Magi deceived by Herod's apparent desire to worship this child, or were they suspicious of his motives? Did they think Herod's intentions were honourable, or realise that he would go to 'worship' the child with a dagger up his sleeve? Whatever the case, they set off for Bethlehem. And as they did so, 'the star they had seen in the east went ahead of them until it stopped over the place where the child was' (v.9). They were 'overjoyed' (v.10) to see the star again, presumably because it hadn't been visible for a while. Its reappearance must have confirmed to them that they were on the right track.

The Magi found the 'house' (v.11) where the family were living. No longer were Mary and Joseph in a stable. It seems they had decided to stay in a house in Bethlehem. They probably did this initially to be near Jerusalem for the required ceremonials, as their home town of Nazareth was a good seventy miles to the north, but then decided to stay on in Bethlehem rather than return back home. Maybe God had told them to remain there, in view of what happened later (vv.13–15), as Bethlehem was much nearer to the safety of Egypt.

Also, the fact that Jesus is described as now being a 'child' (v.11) shows that the traditional view of the shepherds and the Magi bumping into each other in the stable on the night Jesus was born cannot be correct. It seems that the Magi came some time later, visiting the 'child' Jesus in the 'house' where He was now living – maybe up to as long as two years later, given Herod's subsequent actions (v.16). Interestingly, the Church has always celebrated the coming of the Magi at a different time in the calendar: namely on January 6th at the feast of Epiphany.

Significant gifts

Joseph must have had a bit of a shock when he went to the door and opened it! What a sight would have met his eyes! There were all these well-dressed strangers with their servants and baggage and animals, no doubt telling him that they'd come to see the child who had been born king of the Jews. Maybe Joseph had heard about their arrival in Jerusalem on the grapevine; and now they were all standing outside his door. He and Mary must have watched open-mouthed as these rich and powerful foreigners came into the house and 'bowed down and worshipped' the child Jesus.

Significantly, the first gift the Magi brought to Jesus was their worship. They knew this king was special, but they probably didn't know why. It seems likely that these Magi were all Gentiles, maybe even drawn originally from different parts of the world. So here we have a beautiful picture of the Gentile world coming to worship at the feet of the Jewish Messiah, whose message of God's love, mercy and grace included them too.

Having bowed down and worshipped Him, 'they opened their treasures and presented him with gifts of gold and of incense and of myrrh' (v.11). This indicates to me that these gifts were carefully selected by the Magi from among several possibilities, presumably under the guidance of the Holy Spirit. Those chosen were certainly full of symbolic significance. The gold spoke of the fact that Jesus was a king, who had come to establish God's kingdom on earth. The incense symbolised the fact that Jesus was a priest: the mediator between God and mankind. The myrrh spoke of His suffering and death on the cross. I wonder if the Magi realised the significance of the gifts they presented? And I also wonder what Mary and Joseph did with the gold, incense and myrrh! Did they use these gifts to finance their stay in Egypt or to fund Joseph's carpentry business, for example; or did they just keep them tucked away somewhere to remind them of the wonder of everything that had happened?

What are we giving to God in response to His gift of Christ to us? Like the Magi, should we not first of all give Him our worship, enthroning Him in our lives; and then lay down before Him the gifts and abilities He has given us to be used in His service, as He so chooses?

Aftermath

Any suspicions the Magi may have had concerning Herod's reasons for sending them to Bethlehem were confirmed in a dream, in which they were warned 'not to go back to Herod'. So 'they returned to their country by another route' (v.12).

I wonder how the Magi felt when they subsequently heard about Herod's order to massacre all the young boys of two years old and under in the Bethlehem area (v.16)? Did they feel guilty, realising that it was their failure to report back to Herod concerning the whereabouts of the child which had resulted in that paranoid maniac instigating his killing spree? Did they wonder whether the child they had worshipped had been killed, or had managed to escape? In view of all that had happened, did the Magi realise that God's hand of blessing and protection would be upon this child, to whose feet He had brought them in homage and adoration?

Chapter 3

Divine Appointments

Simeon and Anna

Luke 2:25–38

A man of the Spirit

Like Zechariah and Elizabeth, Simeon and Anna were part of the faithful remnant among the Jews who were earnestly looking and longing for the coming of the Messiah: 'waiting for the consolation of Israel' (v.25), as Luke puts it. Unlike the others, Simeon had received a direct revelation from the Holy Spirit that he would not die before he had seen 'the Lord's Christ', the Messiah, with his own eyes (v.26). Luke tells us that Simeon was 'righteous and devout ... and the Holy Spirit was upon him' (v.25). Up until now, the Holy Spirit usually came upon people on special occasions, but the sense here is that the Holy Spirit was resting upon Simeon continuously, which was rare. Indeed, the Holy Spirit is mentioned no less than three times in Luke's description of Simeon (vv.25–27). Clearly, he was a man who lived his life in a manner that was pleasing to God; who was careful to perform all the religious duties required, walked under the direction of the Holy Spirit and was open to God at all times.

So it was no coincidence that Simeon was in the Temple courts on the very day and at the very time that the baby Jesus passed through in the arms of His parents. Mary and Joseph had brought Him 'to present him to the Lord' (v.22) and to go through the ceremonies prescribed by the Law (vv.23–24). All those who officiated at these ceremonies involving Jesus were in attendance simply because they happened to be on duty at the time; but Simeon was present because he had been 'moved by the Spirit' (v.27) to be there.

In his arms

So who was Simeon? In view of the description we are given, it has been surmised that he must have been a priest, or at least worked in the Temple in some capacity. But there is no evidence for this. Because he was ready and willing to die (v.29), it has been thought that Simeon must have been an old man; apparently, tradition has it that he was 113 years old! But again, the Bible does not substantiate this. However, it does seem more than likely that he was elderly.

Whoever Simeon was, he was there in the Temple courts at the behest of the Holy Spirit. How long he stood there watching all the parents coming and going with their babies, we don't know. Imagine how great his excitement must have been when the Holy Spirit directed him to Mary and Joseph. This was the divine appointment he had been waiting for and anticipating for many years.

Clearly, there must have been something about Simeon that persuaded Mary and Joseph to allow this complete stranger to come up to them as they were walking through the Temple courts, take their precious baby off them and hold Him in his arms (vv.27–28). Perhaps they sensed that the Holy Spirit was resting on Simeon in a special way, and that reassured them. Whatever the reason, Simeon took the baby in his arms, and began to praise God.

Praise and prophecy

His song of praise has become known as the 'Nunc Dimittis', the Latin translation of his opening words. On seeing Jesus, Simeon was now happy to die in the knowledge that he had seen the Messiah promised by God (v.29). After years of waiting he was now at peace, 'For my eyes have seen your salvation' (v.30); he was holding the baby who had come to bring salvation to the whole world (v.31). To the officials, this was just another baby; to Simeon, his eyes opened by the Spirit, this was the promised baby. He even went on to praise God that this salvation extended to the Gentiles (v.32). This was a quite extraordinary statement for a devout Jew such as Simeon to make, because many Jews believed that the Messiah would come just to save His own people. Luke himself was a Gentile, and one of the themes of his Gospel is that God's salvation is for the whole world – and not just for the Jews. Not only will the Messiah be 'a light for revelation to the Gentiles' (v.32), but He will also bring God's 'glory' (v.32) to Israel, as the Jews see the Son of God walking among them.

Having praised and thanked God for the child, Simeon then turned his attention to the parents, who were still in a state of shock and amazement at his words (v.33). Simeon prophesied that Jesus would have the effect of splitting people into two groups: those who were for Him and believed in Him wholeheartedly; and those who were against Him and rejected Him totally. People would not be able to remain neutral about Jesus. Some would 'rise' while others would 'fall' because of Him (v.34). Those who rejected God's 'sign', as Simeon called Jesus (v.34), would speak out against Him and oppose Him: thus 'the thoughts of many hearts will be revealed' (v.35).

Then Simeon looked straight at Mary and said, maybe with tears in his eyes, 'And a sword will pierce your own soul too' (v.35). The word 'sword' in the original Greek is *rhomphaia*, indicating a large rather than a small sword, and the sense of the verb is 'constantly keep on piercing'. This picture accurately predicted the intensity and frequency of sorrow and suffering Mary would endure as the mother of the Christ, culminating in His death on the cross. Those words must have made their encounter with Simeon a bittersweet experience for Mary, who must have wondered what it all meant.

Making known

'… at that very moment' (v.38), an elderly lady appeared on the scene. Isn't God's timing always perfect?! Her name was Anna, which means 'gracious'. She had been widowed after seven years of marriage, and was now very old indeed (vv.36–37). Luke describes her as 'a prophetess' (v.36), which indicates that she was very close to God, could interpret His message and was not afraid to speak out His truth. Her devotion to God was shown by the fact that: 'She never left the temple but worshipped day and night, fasting and praying' (v.37). She too must have been led by the Spirit and brought to this divine appointment. Her initial reaction on seeing the child was the same as that of Simeon: 'she gave thanks to God' (v.38). Their praise was inspired by the Holy Spirit and must have sounded sweet to God.

In Jewish culture, the wisdom and experience of the elderly was highly valued, which would have given extra weight to what Simeon and Anna said. Do we tap into the vast reservoir of wisdom and experience of the elderly Christians in our churches? Do we give them opportunities to contribute? Or, as often happens in the world, do we ignore them and marginalise them?

Notice that Anna didn't just praise God; she also made known what God had done. She had clearly recognised the baby as the promised Messiah, because she went out of the Temple and 'spoke about the child to all who were looking forward to the redemption of Jerusalem' (v.38); in other words, to those who were anticipating the coming of the Messiah and what He would do.

And shouldn't our lives include those same elements: praising God, and telling others what He's done? After all, how are people going to know about God's salvation if we don't tell them? Simeon and Anna both had divine appointments. Dare we pray that God will give us divine appointments today with people with whom we can share our faith – telling them what God has done for us?

Chapter 4

The Sceptic

Nathanael

John 1:45–51
(Other bit part player appearing: Philip)

Prejudice

Nathanael was sitting under a fig tree (v.48), presumably in the garden of his home in Cana (John 21:2), when his friend Philip, who lived in nearby Bethsaida, arrived. As a devout Jew (v.47), Nathanael had no doubt been spending time there in prayer and in study of the Scriptures. It must have been clear to Nathanael immediately Philip appeared that he was very excited about something. No doubt out of breath in his haste to find Nathanael, Philip blurted out the reason for his visit: 'We have found the one Moses wrote about in the Law, and about whom the prophets also wrote – Jesus of Nazareth, the son of Joseph' (v.45).

If Philip had not mentioned the last part, Nathanael's sceptical reaction would probably have been more positive. Interested though he surely would have been in Philip's excited assertion that he had met the Messiah, for whose coming no doubt Nathanael prayed daily, the fact that Philip had gone on to say that this man came from Nazareth caused all the old prejudices about that town just a few miles to the south of Cana to rise up within him. 'Nazareth! Can anything good come from there?' (v.46) he exclaimed; his question laced, no doubt, with a good deal of sarcasm.

Despised by the Jews because a Roman garrison was based there, Nazareth also had a reputation among some, including it seems Nathanael, for moral laxity and lack of religious observance. Added to which, the district of Galilee as a whole, in which Nazareth, Cana, Bethsaida and Capernaum all lay, had produced many hotheads and false Messiahs over the years. No wonder Nathanael was sceptical of Philip's claim! A devout, patriotic Israelite such as Nathanael would also have known that the Scriptures said the Messiah would be born in Bethlehem in the district of Judea (Micah 5:2), not Nazareth in Galilee.

'Come and see'

Nathanael must have felt sorry and not a little disappointed that his friend Philip had apparently been so easily deceived. Philip, on the other hand, must have felt saddened at Nathanael's dogmatic scepticism. How could he overcome his friend's prejudice? Philip obviously realised that prejudice is often the result of lack of knowledge and understanding of people, so instead of trying to argue him into changing his attitude (which he probably wouldn't have succeeded in doing anyway), he invited Nathanael to 'Come and see' (John 1:46); to come and meet Jesus for himself, and then make up his mind.

To his credit, Nathanael agreed to do this, when he could easily have refused and stalked off to resume his position under the fig tree again. Had he done so, Nathanael would have missed the opportunity of meeting with Jesus and of becoming one of His chosen twelve disciples. Are there times when we miss out on being involved with what God is doing because of our prejudices or preconceived ideas? Do we tell others the good news that we have met with Jesus and try to bring them to see for themselves?

None of the lists of the Twelve include the name Nathanael,

but it seems highly likely that Nathanael and Bartholomew were actually the same person, since he and Philip are linked together in the list of names (Matt. 10:3) and the Synoptic Gospels don't mention Nathanael at all. It wasn't unusual in those days for one man to be known by two different names.

Convinced

When Jesus saw Philip bringing his friend to Him, He said of Nathanael, 'Here is a true Israelite, in whom there is nothing false' (John 1:47). Nathanael's devotion was known to God, and he deserved to be called a proper 'Israelite'; the sort of man commended by the psalmist when he said: 'Blessed is the man ... in whose spirit is no deceit' (Psa. 32:2). Nathanael was shocked and amazed that Jesus knew all about him before they had even met, and was intrigued to know how. The answer Jesus gave left him even more mystified and amazed: 'I saw you while you were still under the fig-tree before Philip called you' (John 1:48).

It does come as a bit of a shock when we first realise that God knows all about us; that nothing we say or do is hidden from Him (Psa. 139)! Maybe we need to remind ourselves of that fact every day, and allow it to inform and affect our lifestyle. After all, is not each one of us accountable to God (Heb. 4:13)?

By now, Nathanael was totally convinced that Jesus was indeed the promised Messiah, declaring emphatically: 'Rabbi, you are the Son of God; you are the King of Israel' (v.49). Jesus' reply to this indicated that Nathanael's confession of faith was just the beginning of what God had in store for him: 'You believe because I told you I saw you under the fig-tree. You shall see greater things than that' (v.50). In other words, 'Nathanael, you ain't seen nothing yet!'

Isn't it good to be reminded that finding Jesus as our Saviour is but the start of a lifelong walk with God, with all the exciting possibilities that brings? In the wonderful words of the apostle Paul reflecting Isaiah 64:4: 'No eye has seen, no ear had heard, no mind has conceived what God has prepared for those who love him' (1 Cor. 2:9).

Jacob's ladder

Jesus then told all those present that they would 'see heaven open, and the angels of God ascending and descending on the Son of Man' (John 1:51). This is a clear reference to the dream of Jacob, the first Israelite (Gen. 28:12; 32:28), except here Jesus used the ladder that Jacob saw as symbolic of Himself as the link between heaven and earth. This was not something His disciples would actually 'see' with human eyes, like the Transfiguration; it was a spiritual insight they would gain into who Jesus really was, and why He had come.

I wonder if Nathanael's eyes had been opened to these truths by the time he stood on the shore of the Sea of Galilee, watching the risen Christ cook breakfast for him (John 21:1–13)?

Chapter 5

The Clash of the Kingdoms

A man with an evil spirit

Mark 1:21–28

Sin city

Somewhere in the city of Capernaum, a man was getting ready to go to the synagogue, as he did every Sabbath day. Rumour had it that Jesus of Nazareth, who had apparently turned water into wine recently at a wedding in the nearby town of Cana (John 2:1–11), was going to be there, and that had stirred something within him. He would have also heard that, when Jesus had attended His local synagogue in Nazareth the week before, there had been a riot, and He had been driven out of the town. The man must have wondered what Jesus had said, and whether He would repeat it in Capernaum that day.

Capernaum was a very wealthy city, but it was also very decadent and full of sin. It was the headquarters for many Roman soldiers. The result of this was that the city was subject to pagan influences from all over the Roman Empire. It was certainly a place where the kingdom of Satan was well established.

I imagine the man making his way through the streets of the city in the direction of the synagogue, joining with the ever-increasing numbers of his fellow Jews as he neared the building. As he passed groups of Roman soldiers patrolling the streets, he would have felt the hatred of them rise within him, as it did within the heart of every self-respecting Jew. The exception to this emotion was one of the centurions stationed there, who ironically had actually paid for the building of their splendid synagogue (Luke 7:5; see Chapter 11), and was consequently held in high esteem by the Jews of the city.

Teaching with authority

I imagine the man entering the synagogue, greeting those around him, and taking his customary seat. There must have been a great sense of anticipation in the place which, no doubt, was absolutely packed. He must have looked around, wondering which of the unfamiliar faces was actually this Jesus.

The familiar service began. And then, at last, the leader invited Jesus to come forward, and He 'began to teach' (Mark 1:21). The more Jesus spoke, the more the man must have felt conflicting emotions rising within him. Like the rest of the congregation, he was used to going along to the synagogue week by week and hearing the rabbis arguing over the finer points of what the Law said. If a person asked them a question about the Law, they would usually quote a particular teaching, then back up what they had said by referring to what some other rabbi had stated in the past – a bit like lawyers do today. They did this to give their words more authority.

But Jesus wasn't doing that at all. His teaching didn't consist of arguing about nuances of meaning that were over the heads of most people. And, when Jesus was asked a question, He gave a straight answer without basing support for what He was saying on the teaching of other rabbis. No wonder the people were 'amazed at his teaching' (v.22)! It was so different, 'because he taught them as one who had authority, not as the teachers of the law' (v.22). Jesus was standing there, saying things the man had never heard before, with an authority that could only come from ...

Suddenly, along with the amazement he felt like everyone else, there must have been a rising tide of fear and hatred inexplicably taking over his whole being, consuming him, bursting out uncontrollably from within him, screaming: 'What do you want with us, Jesus of Nazareth? Have you come to destroy us? I know who you are – the Holy One of God!' (v.24). Some Jews thought that when the Messiah came He would destroy the demons. This would indicate that the kingdom of God had arrived. The evil spirit within this man obviously knew this too (v.24).

To the rescue

Sometimes mental illness is mistaken for demon possession, and vice versa. This man was clearly demon-possessed, because he revealed a knowledge of who Jesus really was. He was under the control of the evil spirit. The irony of this outburst is that the evil spirits knew and acknowledged the true identity of Jesus, whereas the Jewish religious leaders, who should have recognised it, failed to see it or refused to accept it.

The next thing the man knew, he was being shaken violently and uncontrollably, and his voice was emitting a shriek that was not of his making (v.26). He probably finished up in a heap on the floor. It was at this point that he must have felt a great sense of release and peace flooding his whole being. Jesus had come to his rescue. Jesus had silenced the demon because He wanted people to come to an understanding of who He was by listening to His words and observing His actions (not because of some demon telling them). But, more importantly for the wellbeing of the man himself, Jesus had cast the demon out of him (v.25).

Point of entry

How had the man got himself into this state of being possessed by a demon? Given the pervading culture in Capernaum, there would have been plenty of opportunity for occult involvement. It seems likely that, as with anyone who finds himself or herself in such a situation, he had opened a door through which Satan could enter his life by getting involved in activities such as astrology, witchcraft, levitation, spiritism or using Tarot cards or Ouija boards.

Today, such experiences are more widespread than we might think, as people are sucked into the often fascinating and seemingly harmless world of evil. But, praise God, because of what Jesus did on the cross, in and through His name we can be released from any harmful effects of being involved with the occult (see Chapter 36).

A powerhouse or a talking shop?

The reaction of the congregation is understandable: 'The people were all so amazed that they asked each other, "What is this? A new teaching – and with authority! He even gives orders to evil spirits and they obey him"' (v.27). We have already seen why they were amazed at Jesus' teaching, but now they had seen His authority confirmed in power.

The apostle Paul wrote: 'For the kingdom of God is not a matter of talk but of power' (1 Cor. 4:20). Doesn't that apply just as much today as it did then? Unfortunately, in my experience, many churches have become a talking shop rather than a powerhouse. People are drawn to God in many ways, but is not one of the most magnetic of these when they see evidence of the power of God at work?

Chapter 6

Touching the Untouchable

A man with leprosy

Mark 1:40–45

The dreaded disease

At the time of Jesus, leprosy was an incurable disease, and everybody dreaded catching it. The skin of a person with leprosy became covered with the most awful sores, and the flesh withered away, drastically altering their appearance. If that wasn't bad enough, it could be as long as thirty years before the leper actually died of the disease.

There were social and religious consequences too. Because it was such a contagious disease, no one was allowed to touch a leper, and lepers were not allowed to mix in society. The Law of Moses, by which the Jews lived, contained clear instructions about skin diseases and rules for those who suffered from them (Lev. 13:1–46; 14:1–32). The attitude to leprosy then was a combination of fear and disgust. Lepers were outcasts who often lived in colonies outside the towns and cities. Food would sometimes be left for them outside the city walls as the gates were locked for the night.

What an eerie sight it must have been to see these dishevelled, disfigured outcasts approaching the city walls, squabbling over the food, and then shuffling off again into the night.

Lepers were also regarded as being outside God's chosen people; so they not only became social outcasts but religious outcasts as well. Touching a leper for whatever reason made you religiously unclean, and you had to take certain prescribed steps before you were considered fit to worship God once again.

Desperation and faith

The man would probably have lost count of the number of years he had been exiled from society in this leper colony. He must have wondered how much longer he could survive. The older he got, the harder it seemed to become. But then, one day, as he was shuffling along the road in his torn rags, his straggly hair dirty and unkempt, the lower part of his face covered, shouting 'Unclean, unclean!' – all as prescribed by the Jewish law (Lev. 13:45–46) – and dodging the rocks being thrown at him to keep him away, it seems he overheard a group of people talking about someone called Jesus of Nazareth. I imagine him listening, as he stood at a distance, and hearing that this Jesus had healed many people of their diseases. Rumour had it that He was coming to town the next day (Luke 5:12).

On hearing this, a desperate hope must have formed a question in his mind: 'If Jesus can heal people of their diseases, why can't He heal me of mine?' Perhaps he had wrestled with this thought all that night, juxtaposing his growing faith that Jesus could heal him against the likelihood that Jesus probably wouldn't even come near him, let alone have time for him, despised outcast that he was. And there was another complication: if Jesus were in the town (and he, as a leper, was forbidden by the Law to enter a town), how was he going to get near Him? And yet … how could he let an opportunity like this pass him by?

Desperation and faith are a powerful mixture, and they propelled this leper through the social and religious restrictions of the day to the feet of Jesus, without so much as an 'Unclean!'

falling from his lips. There he knelt and begged Jesus, saying, 'If you are willing, you can make me clean' (Mark 1:40). The shocked crowd must have been torn: did they cover their faces and get as far away as possible from this contagious creature or stay right where they were to see what Jesus would do?

As he knelt there, the leper must have been fearful as to how Jesus might react to the temerity of his actions, particularly as leprosy was widely regarded as God's punishment for sin. Would this Jesus be willing to heal him or would He reject him as well?

When we come to God with our needs, whatever they may be, doesn't He expect us to show similar qualities of humility and expectancy? As we come, is it not important to remember that faith expects but does not demand, and that healing comes within the sovereign will of God?

Shocking response

What happened next must have shocked the leper as much as it would have shocked the crowd who remained. He was suddenly aware that Jesus was reaching down and putting His hand on him (v.41); this man from Nazareth was actually touching him! What a glorious feeling of unspeakable joy must have surged through the leper's whole being as he felt the gentle hand of Jesus laid upon him. Here, at last, was someone who saw past his physical condition and saw him as a person. Here, at last, was someone who cared about him and accepted him, disgusting as he was. No one is too disgusting for God to touch.

The leper would have known full well that, by touching him, Jesus was breaking the Jewish law and making Himself religiously unclean. What a wonderful picture this is of what Jesus would do on the cross. He who was holy and sinless would become unclean for us, taking our sin upon himself, so that we might be cleansed from the leprosy of our sin (1 Pet. 2:24; 1 John 1:9).

It could be argued that Jesus didn't need to actually touch the man to heal him: the spoken word would have been enough. But Jesus is always concerned about the whole of us, not just our bodies. This man needed more than physical healing: he needed to feel accepted. And that was the importance of the touch. Are we prepared, as individuals and as churches, to reach out and touch those regarded as untouchable?

'Be clean!'

The surprise and wonder of feeling the touch of Jesus' hand must have caused the man to look up into His face. And then Jesus spoke words to him that must have thrilled him to the core: 'I am willing … Be clean!' (Mark 1:41). He could hardly believe his ears. Jesus was actually willing to heal him, an outcast and a reject. Could he believe it? Dare he believe it? 'Be clean!' The words must have rung in his ears. Could it be true? The incurable cured?

I imagine him tentatively folding back the sleeve of his cloak, scarcely daring to look at his arm; lowering his face cloth and gingerly touching the skin of his cheeks to see whether it felt any different. And his joy at discovering that it did!

Keep quiet

But before he could leap to his feet with the excitement of it all, Jesus spoke to him again. He probably noticed that the tone of Jesus' voice had changed from that of gentle compassion to being rather stern (vv.41,43): 'See that you don't tell this to anyone. But go, show yourself to the priest and offer the sacrifices that Moses commanded for your cleansing, as a testimony to them' (v.44).

On hearing what Jesus said, various thoughts must have gone through his mind. Surely Jesus couldn't be serious about that first bit? Fair enough to tell him to go to the priest, who would give him a thorough examination and then pronounce him clean, and to offer the special sacrifices – that was required by the Jewish law. But how could Jesus possibly expect him to keep quiet about what had happened to him? Everyone he knew would notice for a start! He would have had no idea that Jesus said these words to many people he healed, in order to prevent rumours that He could be the promised Messiah from spreading widely at that time. All he knew was that in a moment of time his life had been completely transformed. He had been cleansed of his affliction and could look forward to being welcomed back into society. He would be able to go to the synagogue again; even to the Temple in Jerusalem! How could Jesus expect him to keep his joy to himself? No way! Not a chance! And off he went, telling everybody what Jesus had done for him (v.45).

New challenge

As he ran off to see the priest, did it cross the man's mind for one moment that he was about to face a new challenge? He was going to have to adapt to a completely new lifestyle. Just think for a moment of the many ways in which his life was going to change due to the cleansing he'd experienced: the places he would go to, the people he would associate with, and the way he would spend his time would all be very different to his previous life.

When we experience cleansing from the leprosy of sin, doesn't this also bring with it the challenge of a completely new lifestyle? Perhaps now is the time to prayerfully consider the places we go to, the people we associate with and the way in which we spend our time. Are they in keeping with what God would want of us?

Acceptance

I wonder how readily the community accepted the man into their midst? I imagine that there would have been a certain amount of suspicion, reservation and caution in the air. I can just see people huddling together in their little groups, pretending not to stare at him, and asking one another in whispers whether it really *is* the leper whom they used to know and so assiduously avoided. They knew it was of course. They had been there when the priest pronounced him fit to re-enter society, assuring them that a thorough examination had taken place and that the appropriate sacrifices had been made. And yet … knowing was one thing; accepting was quite another.

Don't we also have to face the same challenge as people's lives are transformed and they are brought into the Church?

The question is: how ready are we to accept people fully into fellowship? Are we as prepared to do this as Ananias was with Saul, the arch persecutor of the Early Church (see Chapter 32)?

My prayer is that God will make the Church a community where all transformed 'lepers' are welcomed and accepted.

Chapter 7

Who needs Physiotherapy?

A paralysed man

Mark 2:1–12

What are friends four?

Isn't it good to have friends who care? This particular paralysed man, who lived in Capernaum, was fortunate enough to have a group of them (v.3). Presumably they came and tended to his needs every day. But today was different. They must have told him excitedly that Jesus of Nazareth was back in town (v.1), and how they were determined to take him to Jesus. Seeing what Jesus had done on His previous visit had obviously stirred up their faith to the point where all of them believed that Jesus could and would heal their friend. And together they put their faith into action; four of them carrying the paralysed man as he lay on his mat to the house where Jesus was teaching (v.3).

What a challenge this is to us: to be an inspiration and encouragement to those around us who are in need, not only physically but also spiritually and emotionally. So often we think that it is the responsibility of the individual to have faith. While that is obviously very important, is it not just as important for us to have faith on behalf of that person too, and to get alongside them, supporting their faith?

There's a hole in my roof ...

The trouble was, the friends found that: 'So many gathered that there was no room left, not even outside the door ...' (v.2). Isn't it amazing how many obstacles occur when we try to bring people to Jesus? I can imagine the groans coming from the group of friends as they rounded the corner and saw all the people piled outside the house. Some of them were probably of the opinion that they might as well turn around and take their paralysed friend back home straight away – on the grounds that they could always try again another time. And then one of them had a bright idea.

In those days, houses were built of stone. They had flat roofs which were usually made up of a thick layer of mud or clay mixed with straw, packed with a stone roller, and supported by mats of branches across wooden beams. There was a stairway outside which led on to the roof. So for the four friends it was simply a matter of carrying the paralysed man up the stairs and on to the roof. I wonder what he had to say about all this?

Once that had been achieved, it was a relatively easy task to pull up part of the roof and make a hole large enough through which to get their friend to Jesus. Mark tells us: '... they made an opening in the roof above Jesus and, after digging through it, lowered the mat the paralysed man was lying on' (v.4). This just shows how determined they were to get their paralysed friend to Jesus.

It must have been quite a comical scene. There was Jesus in full flow, as He '... preached the word to them' (v.2), when suddenly lumps of mud, bits of straw and chips of wood started dropping down on Him. I imagine the people who were listening not only being distracted by this, but wondering whether to laugh or pretend it wasn't happening. The way I see it, Jesus stopped talking, looked up, and then, with a broad smile on His face, moved out of the way as the mud, straw and wood continued to rain down from above. I don't suppose the owner of the house was best pleased about what was happening though. Whatever was he going to write on his house insurance claim form?!

Eventually the hole was big enough for the paralysed man, still lying on his mat, to be lowered through (presumably by means of ropes – which one of the friends would have had to go and get) and down to where Jesus was standing.

Pardon?

Mark's account continues: 'When Jesus saw their faith …' (v.5). No words of faith were expressed here, neither from the friends above nor the paralysed man below. Nobody said anything. It was the action they'd taken, and the lengths they'd gone to, which spoke out their corporate faith far more eloquently than words could ever have done. And Jesus always responds to faith.

But His response can't have been anything like what the paralysed man was expecting. Mark tells us that Jesus '… said to the paralytic, "Son, your sins are forgiven"' (v.5). At which point I imagine the man looking at Jesus with a puzzled expression on his face, and thinking: 'Pardon? That's not what I was expecting to hear! "Be healed" was more what I was hoping for.'

In my experience, there are often times when we come to God in faith and His response is nothing like what we were expecting or hoping for. But isn't that because God is sovereign and supernatural? I believe that God deals with us according to His own sovereign ways, time and will; and with His supernatural knowledge He knows exactly what the root of the problem is, what the real need is, and what must be tackled first. Isn't it true to say that, in the case of all of us, our deepest need is for God's forgiveness?

Jesus was emphasising both to the paralysed man and to the crowd that having your sins forgiven was more important than being physically healed. At which point the man must have thought: 'Pardon? Can my sins really all be pardoned? Can I really be forgiven for all the wrong things I've done?'

Sickness and sin

Engrained in Jewish culture was the belief that sickness was sometimes caused by sin. Indeed, one contemporary Jewish rabbi is reported to have said that ' ... there is no sick man healed of his sickness until all his sins have been forgiven him'. It's more than likely that the paralysed man believed this, thinking that he was ill because God was punishing him. Jesus would have known this, and therefore He tackled this fundamental issue first. Jesus was always concerned for the whole person.

What joy Jesus' words must have caused to rise within the man! God was not angry with him; he was not living under God's judgment; he was being accepted into the family of God. Jesus even called him 'Son' to emphasise the point (v.5). This was a further indication that none of us is rejected by God on account of our sin: God's forgiveness extends to each one of us and we are welcome in His family, where He is our loving Father.

Blatant blasphemy

Mark doesn't tell us what the reaction of the crowd was to these words of Jesus. My guess is either stunned silence or gasps of amazement followed by low whispers, as the news rippled out to the crowds in the street outside. Then the paralysed man realised that Jesus was no longer speaking to him, but to the teachers of the law. I'm sure he had no idea that they were sitting there thinking, 'Why does this fellow talk like that? He's blaspheming! Who can forgive sins but God alone?' (v.7). But Jesus knew what was going through their minds, and asked them what must have seemed to the paralytic to be a rather strange question involving him: 'Which is easier: to say to the paralytic, "Your sins are forgiven," or to say, "Get up, take your mat and walk"?' (v.9). I imagine Jesus pausing at this point to let the significance of His question sink in – and the man lying there on his mat thinking, 'What's this all about? Am I going to be healed, or am I just the object of a religious debate?'

It could be said that both statements are just as easy to say; so what point is Jesus making? It's all about proof. Can it be proved that a person's sins have been forgiven? Obviously not: it's a matter of faith. Can it be proved that a paralysed man has been healed? It certainly can: it's a matter of sight. So in that sense it is easier to say 'Get up and walk', because that can be seen to have happened and be conclusively verified. That is why Jesus linked the two conditions together by saying: 'But that you may know that the Son of Man has authority on earth to forgive sins ...' and then addressing the paralytic: 'I tell you, get up, take your mat and go home' (vv.10–11).

The fact that the paralytic would be healed, which could be seen, would show that he had also been forgiven, which couldn't be seen. It was a visible sign of an invisible truth. The proof of the forgiving was in the healing. Jesus was stating quite categorically that just as He could heal, so He could forgive. And this meant that any charge of blasphemy was completely unfounded.

Crisis of faith

Meanwhile, back on the mat, the paralysed man was suddenly aware that Jesus had turned His attention away from the teachers of the law and back to him. Had he heard what Jesus had said correctly? Had He really told him to '... get up ...' (v.11)? Up until now, it had been his friends who'd been putting their faith into action. Now it was his turn. How was he going to respond to Jesus' command? This was a crisis point for him: a crisis of faith.

He could have just laid there on his mat, looking up at Jesus, thinking to himself, quite reasonably: 'Get up? I can't get up: I'm paralysed. How can I possibly get up? And even if I do try to get up, I'll probably just fall flat on my face, and all these people will laugh at me. I'll be the butt of jokes for years to come. On the whole, I think I'll just stay where I am after all.' And the chance for healing would have passed him by. The opportunity to have his life transformed would have gone, probably for ever.

But he didn't. He responded by putting his faith into practice. He obeyed Jesus, even though he probably still had doubts and fears in his mind; even though it would have taken all the courage he could muster to begin to move those atrophied limbs.

What a wonderful experience he must have had of the power of God surging through his paralysed body as he began to move in response to Jesus' command! And the more he moved, the more he found he could move, until he was on his feet in front of them all. Mark simply says: 'He got up ...' (v.12). But, as we have seen, it wasn't quite as simple as that.

The amazing thing is that he required no physiotherapy whatsoever! No weeks and months of painful exercise were needed to restore his body to full working order. So triumphantly had he come through his crisis of faith that not only could he get up, but he could stand, bend fully down to his mat lying there on the ground, use his arms to roll it up, and walk unaided all the way home. He was completely cured, with all his muscles, joints, bones, sinews and tendons working perfectly and painlessly. No wonder 'This amazed everyone ...' and resulted in spontaneous praise (v.12)!

In my experience, there are times in our lives when we too come to a crisis of faith: a point where God speaks to us quite clearly and requires us to take a step of faith. Or it may be that a situation arises over which we have no control and God tells us to have faith in Him – because this did not take Him by surprise and He is in control.

The question is: How do we respond at the crisis point? Like the paralysed man, are we prepared to trust and obey?

Spiritual paralysis
And is it not possible for us to be perfectly healthy physically, and yet to be paralysed spiritually? In my experience, our attitudes to others can cause this to happen to us, as can wrong habits, past events and present circumstances. Are we prepared to come to God and humble ourselves before Him, knowing that we are going to hear those wonderful words: 'Get up!' and experience the release only He can give?

Sometimes it can be so difficult and painful that, like the paralysed man, we need the support and help of friends to bring us to God in the first place. And He may require us to take certain courses of action, which may not be easy; but this is an essential part of our rehabilitation process. Unlike the paralysed man, we may require physiotherapy to restore us to being a person who, in every sense of the word, is fit for the Master's use.

Chapter 8

From Darkness to Light

Nicodemus

John 3:1–16; 7:50–52; 19:39–42

'At night'

Nicodemus must have been doing a lot of thinking about this man called Jesus. As a Pharisee (3:1), Nicodemus was a learned teacher; in fact, a literal translation of verse 10 would indicate that he was the teacher of the Jews. Many Pharisees were implacably opposed to Jesus because He continually challenged their teaching and lifestyles, thereby undermining their authority. But Nicodemus seems to have had a different attitude and to have been a genuine seeker after truth. Like Nicodemus, are we still open to be taught by God, no matter how knowledgeable we consider ourselves to be?

His curiosity about Jesus seems to have been aroused by the miracles He performed (v.2). Whereas many of his colleagues on the Sanhedrin, the Jewish ruling council (v.1), attributed these miracles to the fact that Jesus was in league with the devil (Luke 11:15), Nicodemus did not. He firmly believed that Jesus was 'a teacher who has come from God' (John 3:2), as he told Jesus to

His face when he met Him. It seems that Nicodemus had not only seen and heard what Jesus was doing, but he had also heard what Jesus was saying. Rather than rejecting Jesus' teachings out of hand like many of his fellow-Pharisees, Nicodemus wanted to know more. So he came to Jesus 'at night' (v.2). Most likely this was because he wanted to have a long, uninterrupted conversation with Jesus, which would have been impossible during the day. But it may have also been that Nicodemus wanted to keep his visit to Jesus a secret from his colleagues.

Shocked

As he came, Nicodemus may have been thinking that it would be interesting to hear what Jesus had to say on subjects the rabbis were constantly debating, such as the qualifications for eternal life, or which of the commandments was the greatest. Or, more likely in view of the subsequent conversation, Nicodemus had it in mind to discuss the kingdom of God with Jesus. He may even have begun to wonder whether Jesus was the One who had come to restore God's kingdom on earth, as the Scriptures taught. Undoubtedly he would have been longing for the kingdom to come because, as both a Jew and a Pharisee, he would have assumed that he had the right to enjoy its benefits and blessings to the full. Was he in for a shock!

Having expressed his admiration for Jesus (v.2), Nicodemus was probably just about to pose his first question, when Jesus came out with a statement that must have taken the wind right out of his sails and shocked him to the core: 'I tell you the truth, no-one can see the kingdom of God unless he is born again' (v.3). It seems that Jesus not only knew what was in Nicodemus's mind, but also recognised Nicodemus as a searcher after truth, because He used the phrase 'I tell you the truth' three times during their conversation (vv.3,5,11).

Nicodemus must have taken a little while to recover his poise as he pondered what Jesus had just said. 'Born again, born again? What sort of ridiculous notion is that?' he must have thought to himself, and proceeded to challenge it with words probably laced with sarcasm: 'How can a man be born when he is old? Surely he cannot enter a second time into his mother's womb to be born!' (v.4). Nicodemus may have been theologically well educated and a leading teacher of his generation, but he lacked spiritual insight. He didn't realise that Jesus was talking about a supernatural birth.

In my experience, we encounter similar difficulties when we try to explain to people that they need to be 'born again'. Many remain convinced that their background, church attendance, doing good works, living moral lives, and so on, are what is required to enter the kingdom of God. How we need to continue to pray that God will open their eyes to see the truth.

Astonished

Nicodemus may have been surprised to find that Jesus had more to say on the subject. Again, Nicodemus heard Jesus saying that He was telling him the truth, and then Jesus went on to develop what He had already said: '… no-one can enter the kingdom of God unless he is born of water and the Spirit' (v.5). Nicodemus must have been beginning to get irritated by Jesus repeating the word 'no-one'. He must have realised that 'no-one' included him, and this was challenging everything he'd been brought up to believe about the kingdom of God and its entry qualifications. Perhaps it was starting to dawn on him that neither his ethnicity nor his devoutness was going to gain him a place in the kingdom of God.

Then Nicodemus heard Jesus talking about the fact that, just as we are born naturally, so we need to be born spiritually (vv.5–6) in order to enter the kingdom of God. The astonishment Nicodemus was feeling as he listened to all this must have showed on his face at this point, because Jesus looked at him and said, 'You should not be surprised at my saying, "You must be born again"' (v.7). Nicodemus must have been thinking, 'But I am surprised; in fact, I'm totally gobsmacked!' – or words to that effect.

And then, Nicodemus was aware that Jesus had changed the illustration from one of birth to that of the wind: 'The wind blows wherever it pleases. You hear its sound, but cannot tell where it comes from or where it is going. So it is with everyone that is born of the Spirit' (v.8).

Nicodemus would have known that wind was a symbol of the Spirit of God, and may well have recalled the prophecy about the dead bones, where the wind of the Spirit came and brought the bones to life (Ezek. 37:1–14). But none of this seemed to be making any sense. By now, his mind must have been spinning with bewilderment, and he found himself spluttering: 'How can this be?' (John 3:9). He had come in the dark – and he was still in the dark!

Now it was Jesus' turn to be astonished: 'You are Israel's teacher, and do you not understand these things?' (v.10). Nicodemus knew all the facts recorded in the Scriptures, but he was struggling to comprehend the truths they expressed. At this point, Nicodemus must have sensed a certain bemusement creeping into Jesus' voice at his inability to believe and accept the truth that he was being told (vv.11–12).

'Lifted up'

But Jesus hadn't given up on Nicodemus yet, and brought into play an illustration from the Scriptures with which he would have been very familiar: the serpent on the pole (Num. 21:8–9). This incident served as a picture of man's sin being punished, but God's grace providing a remedy for sinfulness. Any person who had been bitten by a snake could look to the brass serpent, which had been 'lifted up' (John 3:14) on a pole for all to see, believing that God would heal them if they had the faith to obey. It was a case of 'look and live'!

Nicodemus then heard Jesus explaining the truth of the event that this incident prefigured: that He Himself 'must be lifted up, that everyone who believes in Him may have eternal life' (vv.14–15). This must have puzzled Nicodemus even more. How was Jesus going to be 'lifted up'? And if He were, would he, Nicodemus, be there to see it? What exactly did Jesus expect him to believe? And did this 'everyone' actually include the

Gentiles as well as the Jews? (That last thought would have been really shocking to Nicodemus.)

Whether or not Jesus spoke the remainder of this passage to Nicodemus is unclear, because Jesus always referred to the first Person of the Trinity as 'Father', not as 'God'. However, I would still like to think that Nicodemus was the first person to hear those oft-quoted words: 'For God so loved the world that he gave his one and only Son, that whoever believes in him shall not perish but have eternal life' (v.16). Why not thank God for the day when you realised that 'whoever' included you!

Changed

Nicodemus went away into the darkness with much to ponder. Being the kind of man he was, he must have thought deeply about everything Jesus had said. Perhaps then he began to wonder if, when Jesus talked about being 'born of water', He was speaking of something more than natural birth. Maybe Jesus was making a connection between what He was saying about being 'born of water' and what Nicodemus had undoubtedly heard John the Baptist teaching about being baptised in water as a symbol of repentance of the heart (Luke 3:3–9). Did Nicodemus then make the step of realising that repenting of one's sins before God enabled one to be born spiritually? Perhaps he remembered what he'd read in the Scriptures about God's promise: 'I will sprinkle clean water on you, and you will be clean; I will cleanse you from all your impurities … I will give you a new heart and put a new spirit in you' (Ezek. 36:25–26). Did Nicodemus also realise that Jesus had used the illustration of the wind to explain that the new birth is not only a necessity, but also a mystery?

Certainly something fundamental must have happened to change his thinking, because the next time we read about Nicodemus he was defending Jesus in the Sanhedrin. It seems that he had become a secret believer. As his colleagues discussed ways and means by which they could get rid of Jesus, Nicodemus courageously confronted them with a question carefully framed to point out that they were in danger of breaking the law: 'Does our law condemn a man without first hearing him to find out what he is doing?' (John 7:51). The anger that his stance must have brought down upon him from many of his fellow Pharisees can only be imagined. Here was one of their own defending this Jesus: unbelievable! His reputation must have been severely damaged by his stand. Are we prepared to stand up courageously for Jesus, even though it might cost us our reputation and standing?

Maybe it was only when he saw Jesus 'lifted up' on the cross that Nicodemus finally understood the meaning of the serpent on the pole. Here we see the complete change that had taken place in his life. He went with Joseph of Arimathaea, a leader of the Sanhedrin and a secret believer like Nicodemus, to bury the body of Jesus (John 19:38–42). Nicodemus had brought with him 'a mixture of myrrh and aloes' which weighed 'about seventy-five pounds' (v.39). Apparently, this was the amount used in royal burials. Does this mean Nicodemus had come to realise that Jesus was indeed the Messiah, the King of the Jews, and was acknowledging this at His burial?

What a beautiful, poignant picture we have here of the two secret believers tending to the body of Jesus. The time for secrecy was over for both of them. 'Taking Jesus' body, the two of them wrapped it, with the spices, in strips of linen' (v.40). Between them, Nicodemus and Joseph of Arimathea then carried the body and laid it in the tomb. Little did they know what they would witness three days later!

Chapter 9

The Sinner of Sychar

The Samaritan woman

John 4:4–30,39–42

Despised

She came to the well, as she always did, in the heat of the midday sun (v.6). Fetching water from the well was 'woman's work' and was usually done in the cool of the early morning and the late evening. But she knew that if she came at those times she would be given a hard time by the other women of the town. It was bad enough being ostracised in the streets of Sychar, without suffering the indignity of being publicly excluded from the female community gathered at the well. She knew very well why they despised her: she had already gone through five husbands, and was currently living with a man who was not her husband – not the sort of behaviour to gain her acceptance into polite female society.

As she approached the well carrying her water jar, she noticed that a man was sitting there. No doubt her curiosity was aroused: 'What is he doing there? What does he want?' she must have thought to herself. Then suddenly she realised that this man was not a Samaritan; he was a Jew!

Deep hatred

The Jews and the Samaritans hated each other with an intensity and bitterness that ran very deep. There were two main reasons for this, and they both went way back into history. The first reason for the hatred was that the Samaritans were descended from Israelites who, in Jewish eyes, had contaminated themselves by intermarrying with Assyrians and other Gentiles after the Assyrian occupation of the northern kingdom of Israel in the eighth century BC. At that time, Palestine was divided into two kingdoms: the southern one being the kingdom of Judah, from which the word 'Jew' comes. Since the Israelites in the northern kingdom had defiled themselves in this way, the Jews maintained that they were the only true pure descendants of their father, Abraham.

By the time of Jesus, Israel had been reduced in size to two districts: Galilee in the north and Samaria. The kingdom of Judah was now primarily limited to the province of Judea. Most of the descendants of the Israelites who had intermarried with foreigners were now living in Samaria, and were therefore known as Samaritans.

The second reason for the hatred was that, although the Samaritans were Jewish by religion, they had broken away and built themselves a temple on Mount Gerizim. This was blasphemy to the Jews, because the Scriptures said there was to be only one temple, and that was to be at Jerusalem. The Samaritans also maintained that Mount Gerizim was where Abraham went to sacrifice Isaac (Gen. 22:2); that it was where Jacob had his dream (Gen. 28:10–17); that it was the place where God chose to place His name (Deut. 12:5); and that it was the mountain on which Moses had commanded an altar to be built, rather than the adjacent Mount Ebal as the Jews believed (Deut. 27:4–6). These disputes were still being hotly contested during the time of Jesus (John 4:19–22).

So, as far as the Jews were concerned, the Samaritans were both physical and spiritual half-breeds: an attitude which the Samaritans fiercely resented. This mutual hatred had been festering for centuries. The situation was so bad that if a Samaritan saw a Jew walking down the street towards him, he would cross over to the other side – and vice-versa.

'Living water'

'I'll just ignore him,' she must have thought. 'I'll draw the water I need and get away from here as quickly as possible.' But then, to her horror, the man spoke to her and asked, 'Will you give me a drink?' (John 4:7). What was she to do now? She must have wondered why this Jew would want to use the well bucket, which she knew he would have considered to be contaminated (v.9, see NIV note), to get a drink of water. She obviously felt that she couldn't just ignore his request; but she didn't see how she could comply with it. She may well have been annoyed at the temerity of this Jew in speaking to her at all. He must have known the social convention just as she did; but clearly he needed reminding of it, so she replied, probably somewhat testily, 'You are a Jew and I am a Samaritan woman. How can you ask me for a drink?' (v.9). 'That'll shut him up!' she must have thought.

But it didn't; on the contrary, the Jew seemed to want to engage her in conversation. She noticed that he didn't answer her question at all, but said instead, 'If you knew the gift of God and who it is that asks you for a drink, you would have asked him and he would have given you living water' (v.10).

'Living water, living water; what does he mean?' she must have asked herself, uncomprehendingly. Maybe she thought he was talking about running water from a stream; but there were no streams nearby. Surely he couldn't be claiming to be able produce water himself? And, in any case, he hadn't got a bucket. Bearing all this in mind she replied, 'Sir, you have nothing to draw with and the well is deep. Where can you get this living water? Are you greater than our father Jacob, who gave us the well and drank from it himself, as did also his sons and his flocks and herds?' (vv.11–12).

What the man said in reply must have both amazed and excited her: 'Everyone who drinks this water will be thirsty again, but whoever drinks the water I give him will never thirst. Indeed, the water I give him will become in him a spring of water welling up to eternal life' (vv.13–14). Not surprisingly, the fact that Jesus was speaking of spiritual things escaped the woman completely, as she would have been preoccupied by the provision of her physical needs. Sadly, in my experience many people suffer from exactly the same condition: they are totally unaware that there is a spiritual dimension to life. They are only half alive.

It must have seemed to her that this man was making her an offer she just couldn't refuse: magical water that would mean her never having to come to the well in the heat of the day again. She could hardly wait! 'Sir, give me this water so that I won't get thirsty and have to keep coming here to draw water' (v.15), she blurted out excitedly.

Stunned

She must have been expecting Jesus to say something like, 'OK then; this is what you do.' But instead, to what must have been her great disappointment and consternation, the man changed the subject completely. 'Go, call your husband and come back' (v.16), He said. What was she going to do now? She certainly wasn't going to air her personal circumstances in public to this Jew. So she simply replied, 'I have no husband' (v.17), which was perfectly true!

She must have been absolutely stunned by what Jesus said next: 'You are right when you say you have no husband. The fact is, you have had five husbands, and the man you now have is not your husband. What you have just said is quite true' (vv.17–18). Was that a gentle smile she saw on His face as He spoke those words?

Worship

I imagine that there was a lengthy pause while the bewildered woman came to terms with what she had just heard. 'How can he possibly know the intimate details of my personal circumstances?'

she must have asked herself worriedly, and with a creeping sense of fear. She could come to only one conclusion: 'Sir, I can see that you are a prophet' (v.19). She clearly wanted to get Jesus off this personally embarrassing subject as quickly as possible, so she tried to deflect Him by raising one of the bones of contention between the Samaritans and the Jews: 'Our fathers worshipped on this mountain [meaning Mount Gerizim], but you Jews claim that the place where we must worship is in Jerusalem' (v.20). And how often do we do the same – trying to deflect what God has spoken to us about, particularly when it's something we'd rather not face up to and deal with in our personal circumstances?

In His reply, Jesus made it clear to the woman that what matters when we worship God is not where we are but our attitude of heart (vv.21–24). God is looking for those who will worship Him 'in spirit and in truth'. It seems to me that worshipping God 'in spirit' means allowing our spirit to be inspired by the Holy Spirit in expressing our worship to God; and that we worship God 'in truth' when the words on our lips match the reality of our lives. Does our lifestyle conform to God's Word in such a way that we can be said to worship God with integrity and 'in truth'?

The Messiah

In spite of her general ignorance on spiritual matters, there was one truth that this woman did understand: 'I know that Messiah ... is coming. When he comes, he will explain everything to us' (v.25). Jesus had already told her that 'salvation is from the Jews' (v.22), and He now followed that up with yet another pronouncement that must have stunned this Samaritan woman: 'I who speak to you am he' (v.26).

This seems to have been a turning point in the life of this sinful woman. The words were hardly out of the man's mouth when she was aware that more Jews had arrived at the well (v.27). As she left the scene and made her way back to the town, leaving her water jar behind in her excitement (v.28), she must have been turning over in her mind all she had heard. Had she really met the Messiah, God's Holy and Anointed One? Yet not one word of condemnation had fallen from His lips about her sinful state; He had accepted her just as she was, and had even promised to give her 'living water' – whatever that meant.

Normally when she was in town she would have kept herself to herself; but not today! She spoke boldly to everyone she met, saying, 'Come, see a man who told me everything I ever did. Could this be the Christ?' (v.29). The citizens of Sychar must have been impressed by the woman's enthusiasm and maybe even sensed that something amazing had happened to her, because we read: 'They came out of the town and made their way towards him' (v.30).

We are not told what passed between Jesus and the Samaritans, but it must have impressed them greatly, because 'they urged him to stay with them, and he stayed two days' (v.40). Over that time, many of the townspeople 'became believers' (v.41). The woman's testimony had played a crucial role in bringing them to belief in Jesus (v.39); so much so that they wanted to hear Him for themselves and became convinced that Jesus was indeed 'the Saviour of the world' (v.42).

Personal evangelism

This despised woman's willingness to testify about Jesus puts us all to shame, I'm sure. And what an unlikely person she was for Jesus to choose as His witness to the people of Sychar! How often are we surprised at whom God chooses to carry out His particular purposes? Jesus knew that she would be coming to that well and had booked her a divine appointment. Her life would never be the same again.

As the woman's testimony showed, personal witness is very powerful and effective in bringing people to Jesus. Indeed, we can learn valuable lessons about how to evangelise from examining Jesus' technique as He sought to share with this Samaritan woman. For example, this was a divine appointment – and praying for such encounters is surely a good place to start. And when the opportunity came Jesus took it. He was gentle and courteous. He got alongside her and spent time with her. He started where she was at with a topic she understood and which was on her mind – water – and used it to get His message across to her. With Nicodemus, Jesus had talked about the kingdom of God because He knew it was a topic that interested him (see Chapter 8); it wouldn't have connected with this woman though! The apostle Paul also learnt to be flexible like this when talking to people (1 Cor. 9:20–23).

May we take all these lessons to heart as we seek to develop our personal evangelism and give testimony to the fact that, like this woman, we have met with Jesus and He has changed our lives.

Chapter 10

Help! I need Somebody

The lame man at the pool

John 5:1–15

Helpless and hopeless

The lame man woke to another day of helplessness and hopelessness beside the pool of Bethesda in Jerusalem. And he wasn't the only one lying there in the shade of the colonnades which surrounded the pool that Sabbath day: 'Here a great number of disabled people used to lie – the blind, the lame, the paralysed' (v.3). The best he could hope for was that some kind passers-by would toss him coins or pieces of bread – unless … unless this would be the day that the angel would come and stir up the waters of the pool (vv.4,7). That's why they were all there, waiting, hoping.

Thirty-eight years he had been there, waiting and hoping. But every time the waters were stirred, someone else had got into the pool before him and been cured, while he had lain there, watching. After all this time, he must have lost hope and resigned himself to the fact that he was never going to get into the pool

71

first, because he had no one to help him (v.7). By now, he had probably got used to the idea that he would spend the rest of his life (if such it could be called) lying there, begging. 'After all,' he may have reasoned, 'begging has provided for my needs for thirty-eight years – so perhaps it isn't such a bad existence; things could be much worse for someone in my condition.'

Stupid question

And then, suddenly, he was aware of this person looming over him. Perhaps he sat up and proffered his outstretched, cupped hands to the stranger in anticipation of money or food. But the stranger didn't seem to have anything to give him. Disappointment must have registered on the lame man's face as he looked at the stranger, and then laid himself down again. But he was aware that the stranger was still standing there, and he heard Him speak extraordinary words: 'Do you want to get well?' (v.6).

'What a stupid question to ask!' the lame man must have thought, as he sat up again to look the stranger in the eye. '"Sir," the invalid replied, "I have no-one to help me into the pool when the water is stirred. While I am trying to get in, someone else goes down ahead of me"' (v.7). I'm sure it never occurred to the lame man for one moment that this stranger could heal him. Why should it? The only way he thought he could be cured was by means of the pool; and that was out of the question. And how often do we find ourselves falling into the same trap of limiting God by thinking that He can only act in one particular way? Are not His ways higher than ours (Isa. 55:8–9)?

The 'house of grace'

It seems that Jesus thought the lame man did want to be cured, because He said to him, 'Get up! Pick up your mat and walk' (John 5:8), despite the man's stated belief that healing could only happen by means of the water in the pool. I imagine the invalid gawping in astonishment at the words he'd just heard. If the stranger had said that He would help him into the pool to be cured that would have been understandable. 'Get up! Pick up your mat and walk' was surely not what he was hoping to hear. And why should he do what the stranger had said anyway? Who was He to be giving out commands?

Suddenly, the lame man must have been aware that something was happening in his legs. He may not have realised that he was experiencing God's healing power, but he must have known he'd been healed, because 'he picked up his mat and walked' (v.9). Jesus usually healed in response to a person's faith; but here none was expressed by the lame man. Which just goes to show that God's grace is freely given and does not depend on our response, nor on what we do or say (Eph. 2:8). At Bethesda, which some say means 'the house of mercy' or the 'house of grace', God showed His mercy in a wonderful act of immediate grace to this lame man, and brought about a dramatic change in his life.

Rules rule OK!

By the time the man had managed to get to his feet, Jesus had disappeared into the crowd (v.13). The man must have wondered what to do next. It seems that he decided to go to the Temple, presumably to give thanks to God and to offer the appropriate sacrifices (v.14). He was on his way there, carrying his rolled-up mat, when he was accosted by some Pharisees. They said to him, 'It is the Sabbath; the law forbids you to carry your mat' (v.10).

Down the years, the scribes had added hundreds of rules to the Torah given by Moses. This collection of rules, known as the Mishna, had been drawn up to interpret what the Law of Moses actually required. So, for example, the Torah forbade work on the Sabbath. But what exactly was meant by the word 'work'? The Mishna contained a list of thirty-nine activities which were classed as 'work' and were therefore forbidden on the Sabbath. One of these was carrying a mat. A man who had been lame for thirty-eight years was now walking; but the Pharisees were more concerned about the observance of their nit-picking rules and regulations than rejoicing at God's mercy and grace in the performance of this miracle!

The man could well have been flustered by such an accusation;

but he wasn't, and replied in a very disarming way by simply telling them what had happened: 'The man who made me well said to me, "Pick up your mat and walk"' (v.11). At this point I can see the hackles of the Pharisees beginning to rise as they angrily demanded to know: 'Who is this fellow who told you to pick it up and walk?' (v.12). The man answered truthfully that he 'had no idea who it was' (v.13); at which point the Pharisees appear to have allowed the man to continue on his way.

At the Temple

While he was at the Temple, the man bumped into the stranger again, who engaged him in conversation: 'See, you are well again. Stop sinning or something worse may happen to you' (v.14). Jesus wanted the man to realise that, thrilled as he was to have been physically healed, it was more important that he should experience the even greater thrill of the miracle of the forgiveness of sins and be healed spiritually.

It seems that during their conversation, the man asked Jesus who He was, because he subsequently 'went away and told the Jews that it was Jesus who had made him well' (v.15). Whether it was because he was afraid of the Pharisees we don't know. But the result was that they 'persecuted' Jesus because He was 'doing these things on the Sabbath' (v.16).

Ensnared

This lame man had been ensnared by his illness for thirty-eight years.

In my experience, there are many ways that we can feel ensnared: for example, by illness, like this man, or by the circumstances or situations in which we find ourselves. When this is the case, it's easy to feel helpless and to lose hope. We may forget that God is with us and can use these hardships to make Himself known to us in a deeper way, and to cause us to become a source of ministry to others.

But then, is it not possible for the God of the impossible to intervene in our lives today and bring about a dramatic change?

Do we still long for that, or have we accommodated the situation to the point that, long ago, we allowed ourselves to lose hope? Whatever hardships we face, may God help us to retain the faith and belief that He is able to release us from them at any moment; provided, of course, that we still want to be released.

Chapter 11

A Man with Authority

The centurion

Luke 7:1–10

Rome rule

The Roman centurion must have been worried, and getting more worried by the minute. One of his servants, whom he 'valued highly' (v.2), was going downhill fast. Presumably he had been very ill for a while, but was now 'about to die' (v.2). There is no doubt that the centurion would have had the best doctors treating his servant; but all their medicines and remedies had been to no avail. The centurion must have wondered what more he could do. And then he had an idea.

The centurion was a military officer in the occupying Roman army, stationed at the fortress in Capernaum. As the word implies, he would have been in charge of a company of a hundred soldiers. Not surprisingly, most of the Jewish people hated the Romans, resenting their presence and the strict control with which they ruled. Some went beyond resentment and formed themselves into terrorist groups, the most notable of which was the Zealots. They were committed to driving the Romans out of Palestine by force, and acts of terrorism were part of their campaign.

In his capacity as a centurion, this man would undoubtedly have received regular reports on the activities of such groups of potential troublemakers, particularly their leaders, many of whom proclaimed themselves as 'messiahs'. Roman policy was to deal ruthlessly with such individuals. Recently, a man known as Jesus of Nazareth had appeared on the Roman radar because He was attracting large crowds. But this Jesus had never claimed to be a 'messiah' – though the centurion would surely have been aware that there had been talk, due to the miracles that He had performed (v.3). In his desperation, he must have begun to wonder whether Jesus would be prepared to perform another one – and heal his servant. So he decided to make Jesus aware of the situation and see what happened.

Searching

Throughout this incident we cannot help but be impressed by the centurion's humility. He was a man of power and status; a representative of the mighty forces of Rome; a cut above all other races. And yet, he humbled himself before this Jewish itinerant preacher. Questions like: 'Whatever will my household think?' 'Whatever will my fellow officers have to say about it?' don't seem to have bothered him. He did not allow any obstacles to stop him from coming to Jesus. What are the barriers that stop us from coming to God?

Actually, this centurion's fellow officers probably wouldn't have been all that surprised, because they knew that he had gone out of his way to find out about the Jewish religion and to understand the culture and beliefs of the Jews. He had even gone to the extent of building a synagogue for them (v.5).

This makes me think that here was a man who was searching for the truth. Having failed to find it in the various religions he had met during the course of his service across the Roman Empire, he believed he had now found what he was looking for in

Judaism. Praise God, He always meets with those who diligently seek after Him (Acts 17:16–34).

Unworthy

Embracing Judaism and building the synagogue had made the centurion very popular with the Jews in Capernaum; a very unusual position for a Roman to find himself in! So he decided to call in a few favours.

Why didn't the centurion go straight to Jesus himself? Perhaps he wanted to show Jesus due deference and respect. Maybe it was because he felt that, being a Gentile, he wasn't worthy enough to approach Jesus personally (Luke 7:7), and that Jesus would be more likely to listen to the Jewish elders than to him. So it seems that the centurion sent for them, explained the situation and asked them to approach Jesus on his behalf. The fact that they agreed to do this (v.3) is evidence of the esteem in which the centurion was held by the townspeople.

Of course, none of us is worthy enough to approach God. We are sinful; God is holy. But God in His great mercy has made it possible for us to approach Him (Heb. 10:10; 4:16).

Undeserving

The Jewish elders were highly respected members of the community, who combined the present-day roles of magistrate and town councillor, though they were not necessarily rulers of the synagogue. Luke tells us that, when they found Jesus, they pleaded earnestly with Him on the centurion's behalf: 'This man deserves to have you do this, because he loves our nation and has built our synagogue' (Luke 7:4–5). So Jesus set off for the centurion's house.

Word got back to the centurion that Jesus was on His way. At this point, the accounts given in Matthew and Luke differ. In Matthew's account, the centurion went to meet Jesus and spoke to Him directly. Luke, being a Gentile himself and writing with Gentiles in mind, was keen to emphasise the continued politeness and consideration that this Gentile showed towards Jesus, so he put the centurion's words into the mouths of friends. What is really important are the words that are actually spoken.

Having studied the Jewish religion, including its customs and practices, the centurion knew that, according to the laws of the rabbis, Jesus would defile Himself by going into the house of a Gentile. As a result, He would need to undergo a process of cleansing. Not wanting Jesus to defile Himself by entering his house, the centurion's message to Jesus is: 'Lord, don't trouble yourself, for I do not deserve to have you come under my roof' (v.6). The elders might have thought that the centurion was a deserving case, but he knew better.

This serves to remind us that we are all undeserving of God's love, mercy and forgiveness. We can do nothing of ourselves to merit it, nor can we do anything to earn it: it is possible only through the grace of God (Eph. 2:8–9). Jesus had to defile Himself to bring about our salvation by taking our sins upon Himself, so that we could be made righteous and acceptable in God's sight (2 Cor. 5:21). Isn't God's grace just so amazing?!

Amazed

But it was the next part of the centurion's message that caused Jesus Himself to be amazed: 'But say the word, and my servant will be healed' (7:7). Although the centurion knew he had authority and power, he recognised that Jesus had greater authority and greater power. He also realised that his authority and power were temporal and of this world, but that Jesus' authority and power were eternal and not of this world. However, the centurion did see a similarity between them: both of them had only to command to be instantly obeyed. He realised that Jesus didn't even have to see the person who needed healing: just to speak the word of authority was enough.

The centurion's grasp of the reality of the situation, and his statement of faith which resulted, left Jesus 'amazed' (v.9). So amazed, that He commented on the man's great faith to the crowd, commending it to them all by saying that He had not found such depth of faith anywhere among the Jews (v.9). As a

Gentile, these words would have been music to Luke's ears, as they showed unequivocally that Jesus responded to faith expressed by Gentiles just as readily as to faith expressed by Jews.

Having sent his message to Jesus, I imagine the centurion returning to the bedside of his servant, looking and hoping for some indication of a change for the better. Then, suddenly, it happened! In an instant the servant was restored to full health and strength (v.10). The servant had been healed by Jesus due to the centurion's expression of faith, and not because the centurion in any sense deserved to have his requests answered as a reward for studying Judaism or building the synagogue, as the elders thought he might (vv.4–5). Likewise Jesus does not answer our prayers in response to our 'good works' but in response to our faith in His goodness, love and authority.

The irony is that Jesus should have been able to find such faith among the Jews. For centuries God, through their religious customs and practices and through the teachings of the prophets, had been preparing them for the coming of the Messiah, so that they would recognise Him and understand what He was doing when He came (vv.18–23). And here was this Gentile, with none of these advantages, having greater faith in Him than any of them!

Interestingly, Jesus is only described as being 'amazed' on one other occasion besides this one. That was when He was rejected by His own people in His home town of Nazareth, where He was '... amazed at their lack of faith' (Mark 6:6). So here He was amazed on account of such belief, whereas at Nazareth He was amazed on account of such unbelief. Dare we ask ourselves which of the two Jesus sees when He looks at us?

Chapter 12

The Weeping Widow

The widow of Nain

Luke 7:11–15

Too much to bear

The day she would have been dreading had dawned. Today was the day when her son would be buried. She must have wondered how she was going to get through it. She had already experienced the pangs of bereavement and the inconsolable sense of loss when her husband had died, leaving her a widow. But at least then her son was there to comfort, support and provide for her. But now he had died prematurely, leaving her completely alone in the world. It was all too much to bear. She must have felt as though life had kicked her in the teeth. She had nothing to look forward to; she was staring destitution in the face.

As she came out of her house to take her place immediately behind the bier, on which her son's body lay wrapped in a sheet, she may well have been surprised to find that a large crowd had gathered outside to accompany her to the burial ground. The townspeople obviously understood the desperate predicament

81

in which the widow now found herself, hence this surge of collective sympathy. They knew that, unless she married again or had family who would take her in, her only means of survival would be through begging on the streets.

The widow must have felt a mixture of emotions at seeing the crowd, which I imagine included gratitude, that they were there to grieve with her, as she certainly couldn't afford to hire mourners to weep and wail, as was customary; and scepticism, wondering if they would come and visit her during the next thirty days (as she sat at home in mourning on the traditional low stool that she had used when her husband died), or stand with her in the synagogue as she said the traditional Kaddish prayer for the dead every week for the next eleven months.

Times of tears

The procession wound its way slowly through the streets of Nain and out through the town gate in the direction of the burial ground (v.12). Suddenly, she was vaguely aware through her streaming tears that there was another crowd of people coming towards them (v.11). In contrast to the noise of weeping and wailing from her son's funeral procession, this crowd was full of the noise of laughter and joyfulness. The next thing she knew, the wailing around her had subsided – and so had the noise from the other crowd. I imagine her wiping her eyes and looking to see why. And then she saw a man walking across from the other crowd towards her. 'Who is he?' she must have wondered; 'And how dare he presume to intrude on my grief?'

And then He spoke words that to her must have seemed oddly inappropriate for the occasion: 'Don't cry' (v.13). To which her response might well have been something like: 'Don't cry! What do you mean, don't cry! You don't understand the situation I'm in at all. I'm destitute, totally bereft of all support, and my future just doesn't bear thinking about. And you're telling me not to cry! As far as I'm concerned, tears are all I've got left.'

In my experience, when we find ourselves in a traumatic situation, it's so easy to be overwhelmed by the circumstances to the point where we are convinced that God just doesn't understand; and we even find ourselves believing He has forsaken us. Be assured that He does understand (Job 23:10), and that He will never forsake us (Heb. 13:5–6). Whenever God sees us in those times of tears, His heart of compassion goes out to us, and He comes to speak words of comfort and reassurance to us (2 Cor. 1:3–4). And not only that: He wants to be actively involved with us, wiping our tears away and giving us His joy in place of our sorrow (Jer. 31:13). He is able to do this, for He is the Lord of every situation. And that is exactly the title used of Jesus here: 'the Lord' (Luke 7:13), because Jesus was well able to do something miraculous in the life of this woman and in the death of her son.

Surely not

Through her tears, the weeping widow must have watched in astonishment as the man turned away from her, strode up to the bier and touched it, with the result that '... those carrying it stood still' (v.14). They were probably completely taken aback that anyone would do such a thing, because touching a bier made you religiously unclean. But, as we saw when Jesus healed the man with leprosy (see Chapter 6), Jesus was not interested in the consequences of His actions for Himself: His only concern now was for the widow (v.13).

Now everyone in both crowds had stopped and was watching intently. The people from the town had no doubt heard about Jesus, but they may not have realised that this was actually Him in person. Indeed, this was His only recorded visit to Nain. Isn't it interesting that it should coincide with this funeral? But then, nothing God does is ever coincidental, is it? The citizens of Nain were probably asking themselves: 'What is that crazy man doing?' – though hardly daring to whisper such thoughts to their neighbour.

And what of the other crowd? Many of them, especially the disciples, had already seen Jesus demonstrate His power over nature, over illness and over evil: but never over death. Surely not. He can't be going to ... I imagine them watching intently, open-mouthed, catching their breath, hardly daring to move ...

Son rise!

The grieving mother could believe neither her eyes nor her ears. Not only had this man touched the bier, but He was also now speaking to the corpse of her son in a very authoritative tone of voice. And what He said must have left her stunned: 'Young man, I say to you, get up!' (v.14). Jesus was about to demonstrate His power over death for the first time.

Imagine the reaction of the bearers when the dead body they had been carrying suddenly sat bolt upright and began to speak (v.15)! I'd love to know what he said, but unfortunately Luke doesn't tell us. How about: 'Would somebody mind getting me out of this sheet?'

And as for his mother: what must her reaction have been? Probably shock and joy in equal measure. She was apparently rooted to the spot, because Luke tells us that 'Jesus gave him back to his mother' (v.15). For me, this conjures up the lovely picture of Jesus helping the young man down from the bier, as the bearers stood there completely dumbstruck, and ushering him into his mother's outstretched arms for the biggest embrace you're ever likely to see!

The economy of God

What encouragement there is for us in this miracle, and what an important lesson there is for us to learn. We can be encouraged that, however desperate our situation might be, God is right there with us. And, as we commit it to Him, He will always bring blessing for us into it and bring glory to His name out of it. He may not always perform the miracle we might want, but I have found that He will certainly minister His supernatural power, strength, courage, peace, wisdom (or whatever else it may be that we need to receive from Him) into our lives, if we ask Him to. Isn't that in itself a miracle of divine grace?

I don't believe that God, who is love (1 John 4:8), deliberately causes us to go through bad experiences or brings traumatic happenings into our lives to teach us something. However, I do believe that, as we submit every situation we go through to God (no matter how devastating it might be), He will wonderfully use it to draw us closer to Himself. Moreover He will use it to help us learn more about Him, to give us opportunities for witness that wouldn't have occurred otherwise, to enable us to minister more effectively to others as a result of what we've been through and for many other purposes.

In my experience nothing, but nothing, we go through is ever wasted in the economy of God. We just need to allow Him the opportunity to recycle it.

Chapter 13

A Lesson in Love

Simon the Pharisee

Luke 7:36–50
(Other bit part player appearing: A sinful woman)

A dinner invitation

It seems likely that Simon the Pharisee lived in Capernaum. As Jesus spent a lot of time in that town, Simon would have had plenty of opportunity to hear what Jesus was saying, and to see the miracles He was performing. He would have undoubtedly been present in the synagogue when Jesus cast an evil spirit out of a man (see Chapter 5), and had probably followed what Jesus was doing with interest ever since.

So Simon decided to invite Jesus to dinner at his place. Why did he do this? Perhaps he wanted to examine Jesus more closely, or to question Him in the hope that Jesus might say something indiscreet, in such a relaxed atmosphere, that he could use as an accusation against Him. Maybe he invited Jesus simply because He was such a popular figure, and Simon could boast to his fellow Pharisees (and anyone else who would listen) that he'd actually had the man in his house. And it would mean that there would be no shortage of people wanting to attend this occasion. Or perhaps he just thought it would be a rather amusing and entertaining thing to do. 'He might even perform a miracle while He's here!' is a thought which could well have crossed Simon's mind. Maybe he even wondered if he should deliberately run out of wine, considering what he'd heard had happened at that wedding in Cana (John 2:1–11)! Little did he know that the occasion was going to backfire on him spectacularly. It was certainly going to be a dinner party Simon would never forget!

Simon must have been delighted when Jesus accepted his invitation (Luke 7:36). However, it's clear that he was determined to keep Jesus 'in his place'; after all, in spite of the fact that He could perform miracles and had the crowds hanging on His every word, He was just a carpenter from Nazareth. Accordingly, Simon instructed his servants that Jesus was to receive none of the courtesies customarily afforded to dinner guests: His feet were not to be washed when He arrived; there was to be no oil put on His head, the mark of an honoured guest; nor was He to be seated at the top end of the table in the places reserved for special guests. Simon himself would not give Jesus a kiss of welcome; nor would he arrange for all the men to line up and kiss Jesus' hands, as would normally happen at the arrival of a rabbi.

Conversation-stopper

Simon must have been congratulating himself on the success of the occasion, when he noticed a woman appear in the doorway carrying a jar. His food must have stuck in his throat and his mouth opened wide as he realised exactly who this woman was: a well-known prostitute of the town (v.37).

It was customary for guests to recline on couches while eating, with their heads nearest the dinner table. They would prop themselves up on one elbow, with their feet sticking out behind them. Imagine Simon's horror when this prostitute made a bee-line for Jesus, came up behind Him, put her jar down, and started sobbing at His feet. What a conversation-stopper! The whole room must have fallen silent, and watched in fascinated disbelief and curiosity as this woman showered her tears on Jesus' feet, wiped them with her dishevelled hair, kissed them repeatedly and poured perfume from her alabaster jar over them (v.38).

What an embarrassing scene this would have been for the host! What could he say? When he did recover his composure, Simon muttered to himself, 'If this man were a prophet, he would know who is touching him and what kind of woman she is – that she is a sinner' (v.39). Was he really thinking: 'This man might claim to be a prophet, but he certainly isn't one. We Pharisees have been right about him all along; he's an impostor'?

Simon was uncharitable, condemnatory, judgmental and 'holier than thou' in his attitude towards this woman. Are we also sometimes guilty of responding in such a way when we see someone we consider disreputable coming to Christ in repentance? Do we support and encourage them in their faith and seek to make them feel welcome in the church – or do we just hope they'll go away?

The two debtors

It seems that Jesus heard Simon's muttering, because Jesus answered him, 'Simon, I have something to tell you'. I try to imagine the tone of voice in Simon's reply, 'Tell me, teacher' (v.40): was it light-hearted, or sarcastic, or intrigued, or faintly amused? Or was Simon expecting Jesus to apologise for the embarrassment His host had been caused by the woman's performance? If so, then he was to be disappointed, because, amazingly, Jesus proceeded to tell him a short story, of all things! Hardly, I imagine, what he was expecting to hear in the circumstances.

The story was about two people who owed a money-lender different amounts: 500 and 50 denarii respectively (v.41). As neither could pay, the money-lender cancelled the debts of them both (v.42). Jesus then delivered the question He had been building up to: 'Now which of them will love him more?' (v.42).

Simon must have thought for a moment. He was probably wondering what this had got to do with anything! Besides which, the answer seemed absurdly obvious – so was there a catch to it?

'In which case,' he may have thought, 'I'd better couch my reply carefully.' So he said, 'I suppose the one who had the bigger debt cancelled'; to which Jesus replied, 'You have judged correctly' (v.43). Simon was probably still wondering why Jesus had told him this story at all. He was to find out soon enough.

You ... she

Simon must have been embarrassed to see Jesus then turn to the woman; but he was about to be embarrassed even more. The next thing he knew, Jesus was asking him, 'Do you see this woman?' (v.44). Simon could see 'this woman' all right; in fact, he was probably sick of the sight of her by now. The nerve of the woman to gatecrash his dinner party and to put on such an appalling, sickening show of emotion! Maybe he even felt jealous, because she had become the centre of attention rather than him.

'But what's He saying now about coming to my house?' Simon must have asked himself with growing incredulity as he heard Jesus' words:

'You did not give me any water for my feet, but she wet my feet with her tears and wiped them with her hair. 'You did not give me a kiss, but this woman, from the time I entered, has not stopped kissing my feet. 'You did not put oil on my head, but she has poured perfume on my feet' (vv.44–46).

I imagine Simon becoming more and more furious as Jesus went through this litany of 'you did not, but she did', and thinking, 'How dare this carpenter from Nazareth compare me, a law-abiding, upright, devout Pharisee, to this woman of the street, this disreputable sinner, this social outcast?' But the coup de grâce was about to hit him right between the eyes: 'Therefore, I tell you, her many sins have been forgiven – for she loved much' (v.47).

Who is this?

It seems likely that the woman's outpouring of love in this extravagant manner was the expression of her joy at being forgiven when she had repented on a previous occasion (v.37).

Jesus confirmed to those gathered at the dinner that her sins had been forgiven, and that it was her faith that had saved her, not the public act of gratitude they had just witnessed (vv.48,50). This really stirred up Simon's guests. 'Who is this who even forgives sins?' they asked each other, perplexed (v.49). Simon may well have heard about Jesus saying 'Your sins are forgiven' before, and must have pondered the implications of Him making such a pronouncement. Indeed, he may have actually been present at the healing of the paralysed man when the issue was debated (see Chapter 7). But it still must have shocked him, and made him wonder how it could be that a woman such as she could receive the grace and forgiveness of God.

Did Simon ever understand that it was because the woman realised her need of Jesus, whereas he didn't; because she had repented of her sin, whereas he hadn't; because she loved Jesus with all her heart, whereas he didn't?

I sometimes wonder if we really and truly appreciate the width of God's mercy to us, the depth of God's love for us, and the size of the debt that we have been forgiven. Are we as grateful to God as the woman was? Is our love for God as extravagant as hers?

Chapter 14

The Legion meet the Lord

The Gadarene demoniac

Mark 5:1–20

Terrified and terrifying

The exiled man lived, or rather existed, about six miles from the town of Gadara near the lake. Near the shore there was a rock wall, out of which had been hollowed a number of caves that were used as tombs. These had become his dwelling place ever since he had been driven out of the town (v.3) – an appropriate abode for such a man, given the Jewish tradition that a tomb was one of the dwelling places of demons. And he had them in abundance; they had possessed him, and turned him into a deranged, demented being, who no longer seemed to have any control over himself.

Not surprisingly his fellow citizens, including his family (v.19), were terrified of him, and didn't know what to do with him. His behaviour in the town had become so outrageous that they decided to throw him out. How he came to be in this state we are not told. It must have taken several of the local men to force him away from human habitation, and to hold him down while they fastened the chains to his wrists and feet in a futile attempt to protect themselves from him (vv.3–4). He was so strong, due to the superhuman strength coming from the demons which possessed him, that 'he tore the chains apart and broke the irons on his feet. No-one was strong enough to subdue him' (v.4). He had become a loathed and fearsome monster.

Alone, desolate and possessed, he must have been a terrifying sight. I imagine him clad only in rags soaked in blood from the deep wounds caused by the chains and the self-inflicted cuts made with sharp stones (v.5); broken chains hanging from his wrists and clinging to his feet; hair flowing, matted and bedraggled; his body dirty and unkempt; night and day running aimlessly up and over the hills that lined the shore, in and out of the tombs, while all the time crying out (v.5), and screaming and moaning unintelligibly. What a tragic sight!

Chains

The demoniac may have been able to break free from the physical chains that bound him, but he was unable to break free from the spiritual chains that kept him in bondage to Satan. Praise God, when we come to Christ, He sets us free from the chains of sin that bind us (John 8:36; Rom. 6:17–18)!

Yet, in my experience, it is possible for us still to be in bondage to Satan. There are all kinds of chains which he will use to restrict us, thereby hindering us from serving God to the full, and being powerful and effective for Him in our daily lives. These chains can affect us mentally, emotionally, physically and spiritually. They include wrong thoughts and attitudes, unhealthy habits, unforgiveness, bitterness, resentment, jealousy, the love of money and possessions, and unrenounced occultic activities.

And I have found that it's so easy to fall into this kind of bondage. It can happen almost without our realising it. But isn't it wonderful to know that through Jesus' death we can be set free, not only from the chains of sin, but also from all the fetters with which Satan would seek to bind us (Luke 4:18)?

Power in the name

Then, suddenly, the demoniac saw a boat approaching the shore from across the other side of the lake. This was not unusual; but his reaction to it was. As soon as the people had disembarked, he found himself running frantically straight towards the man who stood at the head of the group. Maybe, in spite of being possessed, the demoniac somehow realised that this man, whoever He was, could help him – and that's why he ran to Jesus. Or could it have been a case of the demons within him propelling him towards the One to whom they must submit? Whatever the reason, he found himself kneeling in front of Jesus (Mark 5:6), who immediately commanded the demons to come out of him. This provoked the demons so much that the man began to shout 'at the top of his voice' (vv.7–8).

The man found himself yelling, 'What do you want with me, Jesus, Son of the Most High God? Swear to God that you won't torture me!' (v.7). As in the Capernaum synagogue (see Chapter 5), the evil spirit, this time speaking on behalf of all the others, recognised Jesus' true identity, His divinity, and His power and authority. Interestingly, this demon living in Gentile territory actually used the title for God that only Gentiles used (see Dan. 3:26). The superiority of Jesus' power and authority over it was such that the evil spirit was reduced to squirming before Him, pleading not to be tortured.

Although we live in a world that seems to be in the grip of evil, we have no need to fear. God is sovereign: He is in control, and will ultimately deal with evil once and for all (Rev. 20:10). Meanwhile, we can be victorious over anything that Satan brings against us, because Jesus has triumphed on the cross (Rom. 8:31,34–37).

Jesus, by virtue of who He is, had the authority to know the name of the demon so He could exercise his power over it and deal with it directly and effectively. The demon gave his name as 'Legion', saying that there were many of them (v.9). This emphasised, if any further confirmation were needed, what a terrible state this poor man was in. A Roman legion consisted of 6,000 men, and they were notorious for their violence and brutality. Whether the name was an indication of the actual number, or the type of behaviour they caused, is open to debate. What can be said with certainty is that, however great the forces of evil are, Jesus has the power and authority to overcome them – as we have, in and through His name.

A pigtale

The demons repeatedly begged Jesus not to send them 'out of the area' (v.10). They were afraid of being sent into eternal punishment: 'into the Abyss', as Luke puts it (8:31). Instead, they asked Jesus if they could go into the herd of pigs feeding on the nearby hillside (vv.11–12) – another indication that Jesus was in Gentile territory. Jews did not keep pigs: they were 'unclean' animals according to the Law of Moses, and were unfit for human consumption (Lev. 11:7). They weren't even supposed to touch them.

Jesus allowed the demons to go into the pigs, with dramatic results (v.13). I'm sure it wasn't that Jesus didn't care what happened to the pigs. It seems to have been more a case of the demoniac needing to be convinced that the evil spirits had been cast out of him and that he had been delivered from the bondage of Satan.

It's hardly surprising that 'Those tending the pigs ran off' (v.14) after the sights and sounds of what they'd just witnessed! And, human nature being what it is, 'the people went out to see what had happened' (v.14), having no doubt heard the reports given by the herdsmen.

Released and restored

And when the people saw, they couldn't believe their eyes. Mark tells us that there were three aspects to the dramatic transformation of the demoniac that would have been difficult for the people to come to terms with (v.15).

First of all, he was just 'sitting there', whereas they were used to him running all over the place, never still, always on the move;

restless, twitching, panting. Secondly, he was 'dressed', whereas he was normally in various states of undress, clothes torn into rags. Thirdly, he was 'in his right mind', whereas usually he was either yelling at the top of his voice or grunting in an incomprehensible language, cutting himself with stones and behaving in a totally unpredictable manner. And yet, here he was, 'sitting there, dressed and in his right mind' (v.15).

What happened to the demoniac seems to me to be a wonderful picture of each one of us when we accept Christ as our Saviour: we are at peace with God (Rom. 5:1); we are clothed in robes of righteousness (Isa. 61:10); our minds are renewed and our lives are transformed (Rom. 12:2).

A missed opportunity

We might expect that the local inhabitants would have been jumping for joy at what had happened, and praising God for ridding them of this nightmare. Not a bit of it. They just couldn't handle this amazing transformation at all; it blew their minds completely. They were used to the demoniac as he was. They had learnt to cope with his deviance and to accept it as a part of their lives. I imagine them just standing there, gaping, asking themselves: 'What kind of power is this, that can transform a situation like this; that can bring peace into such turmoil; that can deal with such evil?' Even though they had probably heard of Jesus' power already, and some of them may have even seen it at work before (Matt. 4:25), now that it had actually come where they were and dramatically affected their circumstances, they were 'afraid' (Mark 5:15). Not grateful; not thankful; afraid. They didn't know what to think, let alone what to do. Their minds were in total confusion.

In their uncertainty, the people gathered around the herdsmen, who had seen it all unfold before them on the shore below, and got them to go over the events once more (v.16). What happened to the pigs seems to have been the clinching factor. This stranger, they concluded, was obviously a dangerous man to have around. Whatever might He do next? And so 'the people began to plead with Jesus to leave their region' (v.17). They didn't just ask Him politely: they got down on their knees and begged Him to go, so afraid were they.

Whenever Mark uses the word 'frightened' or 'afraid', it always means frightened in a religious or spiritual sense. The Gentiles gathered on that shore realised that something unbelievable and incomprehensible had happened that was outside their control. And that was the source of their fear.

What an opportunity they missed! What further miracles and wonders might they have witnessed had they embraced Jesus and welcomed Him into their villages and towns! But, instead, they allowed their fear of what He might do to dominate their minds, and they missed out on God's blessing as a result. What a tragedy it would be if we were to be guilty of the same kind of thinking in our churches! I wonder if we are?

Plan D

The restored man must have been horrified at the reaction of the townspeople. Seeing Jesus getting ready to leave in the boat, he ran to Him, and 'begged to go with him' (v.18). He obviously wanted to spend his life from now on in the company of Jesus, serving Him, learning more about Him, growing as a disciple. But Jesus had other plans for him.

From the man's point of view, it must have seemed quite clear what Jesus would want him to do; but perhaps he was asking to go with Jesus for the wrong reasons. Maybe I do him an injustice, but what if his real motivation was to escape from this place where, for the rest of his life, he would have to live with the shame of his past hanging over him? I couldn't blame him if it was. The thought of people pointing him out, sniggering behind his back, making rude comments – even avoiding him – might have been too much for him to cope with just at this moment.

Sometimes it may seem obvious what God would have us do. But, before we go ahead and do it, isn't it a good idea to make it a matter of earnest prayer, asking God to confirm it to us in some definite way, so we know that we are not doing it for the wrong reasons? It may be, as in this case, that God in His wisdom has something completely different planned for us: plan D – a Divine plan.

To boldly go

Until this moment, Jesus had been telling those He had healed to keep quiet about what He'd done for them, and not to go around telling everybody (see Chapter 6). But, as He was now among Gentiles, who had no tradition or concept of a coming Messiah, He could allow people to speak quite freely about Him, without concern for the consequences that could ensue had He adopted such an approach back in Galilee and Judea. Obviously, the man would make an extremely effective witness to the power of Jesus, and to the love and mercy of God being extended even to the Gentiles.

I would imagine that the man was rather taken aback when he heard Jesus' Plan D (v.19). His family had probably disowned him long before, although they might have taken him food. Now Jesus was commanding him to go back home and tell them what God had done for him; and how He'd had mercy on him. Not only were they going to hear about the change: they were going to see it before their very eyes. And seeing it would open the way for them to hear about it.

I find it very challenging to reflect on whether people see the difference God has brought about in me, or whether it's barely perceptible in my daily living. Is it attractive and noticeable enough for them to want to hear what's happened in my life and to desire the same experience of God for themselves? And, so often, as with the ex-demoniac, our witnessing begins at home, which can be the most difficult place.

When the opportunity arises, do I take advantage of it and speak out boldly? I wonder if we dare pray this prayer: 'Lord, give me an opportunity today to speak to someone about You.'

Let's get personal

I'm always impressed by the man's obedience (v.20). He must have been very disappointed to find that Jesus was not going to allow his request. Yet he didn't make the sort of excuses that we are all aware of, and often use, as to why we can't possibly go and tell. And he had more reason than most to make excuses, particularly when we bear in mind the situation he was going to have to face in the community. Nor did he need to attend a host of seminars and evangelism training courses before he could successfully communicate the gospel to people. It was a simple matter of personal testimony: 'tell them how much the Lord has done for you, and how he has had mercy on you' (v.19). I still believe that the most effective resource for effective evangelism is the personal testimony of what God has done for us, how He has had mercy on us, and how our lives have been transformed as a result.

And, because of the man's obedience, the Gentiles of that region heard of the power and mercy of God, and 'were amazed' (v.20). And I don't doubt that the result of their amazement was that many were brought into the kingdom of God and, in due course, became part of the Early Church.

May God help us all to have the same enthusiasm as this man for sharing our personal testimony with others, despite the difficulties we may encounter.

Chapter 15

A Touching Encounter

A woman who touched Jesus

Mark 5:22–34

Alone and afflicted

The woman must have been at her wits' end. I imagine her sitting there, with her head in her hands, sobbing. For the past twelve years she had been 'subject to bleeding' (v.25). What was actually wrong with her isn't clear. It may have been a menstrual problem that had become a constant haemorrhage, leaving her weak and exhausted. According to the Jewish Law, this would make her ritually unclean: an outcast, an untouchable, rather like the leper. This meant that she was not allowed to worship as one of God's chosen people (Lev. 15:25–33).

And if that wasn't enough to put up with, she would also have been shunned by the community, because anyone touching her would have made themselves unclean (Lev. 15:27). Her existence would therefore have been one of miserable isolation.

From riches to rags

During that period of twelve years, she had consulted many doctors, but all to no avail (Mark 5:26). Perhaps it wouldn't have been so bad if there had been some improvement; but in fact she was only getting worse. And now to cap it all, her money had run out, so she couldn't pay for any more consultations.

She must have been quite well off to start with, otherwise she wouldn't have been able to afford the cost of consultations for twelve years. But now she was destitute. This must have been particularly difficult for her to come to terms with, bearing in mind her likely background and status in society. She may even have been thrown out by her family. This woman of independent means was now reduced to being dependent on the means and charity of others. There was no benefits system in place to come to her aid. She had become the sort of person she used to despise. What a bitter pill for her to have to swallow: far more difficult than the ones the doctors had given her.

Resourceless but resourceful

She had reached the end of her resources. Then she heard about Jesus (v.27), and a bold thought formed in her mind (v.28). It was a thought that was full of faith: she was in no doubt that healing would be hers. She had probably heard that Jesus had touched many people as they came to Him for healing. But she didn't want to approach Him in that way, maybe because she was afraid that some people in the crowd would recognise her if she drew attention to herself publicly.

In my experience, fear can so often prevent us from approaching God: fear that God might be angry with us for what we have done or not done; fear of what might happen, or of what might be required of us; fear of what other people might think of us, or say about us; all kinds of fears. When we feel like that, it's good to remind ourselves that God is our loving Father, who longs for us to come to Him, and doesn't want fear to hold us back.

It may be that she didn't want to ask Jesus to make Himself unclean by touching her, even though she may have known that

He had touched a leper. Sometimes we may feel that the very nature of our problem keeps us from God. Isn't it wonderful to know that there is no problem that God is not ready and willing to help with – no matter what our own misgivings may be?

Whatever the reason, she convinced herself that if healing came to those whom Jesus touched, why shouldn't it happen to those who touched Jesus? I imagine her purposefully excusing her way through the crowd to get to the front, at the same time working her way round so that she was directly behind Jesus. Or maybe not quite to the front: just close enough to enable her to stretch out her arm through the front row to touch Jesus' cloak (v.27) and then melt away into the distance.

A ridiculous question

The effect was immediate. The power of God went through her body: the symptoms disappeared, and she was convinced that the cause of the problem had been dealt with too (v.29). This miracle is unique because the woman was cured without Jesus' knowing about her being there. But Jesus did know that someone had touched His cloak in faith, because He felt power go out of Him (v.30). The supernatural power of God within Jesus responded to the touch of this woman's faith.

Was the woman rooted to the spot with the thrill of what had happened to her? Or was she trying in vain to push her way out of the crowd that jostled and heaved around her? Whatever the case, she was suddenly aware that Jesus had stopped and 'turned around in the crowd' (v.30), facing in her direction. The crowd had stopped too, and had probably fallen silent, wondering what was going on. Then she heard Jesus asking a question which must have terrified her and shaken her to the core: 'Who touched my clothes?' (v.30).

'He knows … I don't know how, but He knows! What do I do now?' she must have thought to herself in panic. Meanwhile, she heard the disciples voicing what the crowd must have all been thinking about such an apparently ridiculous question (v.31). There were so many people jostling around and brushing up against Jesus that hundreds must have touched Him. To their surprise, but probably not to the woman's, Jesus persisted by saying, 'Someone touched me; I know that power has gone out from me' (Luke 8:46). Jesus kept looking around to see who had done it (Mark 5:32), with the woman no doubt trying to avoid His eye.

Jesus made such an issue out of this because He was determined that there would be no misunderstanding here. He wanted to make it quite clear that He was not wearing some kind of magic cloak, as some of the wonder-workers of the day claimed to do. Jesus wanted to emphasise the fact that it was the faith of the woman that had brought about her cure, not the fact that she had touched His clothes. That action had merely been a means of expressing her faith.

Confession of faith

By this time, the woman realised that she had no alternative but to confess, and she did so in fear and trembling (v.33). But to her surprise, Jesus did not speak words of anger, but words of peace. He called her 'Daughter' (v.34), in the same way that He called the paralysed man 'Son' (Mark 2:5; see Chapter 7), to reassure her that she had been restored as one of God's chosen people and accepted into His family. With words that must have flooded her being with joy, Jesus confirmed to her that she had been fully cured of her problem. At the same time He made it quite clear, both to the woman herself and to the whole crowd, that it was her faith alone that had caused her to be healed (v.34).

Isn't it comforting and reassuring to know that when we come to Jesus, we will not be greeted with words of anger, condemnation and judgment, but rather with words of peace, love and forgiveness?

Chapter 16

Death of a Daughter

Jairus

Mark 5:21–24,35–43

Do you see what I see?

The crowd in Capernaum could hardly believe their eyes. Wasn't that Jairus, one of the rulers of the local synagogue, pushing his way through their midst towards Jesus? They must have thought he'd come to challenge Jesus on a point of law. But no! Jairus didn't look like a man who was intent on a discussion: the expression on his face said that much, and there were tears in his eyes. And now he was prostrating himself at Jesus' feet. Surely it wasn't happening: the ruler of the synagogue flat on his face before Jesus? What was going on?

Their silent question was soon answered, as the prostrate ruler looked up into the face of Jesus and pleaded 'earnestly' with Him, saying, 'My little daughter is dying' (v.23). Apparently, she was his only daughter, and was twelve years old (Luke 8:42). I can hear the gasps all round the quietened crowd. 'Please come and put your hands on her so that she will be healed and live' (v.23), he asked.

The measure of the ruler

I'm always impressed by Jairus's humility, courage and faith. A man of status in the community, he overcame both his pride and his fear of what others would think of him and say about him, and publicly humiliated himself before this teacher from Nazareth. That is the measure of the man.

I wonder how well we measure up against the yardstick of humility? Are we sometimes too proud to come to God, considering it a reflection on our lack of self-sufficiency? Sadly, God can do nothing for us, or with us for that matter, until we acknowledge our need of Him – however humbling an experience that may be.

Faith at last

True, Jairus was driven by desperation but, nevertheless, what he did took enormous courage for a synagogue ruler, as it was tantamount to treason. And what faith he had. Presumably it stemmed from what he had seen on a previous Sabbath in his very own synagogue, when Jesus had cast an evil spirit out of a member of his congregation (see Chapter 5): not something you'd be likely to forget in a hurry.

Until now, Jesus had been lamenting the lack of faith among the Jews (Luke 7:9). Here at last, though from a most unexpected source, was someone from among His own people who had no doubt that Jesus was able to perform a miracle and heal his daughter. Even though Jesus probably had a strong case for regarding this synagogue ruler as an enemy, He didn't reject him and send him packing. His response to Jairus's faith was immediate. He willingly went with him, accompanied, not surprisingly, by a 'large crowd' who 'pressed around him' (Mark 5:24).

Delay on the way

How must Jairus have felt when Jesus stopped to deal with the sick woman on the way? (vv.25–34; see Chapter 15). Frustration seems an inadequate word to describe the emotions he must have been experiencing. His daughter was literally dying; every second was vital; and the answer to his prayers was standing there asking, 'Who touched my clothes?' and refusing to take another step until the matter was sorted out. Or maybe I do Jairus an injustice. Perhaps he had such faith in Jesus, that getting home as quickly as possible was of no concern to him whatever.

And then Jairus saw some men he recognised coming from the direction of his house and he instinctively knew it was bad news. And he was right. These men certainly didn't spare his feelings as they announced in a cold, matter of fact way: 'Your daughter is dead. Why bother the teacher any more?' (v.35). It was that sort of moment when your heart sinks, and you have that awful feeling in the pit of your stomach. The bottom had just fallen out of his world – and he must have had difficulty holding back his emotions.

Bother to bother

But then Jairus heard Jesus speaking directly to him for the first time, right into the depths of his despair. It seems that Jesus knew exactly how Jairus was feeling and what was going through his mind. Ignoring what the messengers had said, Jesus spoke wonderful yet challenging words to Jairus: 'Don't be afraid; just believe, and she will be healed' (Luke 8:50). Once again, we are reminded how crucial it is for us to allow faith to conquer fear, and to believe that God is able to do the impossible (Eph. 3:20).

In my experience, it's so easy in times of deep despair or great difficulty to adopt the human perspective of the messengers and come to the conclusion that it's not worth bothering God about the situation any more. But I believe God wants us to bother Him, because that shows we have the faith to believe He is able to do something about this apparently impossible situation: and that He not only can, but will.

Rent-a-mourner

Interestingly, Jesus doesn't seem to have waited for any confirmation from Jairus that his faith was undiminished, even though He had now required him to move from a position of believing for the difficult to believing for the impossible. Jesus didn't engage him in conversation, as He did the father of the boy with the evil spirit (see Chapter 19), in order to determine the depth of his faith. He just set off for Jairus's house.

On arrival, Jairus found that his wife had gone ahead and hired professional mourners to weep and wail outside the house (Mark 5:38) – a mark of the wealth of the family. Jairus must have been astonished to hear Jesus tell the mourners quite clearly that 'The child is not dead but asleep' (v.39): in other words, she was not permanently dead. The reaction of the mourners to what Jesus had said was to laugh out loud (v.40). They knew death when they saw it! Jesus ushered the mourners outside, and then turned to Jairus and his wife. Without saying a word, He took them, along with Peter, James and John, into the room where the dead girl lay (vv.37,40). I imagine Jesus asking Jairus's wife where the girl was, then taking them both by the arm, and escorting them into the room.

Getting to grips

I try to picture this moving scene: Jairus and his wife, clinging to each other for mutual comfort and support, tears running down their cheeks, scarcely daring to breathe; their beloved daughter, their only child, lying motionless; Peter, James and John hovering in the background, perhaps remembering what had happened recently on the road outside Nain (see Chapter 12); Jesus approaching the bed upon which rested the body of the girl; bending over the small figure, extending His arm towards her, taking her tiny hand in His; then, while 'gripping her [firmly] by the hand' (v.41, Amplified), gently speaking these words to her: '*Talitha koum!*' (v.41).

These were the actual Aramaic words that Jesus used. The word translated by Mark as 'Little girl' has a very affectionate tone to it, rather like calling a child a 'lamb'. The phrase 'get up' (v.41) actually means 'Arise from the sleep of death!' Jesus just spoke the word, and even death had to release its grip. The girl responded to this command with astonishing alacrity: 'Immediately the girl stood up and walked around' (v.42). I would love to have seen the expression on the faces of her stunned parents!

Practical and impractical

But before the inevitable family celebrations began, Jesus had a couple of things to say to Jairus and his wife. Firstly, Jesus gave them 'strict orders not to let anyone know about this' (v.43), for the same reasons He had given similar instructions to the leper (see Chapter 6). On both occasions, such a command does seem to have been impractical to say the least.

In direct contrast, the second command was surprisingly practical: 'give her something to eat' (v.43). Jairus and his wife must have been impressed by Jesus' concern for the girl's physical welfare. Jesus knew she hadn't had a meal for some time and would, therefore, be feeling very weak. Perhaps Jesus mentioned it because in the euphoria of the moment, such practical considerations may have been overlooked by her parents. And isn't this another lovely example of Jesus' care for, and attention to, the detail of our lives.

Chapter 17

The Fox

Herod Antipas

Mark 6:14–29
(Other bit part players appearing: Herodias; Salome)

Adulterous

The words of John the Baptist must have kept ringing in the ears of Herod Antipas, and been hard for him to put out of his mind: 'It is not lawful for you to have your brother's wife' (v.18). It seems that John had not only confronted him personally on this issue, but was voicing the deep disgust and offence felt by the Jews concerning the adulterous relationship between Antipas and Herodias by condemning it publicly. Herodias was getting so angry about this that she wanted John the Baptist dead (v.19), and no doubt bent Antipas's ear about the matter at every opportunity.

It seems that Antipas and Herodias had met, but probably not for the first time, while Antipas was on a visit to Rome, where he was the guest of his half-brother, Philip – not to be confused with another half-brother, also called Philip, who ruled Iturea and Traconitis, which lay to the north of Galilee. Herodias was niece to both of them, but had married her uncle Philip; Antipas had probably attended the wedding. Antipas was married to the daughter of Aretas IV, an Arabian king. However, his marriage was not working out and, while in Rome, he began an affair with Herodias, which resulted in him divorcing his wife and taking the willing Herodias back to Galilee with him. Such a relationship was contrary to the Law of Moses (Lev. 18:16; 20:21).

The Herods

It is hard to find a good word to say about Herod Antipas. A son of Herod the Great (see Chapter 2), he was self-centred, dissolute, superstitious and without principles – in other words, a typical Herod. Jesus referred to him as 'that fox' (Luke 13:32), which spoke of the cunning and craftiness that characterised the Herods. Antipas basked in the luxurious lifestyle, but above all he had an abiding obsession to be acknowledged as a king by the Romans.

The Herods were descended from Esau, the brother of Jacob, and therefore had a natural antipathy to Jacob's descendants, the Jews (Gen. 25:19ff), even though there was a splash of Jewish blood in their veins. They played at following the Jewish religion when it helped to ingratiate them in the eyes of their subjects, or furthered their ambitions for more wealth and power.

Antipas was appointed ruler of Galilee and Perea by the Romans, and ruled from 4 BC to AD 39. His title was 'Tetrarch', which sounds very grand, but actually means that he ruled over 'the fourth part of the kingdom', which had been divided up by the Romans among the sons of Herod the Great. His brother, Archelaus, was appointed ruler of Judea, but he did such a bad job that the Romans deposed him in AD 6, replacing him with a Roman governor; by the time of Jesus' ministry, this was Pontius Pilate.

Prison visitor

To Herodias's undoubted displeasure, Antipas was not prepared to put John the Baptist to death, but decided to throw him into prison to silence him (Mark 6:17). In spite of John's public outbursts against him, Antipas 'feared John and protected him, knowing him to be a righteous and holy man' (v.20). It seems that John held a particular fascination for Antipas, and that he went to see his accuser in his prison cell, because 'he liked to listen to him' (v.20). I wonder what Herodias made of this?

What did John say to Antipas during those visits that left him 'greatly puzzled' (v.20)? Presumably, John told Antipas to repent of his sinful ways, which is why Antipas might have been 'puzzled', because he had not broken Roman law. It is doubtful whether either morality or religion meant anything to Antipas, in which case he would not have been at all troubled by John's assertion that he had broken God's law. Did they have a conversation and argue; and if so, I wonder whether John thundered at him or spoke gently to him? Or did Antipas just listen and say nothing? Perhaps Antipas simply found John's rhetoric entertaining; or maybe Antipas liked him because he knew John would always tell him the truth.

Dance of death

Meanwhile, Herodias would certainly have been keeping up the pressure on Antipas to put John the Baptist to death. I imagine that this would have led to shouting matches in the palace and a tense atmosphere between them, as Herodias seems to have been the kind of woman who liked to get her own way. But, on this issue, Antipas showed no sign of relenting. Besides his liking for John, this reluctance to give in to Herodias's demand was probably because Antipas did not wish to increase his unpopularity with his subjects by killing a person whom everyone regarded as a prophet and holy man. But then Herodias had a brainwave. An 'opportune time' (v.21) had presented itself.

It was Antipas's birthday, and he decided to throw a banquet 'for his high officials and military commanders and the leading men of Galilee' (v.21). Anybody who was anybody was there. This would have been one of the highlights of the social calendar; and, knowing Antipas as well as she did, Herodias planned to use the occasion to her benefit.

Royal feasts such as this were renowned for their lavishness and catered for every kind of pleasure. Herodias connived with her daughter to take advantage of the character of Antipas. The girl, whom the Jewish historian Josephus names as Salome, was Herodias's daughter by her first marriage. Salome performed a lascivious dance before the assembled throng (v.22), to great acclaim. Herodias knew that Salome would have Antipas drooling at the mouth after such a performance, and it seems she wasn't wrong. As Herodias had anticipated, Antipas, in his aroused and intoxicated state, made a rash offer on oath to the girl: 'Ask me for anything you want, and I'll give it to you … up to half my kingdom' (vv.22–23).

Prompted by her mother (v.24), Salome demanded, 'I want you to give me right now the head of John the Baptist on a platter' (v.25). At that moment, the realisation must have slowly dawned on Antipas that he had been well and truly duped. I try to imagine the look of shock-horror that must have appeared on his face – and the smirk of self-satisfied pleasure on the face of Herodias as she stood waiting in the wings.

Macabre sight

Although he was 'greatly distressed', Antipas knew he couldn't retract his promise and admit to his guests that he had been duped; to have done so would have meant him losing face as well as losing the respect of all present (v.26). 'So he immediately sent an executioner with orders to bring John's head. The man went, beheaded John in the prison, and brought back his head on a platter. He presented it to the girl, and she gave it to her mother' (vv.27–28).

What a macabre sight that must have been! How Antipas must have squirmed as the head of the man he respected, and had determined to protect, passed before his eyes, the blood no doubt still dripping from the neck. At last Herodias had her gruesome prize. Antipas allowed John's disciples to take the body away, and it was placed in a tomb (v.29).

When it came to the crunch, Antipas valued his pride more than doing what he knew to be right. When we are put under pressure by the world, may God help us and strengthen us to do what is right – even if that means losing face or backing down. And is this not also a warning to us to be very careful not to find ourselves in a position where our words or actions compromise our integrity by us behaving inappropriately, thus letting down both God and the gospel witness we represent?

Guilty conscience

It seems that this incident continued to trouble Antipas because, when he heard about what Jesus was doing, he immediately jumped to the conclusion that 'John, the man I beheaded, has been raised from the dead!' (v.16). He was obviously nursing a guilty conscience. But, amazingly – or perhaps not, bearing in mind the Herods' notoriously unstable mentality – Antipas seems to have totally ignored his conscience, and to have conspired to kill Jesus (13:31)!

When Jesus received reports that Antipas wanted to kill Him, He replied, 'Go tell that fox, "I will drive out demons and heal people today and tomorrow, and on the third day I will reach my goal"' (Luke 13:32). Interestingly, it would seem that Jesus' comments were not just aimed at Antipas either, because the word used for 'fox' is feminine: in other words, 'Go tell that vixen ...'. And who else could the 'vixen' have been other than Herodias, the power behind the throne?

Intrigued

When Jesus' words were reported back to Antipas, he must have been intrigued, because Luke tells us that Antipas had been trying to see Jesus (Luke 9:7–9). Imagine his delight, then, when Pontius Pilate actually sent Jesus to him (Luke 23:7–8). He probably didn't realise that Pilate had done this in an effort to fob off the decision about what to do with Jesus on to him. It seems that by now Antipas had become obsessed with Jesus' miracles, and was hoping to see Him perform one (23:8). He would be disappointed, not only on that score, but by the fact that Jesus refused to answer any of his questions (23:9). Perhaps Antipas contrasted this interview with his visits to John the Baptist, who had always had plenty to say to him! In the end, Antipas seems to have got fed up with Jesus, because he resorted to ridicule and mockery, along with his soldiers, before dressing Jesus in 'an elegant robe' and sending Him back to Pilate (23:11).

Antipas had the unique opportunity of personally spending time with both John the Baptist and Jesus; and yet he remained unchanged by either experience. Does the time we spend with Jesus in our daily lives, and worshipping and learning about Him in church, bear the fruit that it should? Are we changed by these experiences, becoming more like Christ as a result? Or, like Antipas, do we remain unchanged?

Exiled

Interestingly, it seems that Antipas had a childhood friend called Manaen, who did become a believer, and is listed as one of the prophets and teachers in the church at Antioch (Acts 13:1). As for Antipas himself, what became of him? He disappears from the pages of Scripture as he dispatches Jesus back to Pilate. But the chronicles of the time do tell us what happened to him.

In AD 36, the Arabian king Aretas, still seething at the way Antipas had treated his daughter, declared war on him. The forces of Antipas were decimated, and, according to Josephus, many people regarded the massacre as God's retribution on Antipas for the beheading of John the Baptist.

The following year, Agrippa, the brother of Herodias, was made ruler of Judea by his friend the new Emperor Gaius (Caligula), who conferred on him the title of King Agrippa I. (This was the same Agrippa who would kill James Zebedee, put Peter in prison, and be struck down by an angel (Acts 12:1–24)). On hearing this, Herodias persuaded Antipas to go to Rome and petition the Emperor to grant him similar status as a king. But when he arrived in Rome to put his case to the Emperor in person, Antipas was no doubt astonished to find himself being accused of corruption, incompetence, and of plotting against the new Emperor by none other than his brother-in-law and nephew, Agrippa! Antipas would have felt particularly sore about this, because for several years Agrippa had lived in the city of Tiberias under his patronage, until the two of them had quarrelled in AD 36. This was obviously a case of revenge! How typical of the soap opera that was the Herods!

In the end, Antipas was thrown out of office by Agrippa's friend, the Emperor. Antipas was banished to Gaul in AD 39 and then to Spain, where he died in exile. Herodias must have loved Antipas, because she chose to go with him into exile rather than accept an attractive offer from the Emperor, made to her because she was his friend Agrippa's sister. As for Salome, believe it or not, she married her great-uncle Philip the Tetrarch, who ruled Iturea and Traconitis. I wonder how long that lasted!

Antipas is remembered as an ineffective ruler, who was more concerned with his own pleasure and status than anything else. He also has the dubious distinction of being remembered as the man who put to death one of the greatest Jewish prophets and the herald of the Messiah, John the Baptist. Will we be remembered for being self-centred like Antipas, or God-centred like John the Baptist?

Chapter 18

A Desperately Seeking Mother

A Canaanite woman

Matthew 15:21–28

Jesus is Lord

She lived in the vicinity of Tyre (v.22), a coastal city of Phoenicia, which lay to the north-west of Palestine. It seems that news of Jesus' miracles had reached Tyre, and there were rumours that Jesus Himself was on His way to the city (v.21). This news must have caused hope to well up within the woman, because she had a problem. She would have undoubtedly tried to deal with this problem by every means available to her, but it seems that none of the measures taken had proved to be the slightest bit successful. Indeed, the problem was just getting worse by the day. It must have caused her heart-rending anguish, because the problem was not with herself – it was with her dearly-beloved daughter, who was possessed by demons (v.22)

This sorely distressed mother had obviously decided that seeking out Jesus was her only hope. And when she found Him, she approached Him, not subtly or sensitively, but desperately, 'crying out, "Lord, Son of David, have mercy on me!"' (v.22). A Gentile she may have been (v.22), but she recognised and acknowledged both the Lordship and Messiahship of Jesus in words to be echoed later by Bartimaeus (see Chapter 23).

It is interesting that throughout their encounter the woman called Jesus 'Lord' (vv.22,25,27). The Greek word translated 'Lord' is 'Kyrios', meaning someone in authority. Like the Roman centurion (see Chapter 11), she realised that Jesus had the authority to deal with her daughter's condition and that He is in control of every situation. Both these Gentiles had an insight into who Jesus is which the Jews had failed to grasp. And is it not important in the pluralistic society in which we live to reaffirm clearly and unequivocally who Jesus is, the Son of the living God, rather than allowing Him to be reduced to the level of the founders of other religions and philosophies?

An anguished cry

Imagine the agony of this mother with a daughter who was 'suffering terribly from demon-possession' (v.22). She was obviously too embarrassed by her to actually bring her to Jesus. Her daughter was probably disruptive, even destructive, and her behaviour was a problem in society. It is quite possible that her husband had left her because of it, as it was unusual in those days for a woman to approach a rabbi. Usually it was the father, as in the case of Jairus's daughter and the epileptic boy (see Chapters 16 and 19). Yet, in spite of the fact that the situation must have been driving her to distraction, she had not rejected her daughter, but continued to love her to the point of desperately seeking help for her.

Few of us have experienced agony like that of this mother, but many of us have already coped, or will in the future have to cope, with heartbreaking situations concerning our own children. If there is one thing I have learnt over the years it is the importance of keeping on loving them, which is very tough going when we don't approve of what's happening or find it difficult to cope with. So often it would be much easier to reject them, and to live as if they don't exist. But should we not be willing to follow the example of the father in the Parable of the Lost Son (Luke 15:11–32), who never gave up hoping, never gave up loving and, I'm sure, never gave up praying?

Persistence pays

Jesus' response to this Canaanite woman is rather surprising: He gave her no encouragement at all. In fact, 'Jesus did not answer a word' (v.23). This is the only time we see this in the whole of His ministry. Usually He encouraged people: here He seemed to be discouraging her. Actually, I think He was paying her a great compliment. He perceived the depth of her faith, but He wanted everyone else to see it too. He knew that her faith was so sure that she would not be put off, but would persist until she was answered. In the end, Jesus complimented her publicly (v.28).

And how persistent she was! Rather than being put off by Jesus' attitude, and thinking 'This is a complete waste of time', she just wouldn't go away. Desperation and faith kept her there. The disciples got sick to the back teeth of her. So much so that they 'came to him and urged him, "Send her away, for she keeps crying out after us"' (v.23). Sometimes our faith is tested too. God just doesn't seem to be responding. How do we react? Do we ask just the once and then give up, or do we persist, as Jesus taught us to (Matt. 7:7; Luke 18:1–8)?

Worthy of worship

When Jesus did finally speak, it was to the disciples, and not to her, although He wanted her to hear and understand the significance of what He was saying (Matt. 15:24). Jesus was making it quite clear that His mission was to the people of Israel, the Jews, and not initially to the Gentiles. This did not mean that Jesus would not respond to Gentiles who had faith in Him, but that the gospel in all its fullness would not be made available to them until after His ascension (Matt. 28:16–20). Even though Jesus seemed to be ignoring her, still the woman was not put off. Her response was not doubt, or even huffiness, but remarkably it was worship: 'The woman came and knelt before him' (15:25). How impressive is that!

Indeed, I find it very challenging too. In the midst of her desperation and distress, with her petition unanswered, she still came to worship. I wonder how often our worship, or lack of it, is determined by our situation or circumstances? For me, it is too often. It's so easy to be influenced by how we are feeling, by whether our prayers have been answered or not, or by the circumstances we find ourselves in. But isn't God worthy of our worship, no matter whatever else may be happening or not happening (Hab. 3:17–18; 1 Thess. 5:18)?

The day of the dog

She pleaded with Jesus once again: 'Lord, help me!' (v.25); and, at last, Jesus spoke directly to her. His reply can't have been at all what she was hoping for: 'It is not right to take the children's bread and toss it to their dogs' (v.26). The Jews called themselves the 'children of God' and often referred to the Gentiles as 'dogs'. Some say this was because, in the opinion of the Jews, dogs were just as likely to receive God's blessing as these pagan Gentiles. Jesus was making the point that the gospel and all its blessings were first and foremost for the Jews, not the Gentiles. Interestingly, Jesus softened the imagery by using the word for 'pet dogs', perhaps to show that the Gentiles were not as far from God's blessing as the Jews thought them to be.

For a moment, the woman must have wondered what Jesus was on about. But then the penny dropped, as she remembered that Jews spoke of Gentiles as 'dogs'. Showing a remarkable calmness and reasoning, considering how emotional she must have been feeling, the woman cleverly extended the imagery Jesus had used. She clearly understood what Jesus was saying, and pointed out that the dogs took advantage of whatever came their way (v.27). In other words she was saying: 'Your priority may be the Jews, but You've come my way, Lord Jesus, and I'm taking advantage of that on behalf of my daughter.'

And now, for the first time, Jesus spoke words of commendation and encouragement as He pronounced healing for her daughter (v.28). What music those words must have been to her ears! She took Jesus at His word, went home expecting a miracle and found that one had taken place. We can only imagine the transformation that occurred in her household on that day when the 'bread' became food for the 'dog'.

Bottom of the class

In those days, women were regarded as second-class citizens. A Gentile woman, who didn't even worship the one true God, was about as low as you could get in Jewish eyes. And yet, Jesus had time for her.

Isn't it wonderful to know that Jesus despises no one? Whoever we are, whatever our background or circumstances, however other people may regard us are of no significance in the eyes of God. Jesus welcomes us, loves us, and has time for us. We are all equal in God's sight (Rom. 10:12; Gal. 3:28).

Unfortunately, the outworking of this principle was not always evident in the Early Church (James 2:1–4); but is the situation any better now? How are we reaching out to those who are poor, helpless, underprivileged and marginalised in our society? May God open our eyes to the opportunities that surround us.

Chapter 19

Father and Son

The father of a boy with an evil spirit

Mark 9:14–29

Disappointed

Like the Canaanite woman in the previous chapter, this man had a child who was possessed by an evil spirit. He too had decided that Jesus was his only hope of getting the problem sorted. But when he arrived at where he thought Jesus was, he found that He had gone (see Mark 9:2), although some of Jesus' disciples were still there.

Though he must have been deeply disappointed that Jesus wasn't around, he was not deterred. After all, hadn't he heard that the disciples themselves had been successfully driving out demons (Mark 6:13)? Surely they would be able to do the same for his son, whom he had brought along with him. But the disciples proved to be unable to cast the demon out of the boy, and had turned aside to argue with some teachers of the law (9:14), leaving the father just standing there, even more disappointed, wondering what to do next.

Delighted

The father must have been delighted when Jesus suddenly appeared on the scene. So were the crowd that had gathered: 'they were overwhelmed with wonder and ran to greet him' (v.15). Spotting the teachers of the law in the crowd, Jesus asked His disciples what they were arguing with them about (vv.14,16). It seems that the disciples' failure to cast the demon out of the boy had been the subject of the debate, because his father answered Jesus' question, and gave Him a vivid description of his son's symptoms and what he considered to be the cause (vv.17–18).

The details he gave would suggest that the boy was subject to epileptic fits. This can be frightening enough today, when we know what's going on. So it is hardly surprising that in Jesus' day they believed that these fits were the attacks of an especially vicious demon. Jesus' subsequent actions show that it certainly was so in this case, but in my opinion it would be a mistake to draw the inference from this that all epilepsy is caused by demon possession.

The father certainly didn't spare the disciples' blushes: 'I asked your disciples to drive out the spirit, but they could not' (v.18). Jesus had given His disciples the authority to cast out demons (Mark 3:15), and they had successfully done this when sent out on a mission (6:13). But not this time. They were obviously puzzled by this, because later on in private they asked Jesus: 'Why couldn't we drive it out?' (9:28).

Corporate faith

The father may well have been expecting words of consolation and encouragement from Jesus; but, instead, Jesus turned away from him and addressed the crowd very severely. He described them as an 'unbelieving generation' (9:19), speaking in the same tone as God had used many times in the past as He criticised his people through the prophets for not putting their trust in Him (Jer. 5:23).

It seems that, for Jesus, the healing of the boy was not just a matter between Him and the father, although that was a very important aspect, as we shall see. Jesus was also looking for faith in the crowd – and He didn't find it. On many occasions we see the importance Jesus attaches to corporate faith.

Do we leave the task of praying for those needing healing of any kind to others, such as the leaders of the church? Certainly, they have a vital role to play (James 5:14), but so, I believe, do the rest of us. In my experience, the power of God to heal is wonderfully released as God's people lift up His name in praise and worship, and join their faith together to pray for the sick and needy. Does God see such corporate faith in the crowd that is our church?

What didn't happen next

When Jesus commanded the boy to be brought to Him, another fit immediately ensued (Mark 9:19–20). Again, it's as though evil cannot help but manifest itself in the presence of God (see Chapter 5).

I'm always surprised, amazed even, at what happened next: or, more accurately, what didn't happen next. Instead of getting right on with the business of dealing with the evil spirit, as I imagine the father would have expected Him to do, Jesus engaged him in conversation, seemingly ignoring the plight of the boy. As he spoke with Jesus, I imagine the father having one eye on his distressed son writhing around on the ground, and wondering when Jesus was going to do something about it.

It appears that Jesus wasn't satisfied with the fact that the father had brought his son for healing; He felt it was important to probe more deeply into the father's thinking. It seems to me that this was for the father's benefit, not His; Jesus already knew where the father was coming from.

Crucial conversation

So Jesus conversationally asked him: 'How long has he been like this?' (v.21). The father explained that this had been happening since childhood, and with dangerous consequences at times. But it was the next clause he used that was the one Jesus had been waiting for: '... if you can do anything ...' (v.22). Jesus picked it up immediately, and quoted it straight back at him: 'If you can?' (v.23). Was there a trace of shocked surprise in Jesus' voice as He said these words? I certainly can't imagine His tone of voice being an indignant one; rather one of gentle firmness that is characteristic of Jesus on so many occasions during His ministry.

It wasn't a question of whether Jesus had the power to heal the son: it was a question of whether the father had the faith to believe that Jesus had the power to heal his son. Jesus' compassion for the man was such that he was determined to strengthen his shaky faith and give him solid grounds for putting his complete trust in Him. So He continued with these mind-blowing words: 'Everything is possible for him who believes' (v.23).

What an encouraging statement that is for us all! Everything is possible because we have an almighty God who can do absolutely anything. When we pray, do we have that assurance fixed firmly in our minds, setting no limits on what God can do, and not doubting for one moment that God is able and willing to deal with that situation?

Rapid response

Thus encouraged by Jesus, the father's response was immediate. All the years of pent-up emotion and anguish, due to his son's condition, came pouring out of him in this exclamation of faith, which was what Jesus had been waiting to hear. The Amplified Bible beautifully captures the father's passionate entreaty: 'At once the father of the boy gave [an eager, piercing, inarticulate] cry *with tears*, and he said, Lord, I believe! [Constantly] help my weakness of faith!' (v.24).

As a parent, my heart goes out to him. He was desperate that any unbelief on his part should not prevent his son from being healed. He wanted him to be made whole more than anything else in the whole world. How often do those of us who are parents wish we could take the pain rather than see our children suffering? We cannot. But what we can do is to ask God to strengthen our faith and, in an echo of the father's words, to help us 'overcome

[our] unbelief', such that we keep believing for a miracle at the hands of the God for whom everything is possible.

The personal touch

This father was about to see his prayer dramatically answered: as Jesus proceeded in His customary way to deal with the evil spirit that was causing the fits, by just speaking the word (vv.25–26). Along with many in the crowd, the father must have thought that his son was dead, as the spirit exited the boy's body with a most violent exhibition, leaving him lying on the ground 'like a corpse' (v.26). His heart must have been in his mouth; but he was about to see the personal touch of Jesus.

Even though Jesus knew that the boy wasn't dead, He didn't just walk away and leave him to recover. He went over to the boy, and 'took him by the hand and lifted him to his feet, and he stood up' (v.27).

What a wonderful picture that is of God's loving care and compassion for each one of us! We can only imagine the father's unconfined joy as he gathered his son in his arms and as the realisation dawned on him that the boy would never suffer in that way again.

Chapter 20

No Condemnation

The adulterous woman

John 8:2–11

Caught in the act

She must have realised that what she was doing was wrong. Adultery was forbidden by the seventh commandment (Exod. 20:14); and yet it seems the temptation was too strong for the pair of them to resist. Then, suddenly, there were men rushing into the house, dragging her outside, and marching her down the street. I imagine her struggling with them, screaming, trying to scratch and kick them as they pulled her along, but to no avail. Among them she would have recognised some Pharisees and teachers of the law (John 8:3). She must have wondered where they were taking her – and why.

Soon, the Temple came into view. The people in the streets must have stopped and stared at the sight and sound of this woman being dragged along, clearly against her will. Many probably followed the hubbub into the Temple courts, and saw the woman being pushed through the group of people listening to that teacher, Jesus of Nazareth (v.2).

When the woman saw Jesus, she may well have known who He was. As she was made to stand before Him (v.3), she must have wondered why the men had brought her to this Jesus. She was about to find out. 'Teacher, this woman was caught in the act of adultery. In the Law Moses commanded us to stone such women. Now what do you say?' (vv.4–5).

Stage-managed

Maybe it was at that moment the woman realised that she had been set up; that this whole incident had been stage-managed; that she was a mere pawn in some game the Pharisees were playing with this Jesus. She must have asked herself why, out of all the women who were guilty of committing adultery in the whole of Jerusalem, was she the only one to be standing under such judgment? And where, she must have wondered furiously, was the man she had slept with? He was conspicuous by his absence, and had clearly been allowed to escape. After all, didn't the Law of Moses decree that, in the case of adultery, both parties were to be put to death, not just the woman (Lev. 20:10; Deut. 22:22)? At the same time, her heart must have been in her mouth, and her eyes full of tears. What would Jesus say? Would He condemn her publicly and compound her shame?

It probably passed her by that the Pharisees were actually seeking to trap Jesus by presenting Him with a dilemma (v.6). On the one hand, if He responded that the woman should not be put to death, He stood open to a charge of breaking the Law of Moses, and would be subject to arrest. On the other hand, if He replied that she should be killed, then the Pharisees would report Him to the Romans, because only the latter could carry out the death sentence (John 18:31). A corollary of such a response would surely have been that all the 'sinners' of society to whom He was reaching out would be likely to abandon Him and His message of God's forgiveness. The Pharisees had undoubtedly planned this confrontation very carefully, and must have felt that they had finally got their man.

The verdict

What happened next must have stupefied all present, including the woman. 'But Jesus bent down and started to write on the ground with his finger' (8:6). Wouldn't we all like to know what He wrote in the dirt of that Temple court?! Was He writing something from the law? Was He listing the sins of the Pharisees? Or was He doing something more symbolic: such as reminding the Pharisees that the commandments they were now seeking to use for their own ends had been written 'by the finger of God' (Exod. 31:18)?

I imagine the Pharisees growing ever more impatient with Jesus not answering their question and seeming to ignore them, so they kept on at Him (8:7). Eventually, Jesus straightened up and, presumably ignoring the woman completely, said to the Pharisees, 'If any one of you is without sin, let him be the first to throw a stone at her' (v.7). The law required that the accusers threw the first stones at the victim (Deut. 17:7).

Are we guilty at times of 'throwing stones' at others? Do we summarily pass judgment on people caught in sin, when we don't know all the facts? Jesus warned us of the consequences of doing this, as only God can judge with justice and fairness (Matt. 7:1–2). Rather, shouldn't our response be one of forgiveness and compassion, remembering that we too are all sinners in God's sight?

Expectation

The woman must have shot a terrified glance in the direction of the Pharisees – but she needn't have worried. As blind to their own faults as they were, even they didn't dare claim that they were without sin. They would also have realised how skilfully Jesus had evaded their trap by upholding the Law of Moses in His verdict, yet ensuring that it could not be carried out, thus avoiding offending the Romans.

So, after what I imagine to have been a rather tense pause in proceedings as the Pharisees weighed up Jesus' words and the woman shuffled nervously from foot to foot, 'those who had heard began to go away one at a time' (John 8:9). During this pause, Jesus had gone back to writing on the ground (v.8).

The woman must have watched the orderly exodus of her accusers with mounting surprise, relief and joy; until, finally, they had all gone, and she was just left standing there all alone (v.9). She must have been wondering what to do next, when Jesus sat up again and looked around. Was that a slightly amused smile she saw on His lips as He asked her, 'Woman, where are they? Has no-one condemned you?' (v.10). I imagine her sense of relief coming through as she replied, 'No-one, sir' (v.11).

But Jesus hadn't finished with the woman. In what I imagine to have been a gentle tone of voice, He continued, 'Then neither do I condemn you' (v.11); at which pronouncement the woman must have felt another wave of joyous relief. But there was more: 'Go now and leave your life of sin' (v.11). How did she react to that command, I wonder? It seems from Jesus' words that this was not the only act of adultery this woman had committed: a lifestyle He did not condone. There may have been no condemnation on the part of Jesus, but there was an expectation: that the woman would repent and change her way of life and behaviour. Whether she obeyed Jesus' command or not, we will never know. The question is: Have we?

Chapter 21

Investigation and Excommunication

A man born blind

John 9:1–38

'Who sinned?'

A blind man sat at the roadside begging, even though it was the Sabbath (vv.8–9,14). It seems likely that his parents had brought him there, and that he still lived with them (vv.20–21). Suddenly, he heard the sound of a group of people approaching. Nothing unusual about that: except this group stopped close by him, and he could just make out what they were saying. He realised that one of them must have been a teacher, because a man in the group asked, 'Rabbi, who sinned, this man or his parents, that he was born blind?' (v.2).

I imagine that the blind man would have been intrigued to hear the rabbi's answer, because he and his parents must have asked themselves this very same question. They probably believed, along with the Jews as a whole, that blindness was a curse from God for sin – a belief implicit in the disciples' question. The sin itself need not have been committed by the person who was afflicted. As in the case of a child born blind, this was seen as being the result of parental sin, although some rabbis even believed that children could actually sin in the womb.

The blind man must have been thrilled with the rabbi's reply: 'Neither this man nor his parents sinned' (v.3). He probably wondered if his ears were deceiving him. I imagine the weight of years of guilt falling off his shoulders and him desperately wanting to tell his parents what this unknown teacher had said. But the rabbi hadn't finished; He had more to say: 'but this happened so that the work of God might be displayed in his life' (v.3). 'What does He mean by that?' the blind man must have thought. He was about to find out in a most unexpected way!

Living in a fallen world unfortunately means that innocent people are going to suffer. I believe that, whatever the reason for our suffering might be, Jesus has the power to help us to deal with it and will give us the strength to cope with it.

Here's mud for your eyes

The blind man was probably still asking himself that question, when he was aware of someone approaching him and putting some substance on his eyes. Little did he know that Jesus had 'spat on the ground' and 'made some mud with the saliva' (v.6). I wonder what His disciples, not to mention the bystanders, were thinking as they watched Jesus engaged in making this extraordinary preparation. They had observed that Jesus usually cured by touch or by word: by mud they had never seen before – and this is the only recorded time it happened.

True, the disciples had seen Jesus use saliva before to bring sight to a blind man in Bethsaida (Mark 8:22–25). On that occasion, the man had been healed in two stages, which is the only recorded miracle where that happened, showing that healing can be gradual as well as instantaneous. But that blind man had been brought to Jesus for healing, whereas this blind man had neither been brought to Jesus, nor had he asked for healing. Faith had not been expressed by him, nor on his behalf. And this is the key to understanding this rather bizarre action of Jesus.

Sent to 'Sent'

I imagine the blind man gingerly touching this strange-feeling application that the stranger had put on his eyes. Then he heard the rabbi telling him to 'Go, wash in the Pool of Siloam' (John 9:7). The pool of Siloam had been built by King Hezekiah (715–686 BC) to allow the inhabitants of Jerusalem access to water within the city walls, which was particularly important during times of siege.

The word 'Siloam' means 'Sent', and it can also be translated 'one who has been sent'; which is exactly what the blind man was. The question was: would he go? By His actions, Jesus had created an opportunity for this man to show his faith – or not. He was given the choice. Either he could stand there, wipe the mud away from his eyes and carry on as if nothing had happened; or he could show his faith by being obedient to Jesus' command, going to the pool and washing as instructed, believing that his sight would be restored if he did.

Did the blind man sit there for a while thinking over this strange instruction, or did he jump up and go immediately? One way or the other, he 'went and washed' (v.7). There is no suggestion that anyone else went with him: he had to have the courage of his own convictions and go alone. Isn't it the case that faith is something we have to put into practice for ourselves, and no one else can do it for us? Others can encourage us and pray for us, but ultimately we have to take the step alone.

And how wonderfully his faith was vindicated. I imagine him slowly and somewhat apprehensively starting to wash the mud off his eyes: and, as he did so, becoming aware of light for the first time in his life as he began to see; and that sight becoming stronger and more defined as shadowy shapes began to take on definite forms, until he could see everything clearly. What a thrill it must have been for him to be able to walk home without any help for the first time in his life (v.7)!

Under investigation

The man must have been surprised at the reaction of his neighbours when he returned home. Some of them were incredulous (v.8), while others were dubious (v.9). He even had to insist that it really was him: 'I am the man' (v.9); at which they demanded, 'How then were your eyes opened?' (v.10). However, the strange explanation he gave, coupled with the fact that he couldn't tell them where this rabbi was, left them puzzled and unconvinced, so they took him to the Pharisees (vv.11–13). And then ensued some lovely moments provided by the simplicity of the healed man's reasoning juxtaposed with the complexity of that of the Pharisees.

The blind man must have been wondering why being healed would get him into trouble with the Pharisees; but, there he was, standing in front of them. Not that he seems to have been cowed by them at all; rather the opposite, as he spoke out with a boldness that may have surprised him. When asked what happened, he replied succinctly: 'He put mud on my eyes, and I washed, and now I see' (v.15).

The man must have been astonished to see the reaction to what he said. The Pharisees started arguing vehemently among themselves, ignoring him completely. Some said that this rabbi, whom they must have suspected was Jesus, could not possibly be 'from God' because he had broken the Sabbath rules (v.16). Others of them reasoned that if Jesus was in fact a sinner, then how could he 'do such miraculous signs?' (v.16).

Eventually, the Pharisees turned back to the man and questioned him about the rabbi, in what seems to me to have been a rather sarcastic manner: 'What have you to say about him? It was your eyes he opened' (v.17). It seems that the man's faith in Jesus and his belief about who Jesus was just kept on growing. He had described Jesus as a 'man' when questioned by his neighbours (v.11). In reply to the Pharisees, he was now convinced that 'He is a prophet' (v.17). Hardly the reply they were hoping for.

Get the parents

The Pharisees, probably taken aback by the man's forthrightness, and not wanting to be further divided over whether Jesus was a prophet or not, then tried to discredit this man's witness to Jesus by casting doubt on whether he was actually blind in the first place (v.18). Which just goes to show that if people don't want to believe, they'll find reasons not to, however unreasonable these might be.

They sent for his parents, who must have been dreading this moment. They were in a difficult position: torn between loyalty to and support for their son on the one hand, and fear of being thrown out of the synagogue if their answers did not please the Pharisees on the other. This was a very real threat, and would mean them being cut off from all social relationships and ostracised by the whole community.

They managed to negotiate the situation quite cleverly. They were loyal to their son by confirming his blindness from birth (v.20), but they put the responsibility for what had happened firmly in his court (v.21). This included what opinion he may have formed about Jesus – saying, in effect, that's down to him, and is nothing to do with us: 'He is of age; ask him' (vv.21–23).

Solid ground

So the Pharisees did ask him, but this time with an explicit command to tell the truth: 'Give glory to God' (v.24). This is almost the identical phrase used by Joshua when confronting a man called Achan about his sin (Josh. 7:19–20). The Pharisees further pressurised the man by going on to say: 'We know this man [Jesus] is a sinner' (v.24). And the word used for 'We' in Greek, the language in which the New Testament was originally written, is emphatic, so the implication was clear. What they were really saying was: *We* know He's a sinner, and *you* had better agree with us.

How must the man have felt now? To his great credit, his response was to speak the truth as requested, simply and boldly, but without being influenced by the implication behind the

Pharisees' statement. 'Whether he is a sinner or not, I don't know. One thing I do know. I was blind but now I see!' (v.25). This was the one irrefutable truth that could not be denied; and it is this fact that the man kept going back to (vv.11,15,25,30). This was the solid ground of experience on which he stood. He couldn't match the intellectual gymnastics of the Pharisees, even if he'd wanted to. But he knew what had happened to him: an experience which no one could deny or disprove.

There are times when we may feel unable to explain the finer points of our faith in a deep theological way: times when we may find it difficult to win an intellectual argument about our beliefs. However, in my experience, a far more effective weapon is the statement of a simple personal faith in Jesus Christ. That is the solid ground on which we stand. So there is no need for us to feel daunted when we find ourselves in similar situations to the one faced by the man born blind. He stuck to his guns, and simply but boldly shared his testimony with them. May God give us the courage to do the same.

Simply logical

However, the Pharisees would not let it rest there. But, in pursuing the matter further, they had come full circle: 'What did he do to you? How did he open your eyes?' (vv.15,26). And by this time, the man was understandably getting just the slightest bit exasperated: 'I have told you already and you did not listen. Why do you want to hear it again?' (v.27). And then, a thought occurred to him; whether mischievous or serious is open to question. Whichever, it is a delightful moment in the proceedings. I only wish I could have seen their faces when he asked them: 'Do you want to become his disciples too? (v.27).

The response of the Pharisees was all too predictable. His question had certainly touched them on the raw, and 'they hurled insults at him' (v.28). Far from daunted by this, he responded to them with a simple logic that cut through their intellectual pretentiousness (vv.30–33). In doing so, he answered their question about Jesus' origin, which seemed to be giving them so much trouble. He started with the fact that 'he opened my eyes', and from that point, his argument proceeded something like this. Such an action could only happen through the power of God; and since God doesn't listen to sinners, it stands to reason that the man doing it must be a godly man. The opening of the eyes of a blind man just doesn't happen; so this must be a miracle. Therefore, the man who did this miracle must have come from God, because only God can do miracles.

Totally disarmed by the man's logical reasoning, and frustrated by their inability to outargue this outcast, the Pharisees resorted to insulting him further, hiding behind their pompous authority, and invoking their ultimate sanction of excommunication (v.34).

When we speak out for Jesus, we may lose friends, be sneered at or even persecuted as a result, just as this man was. But isn't it encouraging to know that nothing can ever take away our salvation or separate us from the love of God (Rom. 8:38–39)?

'He found him'

So there he was, thrown out of the synagogue with all that implied, and all because he dared to speak about what had happened to him. But Jesus heard about it. And not only did He hear about it, but He went looking for him (v.35). What a moving picture that conjures up. In the midst of His hectic schedule, Jesus had time to come right where that man was.

I wonder how the man felt when he saw Jesus? Did he even realise He was the rabbi who had caused him to be healed of his blindness? I'm sure it can't have been long before he did. His heart clearly warmed to Jesus as they talked together, with the result that he willingly confessed his belief in Jesus, acknowledging Him as Lord, and worshipping Him as God (vv.35–38).

And that wonderful time he spent with Jesus, and all the spiritual development that took place in his life as a result, only happened because he was persecuted. And isn't it often in our most difficult times that we most powerfully experience the presence of God and make the most spiritual progress?

Chapter 22

One Thing

The rich young ruler

Mark 10:17–22

Something missing

This rich young 'ruler', as Luke calls him (Luke 18:18), had two great advantages in life: he was extremely wealthy (Mark 10:22), and he had a position and status in society – he would either have been the ruler of a synagogue, or held a judicial position in the local court. But it seems that, in spite of these advantages, he was an unhappy young man. He felt there was something missing in his life: not materially, but spiritually. Although he was a moral and upright person, who sought to obey the commands of the Law of Moses, there was still something missing: he had no assurance of eternal life. Clearly he had discovered that doing good deeds and having high moral standards, praiseworthy as that was, did not answer the question that was bugging him: '... what must I do to inherit eternal life?' (v.17).

He seems to have become convinced that there was something else he needed to do to obtain the reassurance of salvation that he so desperately sought. I imagine him discussing the matter with the Pharisees in the synagogue, and with anyone else who would listen, but getting no satisfactory answer. And then he must have heard about this new teacher from Galilee, Jesus of Nazareth, and gone to listen to Him preaching. He seems to have become convinced that Jesus might be able to answer the question that was troubling him so deeply.

'What good thing?'

At last, he saw an opportunity to put his question to Jesus and, seizing the moment, he 'ran up to him and fell on his knees before him. "Good teacher," he asked, "what must I do to inherit eternal life?"' (v.17); or, as Matthew records the question, 'what good thing must I do to get eternal life?' (Matt. 19:16).

Being able to earn salvation and eternal life was common in Jewish thinking; and still today many people around the world believe that if their good works exceed their bad deeds then they will have earned a place in heaven. Could this be because there is a lack of understanding that we are all sinners in the sight of a holy God, and that nothing we can do will wash away our sin: that only the blood of Christ can do this (1 John 1:7), making us fit to enter into heaven?

Like this young ruler, many think that salvation is a matter of works rather than faith; that it is something to be achieved rather than a gift to be received; that it is all about man's endeavour rather than God's grace. Paul, who would have been brought up to believe this himself, had to spell it out to the church in Ephesus, and indeed to all of us: 'For it is by grace you have been saved, through faith – and this not from yourselves, it is the gift of God – not by works, so that no-one can boast' (Eph. 2:8–9).

Have we accepted God's wonderful gift of salvation through Jesus and unwrapped it in our own lives? Unlike this ruler, have we realised that we are all sinners who need to experience God's mercy, grace and forgiveness (Rom. 3:23–24)?

Exasperation

It seems to me that kneeling at the feet of this itinerant preacher shows how desperate the young man was to get the answer to his question. Perhaps he even thought that flattering Jesus by calling Him 'good' would encourage Him to respond. He must have known that Jewish rabbis did not permit that adjective to be applied to them, on the grounds that only God was truly 'good'. Jesus did point this out to him (Mark 10:18), yet seemed to accept this description as truly applying to Himself. I wonder if the ruler picked up on the significance of this, and realised that he could rely on the truth of what Jesus was saying because He was, in fact, God.

The ruler seemed surprised – or is that exasperation I hear in his voice? – when Jesus answered by referring him to the commandments (v.19), which he was not slow to inform Jesus he had kept since boyhood (v.20). In Matthew's account, the ruler's exasperation continued with the supplementary question, 'What do I still lack?' (Matt. 19:20). Presumably, he was hoping that Jesus would give him another command, obedience to which would bring him the reassurance he was desperately seeking.

Interestingly, the commandments Jesus quoted as the ones he should keep, all deal with our relationships to other people – not our relationship with God. It seems to me that, with masterly technique, Jesus started from where the ruler was at, and with what he understood, in order to bring him to where Jesus wanted him to be: namely, to the point where he could see what was blocking him from having a relationship with God and preventing him from obeying the commandments to put God first in his life.

Hammer blow

The young man probably didn't realise it, but Jesus was so impressed by his sincerity and desire to know, that He 'looked at him and loved him' (10:21), and therefore continued to seek to draw him into a relationship with God. Isn't it true that a mark of God's love for us is that He points out what is wrong in our lives, and disciplines us (Heb. 12:6), in order that our relationship with Him might be maintained? How willing are we to accept God's straight-talking to us, and to yield to His discipline? This young man was about to hear God's assessment of what he needed to do to enable him to have the relationship with God that was necessary – and it would hit him like a hammer blow.

The ruler must have wondered why Jesus was looking at him like that (10:21). I imagine there was a pause before Jesus said, 'One thing you lack ... Go, sell everything you have and give to the poor, and you will have treasure in heaven. Then come, follow me' (v.21). I try to imagine the various expressions that must have crossed the young man's face as he absorbed what Jesus had just spoken to him in such a loving, gentle way: the devastation, the disbelief, the disappointment, all resulting in his downcast demeanour (v.22). He wanted salvation and eternal life, but on his terms, not God's. I imagine him rising slowly to his feet, not looking Jesus in the face but just turning his back on Him, and shuffling away with his head down.

Obviously, selling all his possessions wasn't going to bring him salvation and eternal life. It seems to me that Jesus was putting the ruler in a position where he was forced to look deep into his own heart and decide what his priorities were. The potentially life-changing challenge Jesus presented him with revealed the barrier which prevented him from loving God and becoming a member of His kingdom: his love of money. Possessions were his god, and he wasn't prepared to lay them down, so he couldn't obey the command to 'have no other gods before me' (Exod. 20:3). He was putting his trust in riches rather than in God.

Had he but realised it, Jesus had answered his question, 'What do I still lack?' What was lacking in his life was a relationship with God. How sad it is that 'He went away sad' (v.22), when it could all have been so different.

I wonder what barriers there are in our own lives which are

blocking our relationship with God? Are we prepared to do what it takes to remove them, so we might serve Him fully and love Him with all our heart (Mark 12:30)?

Chapter 23

Blind Man's Faith

Bartimaeus

Mark 10:46–52

It beggars belief

Bartimaeus shuffled his way to a particular spot on the road just outside the city of Jericho (v.46), from where he made his pitch to the passers-by, many of whom were pilgrims making their way to Jerusalem, the Holy City. This poor, blind beggar, probably dressed in little more than rags, sat there along with scores of other beggars with varying disabilities, all against the backdrop of the magnificent city walls. Bartimaeus did this every day: but today was going to be different; a day he would never forget.

Beggars were a common sight along the roads near the cities. They were usually people with some kind of physical disability which prevented them from earning a living. There was no medical help, nor financial assistance, such as disability benefits. The Law of Moses required the community to provide for the needy (Lev. 25:35–38), but this was largely ignored.

Responsibility to others was as unpopular then as it often is now. And the result was beggars everywhere: people without hope in this world.

Passing by

With his acute sense of hearing, Bartimaeus became aware of a noise in the distance. It wasn't the usual chatter of the twos or threes or even small groups of people who usually passed him by, although some did stop and offer him a crust or throw him a coin. No: it was definitely a crowd of people, and a large crowd at that, who were coming out of the city and getting ever closer to where he was sitting.

I imagine that Bartimaeus sensed excitement in the air. He must have thought to himself, 'What's going on? What's happening? This isn't the usual sound of a crowd; there's just something different about it.' Unable to contain himself any longer, he shouted his questions to anyone who would listen (Luke 18:36). Eventually, a reply came back: 'Jesus of Nazareth is passing by' (18:37). Bartimaeus must have thought: 'Jesus of Nazareth? Could it be *the* Jesus of Nazareth? The one who heals the sick, makes the lame walk ... and the blind see?' No wonder he began to shout, 'Jesus, Son of David, have mercy on me!' (Mark 10:47).

Here we see an important principle: Jesus graciously comes where we are and wants us to express our faith by crying out to Him.

Son of David

This is the only place in the whole of Mark where this title is used. Jews believed that when the Messiah came, He would be a descendant of the greatest king in their history: King David. So 'Son of David' became a popular title for the Messiah. However, to voice a title such as this in public risked drawing the attention of the Romans not only to the person doing the shouting, but also to the person to whom it was addressed.

Until now, Jesus had made every effort to keep the fact that

He was the Messiah secret. But on this occasion, Jesus neither rebuked Bartimaeus for having used this title, nor did He tell him to keep quiet about what had been done for him. The time for secrecy was over. Jesus was on His way to Jerusalem, where matters were about to come to a head.

The voices of the crowd

Bartimaeus found himself being told off by people in the crowd: 'Many rebuked him and told him to be quiet' (Mark 10:48). Perhaps some of them were genuinely concerned about him using the Messianic title, and the consequences that might have for Jesus. However, it seems more likely that they were letting their prejudices show. It was as if they were saying: 'You're an outcast, a beggar, an inferior, a nobody. Jesus is far too busy to have time for a down-and-out like you. So just be quiet; accept your lot, and get on with it without making all this fuss.'

The epistle of James is very strong indeed on the subject of prejudice in the Church, showing in no uncertain terms that to discriminate between people or to practise favouritism is wrong (2:1–13). Yet it is so easy to fall into this trap and to find ourselves adopting incorrect attitudes, just as many in this crowd were guilty of doing.

These voices were out to stop his voice being heard. What are the voices that stop us calling out to Jesus? In my experience, it's very easy to find ourselves listening to the wrong voices. So, shouldn't we ask ourselves frequently which voices we are listening to, and why?

Resist and persist

So what was Bartimaeus's response to being treated like this? Did he retreat into his shell, cowed by the crowd? Not a bit of it! Rather, 'he shouted all the more, "Son of David, have mercy on me!"' (10:48).

You've got to admire the man. The rebukes he had received were enough to put most people off, but they just made Bartimaeus even more determined. He refused to be pressurised by those around him, and persisted in crying out for mercy. He didn't care what other people thought about him and his situation. This was an opportunity that might never ever come his way again. Bartimaeus realised the significance of this moment, and seized it with both hands. The Messiah was passing by, and he had the simple faith to believe that the 'Son of David' could do something for him. And his persistence had its reward.

Like Bartimaeus, may we too have the courage to resist and to persist: to resist being pressurised by those around us who would seek to keep us from God, whose voices are constantly there; and to persist in calling out to God in prayer.

Response to the call

It would have been easy for Bartimaeus's plaintive cry to have been lost in the general noise of the crowd. But Jesus always hears the cry of faith. I imagine the crowd falling silent in astonishment as Jesus stopped and said, 'Call him' (v.49). Bartimaeus must have wondered what was happening; and then he heard those around him saying, 'Cheer up! On your feet! He's calling you' (v.49).

Bartimaeus responded immediately and with alacrity, resulting in energetic, even frenzied, action. He threw; he jumped; he came. Away went the cloak with which he would have covered himself, and which restricted his movement. Up he jumped as fast as he could, not taking the usual care that he would normally have done. And he couldn't come to Jesus quickly enough. Suddenly, he was there, standing in front of the One in whom he had placed his hope.

A ridiculous question

And then Bartimaeus heard Jesus asking him what he probably thought was a rather ridiculous question: 'What do you want me to do for you?' Bartimaeus must have thought, 'Isn't it obvious? Do I really have to spell it out?' So he did: 'Rabbi, I want to see' (v.51).

Bartimaeus had to hand the problem over to Jesus of his own free will, and submit it to Him to deal with. It seems to me that there is an important principle here. Jesus never healed anyone against their will. Similarly, God never intervenes in any of our problems unless we hand them over to Him. And, like Bartimaeus, let's also realise that God wants us to be specific in our requests.

Go

Jesus responded straight away. '"Go", said Jesus, "your faith has healed you." Immediately he received his sight' (v.52), and he could see Jesus face to face. Because Jesus stopped, Bartimaeus could go (vv.49,52).

Never having been blind, I can only imagine how wonderful it must be to have your sight restored and to suddenly be aware of a whole new dimension to your life which changes everything. What would Bartimaeus do with his transformed life? Where would he 'go' now Jesus had met with him? He could have gone back to Jericho, with his life changed thanks to his meeting with Jesus, but not going anywhere spiritually speaking. But he made a different choice. Instead, he 'followed Jesus along the road' (v.52).

Isn't being a disciple all about following Jesus on the road? I have found that new experiences in God and learning more about Him are just two of the rich rewards which lie in store for us as we go with God.

Chapter 24

Little, Loaded and Loathed

Zacchaeus

Luke 19:1–10

Up a tree

A little man joined the jostling, excited crowd lining the main street in Jericho. Like everyone else there, he wanted to see this Jesus of Nazareth (v.3). The news of His imminent arrival had spread like wildfire, as had reports that Jesus had healed a blind beggar outside the city (see Chapter 23). The problem the little man faced was that, being small, he couldn't see a thing (v.3). The crowd blocked his view completely, and was so tightly packed that he couldn't push his way through to the front. He was desperate to see Jesus, so he must have stood there for a moment wondering what to do. Then he had an idea.

People joining the crowd would have seen the strange sight of Zacchaeus, the chief tax collector for the district, and most loathed man in the city, running as fast as he could behind those lining the street (v.4). They must have wondered what on earth he was doing! To see a man running at all in those days was an unusual sight and, for a government official like Zacchaeus, it was totally unseemly. And then, to cap it all, he was to be seen scrambling up a sycamore-fig tree like a little boy (v.4). How undignified was that!

Such a tree would have been absolutely ideal for Zacchaeus's purpose: it had a short trunk, making it easy to climb; it was sturdy, and could easily support a man's weight; and it had spreading branches with evergreen leaves, which meant he could remain hidden. As he perched himself carefully on a branch and got his breath back, he must have been congratulating himself on such an excellent vantage point.

What had driven this little man to behave in such an extraordinary fashion? Was it simply curiosity, or were there deeper motivations? Had he found that his huge wealth had not brought him the satisfaction he was seeking? Was he searching for something more meaningful in life? Was he regretting some of the things he had done that had made him the loathed social outcast that he was? Whatever his reasons, he found himself hiding up a tree to see Jesus of Nazareth pass by. Zacchaeus thought he was seeking Jesus; little did he know that Jesus was seeking him!

'Come down'

Zacchaeus must have peered out from between the leaves as he heard the level of noise getting louder and louder. And then, at last, he caught his first glimpse of the man he had been waiting to see. Nearer and nearer He came, with the crowd surging behind and alongside Him in their excitement. I imagine Zacchaeus in his elevated position staring down intently at Jesus as He approached, trying to store the face of this man from Nazareth in his memory. Then, suddenly, something totally unexpected happened: Jesus stopped right by the tree in which he was perched (v.5).

I imagine the crowd falling silent, collectively wondering and whispering as to why Jesus had decided to halt his progress at this particular point. I'm sure Zacchaeus must have been wondering the selfsame thing, when he was suddenly aware that Jesus was raising His eyes up to the tree. He must have caught his breath as he saw Jesus looking straight at him; and then he heard Jesus speak to him by name. 'How does He know my name?' he must have thought – and the thought must have scared him a little. 'Zacchaeus,' Jesus said, 'come down immediately. I must stay at your house today' (v.5).

Beyond the pale

Zacchaeus must have been amazed that anyone would want to come and stay at his house. Being the chief tax collector for the district (v.2), he was shunned by everyone in the city, apart from his team of taxmen. No self-respecting Jew would ever be a tax collector; only Jews who were 'on the make' would defile themselves by working for the Romans, taking money from their kith and kin, and thereby helping the hated occupying power to fund its continuing tyranny. All tax collectors up and down the land were reviled as traitors and 'sinners' by the Jews, and consequently were social outcasts. They were known to be lining their own pockets by extorting more money than the Romans demanded, and keeping the balance for themselves. As chief tax collector, Zacchaeus would have received a cut of his team's ill-gotten gains. No wonder he was loaded! And no wonder he was loathed by the citizens of Jericho. He may have been short of stature, but he certainly wasn't short of a bob or two!

In view of all this, it's hardly surprising that Zacchaeus 'welcomed him gladly' (v.6). I imagine that he could hardly contain his delight! Interestingly, this is the only recorded occasion when Jesus invited Himself to someone's house, and it certainly caused quite a stir among the people of Jericho. They 'began to mutter, "He has gone to be the guest of a 'sinner'"' (v.7).

I'm sure there were many people in that crowd who would have loved to have Jesus as a guest in their home; but He chose Zacchaeus, of all people – to the disgust of everyone else. I wonder if we ever react in the same way as the people of Jericho? Do we sometimes consider that some groups in society are more deserving of God's love and attention than others? Do we feel that certain groups are 'beyond the pale' because of their beliefs, attitudes, behaviour and lifestyle? But, isn't it true that God loves them as much as anyone else, and they too need to hear the good news of Jesus?

Transformation

What a transformation took place in the life of this greedy, grasping little man as a result of having Jesus in his home! Wouldn't we all like to have been a fly on the wall to hear the conversation that took place between them? Zacchaeus wouldn't have needed to be told that he was a sinner, in every respect of the word: he knew that full well. But what he surely didn't realise was that God loved him just the same, and that repentance would bring him forgiveness and acceptance by God.

It seems this is what Jesus must have told him, because of what Zacchaeus said and did next: 'Look, Lord! Here and now I give half my possessions to the poor, and if I have cheated anybody out of anything, I will pay back four times the amount' (v.8). Significantly, Zacchaeus was now calling Jesus 'Lord', which indicates that money was no longer his master – Jesus was. The whole basis and raison d'être of his life had changed fundamentally. The genuineness of his repentance can be clearly seen in his desire to make reparation for his evil deeds. The one-time cheat and fraudster was now keen that the wrongs he had perpetrated were put right, the maximum recompense was paid, and that justice was seen to be done. This reminds us that true repentance will be seen in our actions, and is not a matter of words alone.

Recognising the genuineness of the words of Zacchaeus, Jesus pronounced that, 'Today salvation has come to this house, because this man, too, is a son of Abraham' (v.9). Not only was Zacchaeus 'a son of Abraham' by descent as a Jew, but also he could now be called by that phrase because of his faith in God (Gal. 3:7). Interestingly, the name Zacchaeus means 'righteous one'! Although he had singularly failed to live up to his name, now he had been made righteous in God's sight.

Jesus went on to use Zacchaeus as an example of the 'lost' that he had come 'to seek and to save' (v.10): those 'sinners' who had broken God's laws and were now considered outside of God's kingdom by the rest of Jewish society. Throughout His ministry, the Jews were continually shocked to discover that Jesus had come to save the whole world, which included all those whom the Jews considered to be outcasts, not to mention the Gentiles.

Contrast

It is interesting to compare and contrast Zacchaeus and the rich young ruler (see Chapter 22). Both were rich: one legally so, the other illegally. One was well thought of, the other was loathed. One was religious – a 'good' man; the other was irreligious – an outcast. Both seem to have been seeking something, and looking to Jesus for the answer. But, the one we would have expected to respond positively turned out to be merely a 'hearer' of God's Word, and went away sad and unfulfilled; the other one surprisingly proved himself to be a 'doer', and found the happiness of a life fulfilled in obeying God. The question is: in our lives, are we 'doers' or merely 'hearers' of the Word (Matt. 7:24–27)?

Chapter 25

Chalk and Cheese

Martha and Mary

(Other bit part player appearing: Lazarus)

The family at Bethany (Luke 10:38-42)
Outburst

Martha was thoroughly fed up. She had 'opened her home' (v.38) in Bethany to Jesus, but was getting no help from her sister Mary in preparing a meal. There she was, slaving away in the kitchen, while her sister was just sitting 'at the Lord's feet listening to what he said' (v.39). In the end, Martha could take it no longer. Being the outspoken sort of person she was, I imagine her bursting into the room where Jesus, Mary and presumably her brother Lazarus were in conversation, and blurting out in a very injured, annoyed tone of voice, 'Lord, don't you care that my sister has left me to do the work by myself? Tell her to help me!' (v.40).

It seems that Martha was the eldest of the three, and she was used to taking charge and being in control. She was very hospitable, well organised, eager to please, and keen to do the right thing. She took a pride in her home, her cooking and her practical service to her guests. Mary was somewhat different. For her, hospitality was more about spending time with the guest rather than making sure everything was just right for them. To Mary, conversation was more important than the smooth running of the home. She was a listener, who thought deeply before she spoke or acted. When she did do something, it was often profound, as we will see later. This was so unlike Martha, who couldn't help coming out with her thoughts and feelings on the spur of the moment.

It's not difficult to see how Mary's attitude would have irritated Martha, and vice versa. But, complementing each other as they did, they made a very effective team, though Jesus had lessons to teach them both.

It seems to me that the family of the Church experiences the same tensions as those evident in this family at Bethany. With people of different abilities, attitudes, opinions, expectations, personalities and ways of operating, all interacting simultaneously, is it any wonder that there are problems at times? In my experience, it is vital that we seek to work as a team under the direction of the Holy Spirit, who will knit us together into an effective, cohesive unit that can serve the Lord in the 'Bethany' in which He has placed us.

Priorities

In contrast to Martha's loud, emotional outburst, I imagine Jesus' reply to have been soft and gentle: 'Martha, Martha, you are worried and upset about many things, but only one thing is needed. Mary has chosen what is better, and it will not be taken away from her' (vv.41–42). Jesus didn't reproach Martha for being caught up with the household chores: He understood where she was coming from completely. However, what He did ask her to do was to examine her priorities. Martha needed to spend more time *with* Jesus rather than being so preoccupied with doing things *for* Jesus.

It seems to me that many of us are just like Martha in this

respect. There is nothing wrong in being busy in the work of the kingdom, but is it not even more important to realise the value of spending time with Jesus, as Mary did?

We are not told what happened next. Did Martha stomp off back to the kitchen, or did she take her place at the feet of Jesus alongside her sister?

Lazarus lives (John 11:1-6,17-44)
Love undiminished

Sometime later, Lazarus became ill, and 'the sisters sent word to Jesus, "Lord, the one you love is sick"' (v.3). I would imagine that Martha and Mary expected Jesus to come at once and heal their brother. But He didn't; even though 'Jesus loved Martha and her sister and Lazarus' (v.5), He 'stayed where he was two more days' (v.6). They had no idea that the death of Lazarus was going to present an opportunity for God to show His glory, and for Jesus Himself to be glorified through it (v.4). Martha and Mary were just left wondering why He didn't respond. And are there not times when we too can't see any possible reason why God doesn't respond to our prayers? Could it be that He is working out His purposes in our situation in a way we wouldn't be able to comprehend, even if He told us?

What a test this was of the sisters' love for Jesus. When He didn't come, they must have sat down together and discussed why this might be, without coming up with any satisfactory answers. Why had the One who they knew loved them, failed to respond by coming and healing Lazarus, thus leaving them weeping and mourning the death of their beloved brother? None of it made any sense. And yet, although Martha couldn't resist making a comment to Jesus on the subject when He did finally appear on the scene, there is no hint whatever of a lessening of their love for Him: it remained undiminished.

This raises an uncomfortable question for us. Does our love for God pass this severest of tests, or are we guilty of being the sort of people whose love for God depends on what He does for us? Or can we honestly say that if God never answers another one of our prayers, it will make absolutely no difference at all to our wholehearted love for Him?

Divine compliment

It seems to me that Jesus was so certain of the love of Martha and Mary, so sure it wouldn't falter or melt away when He didn't come and Lazarus died, that He knew He could put them through such a trial as this. What a compliment they were being paid by God Himself, although I'm sure they didn't appreciate it at the time.

And, because the sisters' love was steadfast, enduring and undiminished, they were going to see the power and glory of God made manifest in their lives in a way that they could never have dreamt of. True, their friends and the others present would see it too, but it would affect Martha and Mary personally, and make a dramatic impact on their lives, not to mention on their level of faith.

Arrival

By the time Jesus and His disciples eventually arrived in Bethany, 'Lazarus had already been in the tomb for four days' (v.17). Apparently, many Jews believed that the soul of the deceased lingered near the body for three days following the death, in the hope of returning to it. Now that four days had passed, all hope was gone. Lazarus was definitely and irrevocably dead, to everyone's satisfaction. The Jewish traditions surrounding burial, with or without hired mourners, had been, and were still being, observed. This meant there were still a lot of people around visiting Martha and Mary to comfort them; most of them had come from Jerusalem (vv.18–19). This shows the high regard in which the family was held.

On hearing that Jesus was approaching the village, the two sisters reacted completely differently, but in the way we might expect from what we already know of them. Martha bustled off to meet Jesus, whereas Mary stayed at home (v.20). Not surprisingly, Martha had one or two things to say, whereas Mary was too full of grief to stir herself.

Martha got straight to the point the moment she met Jesus. There followed a conversation between the two of them, the content of which she could never have imagined. "'Lord," Martha said to Jesus, "if you had been here, my brother would not have died"' (v.21). We can only speculate as to the tone of voice in which she delivered these words, but it is hard to imagine that there was not a touch of regret, even mild reproach, in there somewhere.

But Martha followed this statement of fact with a tremendous statement of faith: 'But I know that even now God will give you whatever you ask' (v.22). What did she have in mind when she said this? Was it just a vague faith statement made in hope? Was it a statement made just because she thought that was the sort of thing that Jesus would want to hear? Or did she really have the faith to believe for a resurrection from the dead? Maybe she and Mary had reminded one another of the two previous occasions when Jesus had brought people back to life, and this is what Martha was reflecting here in this specific faith statement.

Superhighway

Jesus reminded Martha of the Jewish hope of the resurrection (v.23). Martha thought that the Day of Resurrection lay a long way into the future (v.24), but Jesus stunned her and everyone else around Him with these amazing words: 'I am the resurrection and the life. He who believes in me will live, even though he dies; and whoever lives and believes in me will never die' (vv.25–26).

When we put our belief and trust in Jesus, we receive the gift of eternal life (John 3:16); so even though our body dies, we ourselves live on and experience eternal life in all its fullness. Praise God, death is not a dead end; it is a superhighway which brings us immediately into the supernatural presence of God (Luke 23:43; 2 Cor. 5:8; Phil. 1:23). What a glorious future awaits us!

Pivotal moment

But before Jesus showed His power over death for the third time, He had a critical question for Martha: 'Do you believe this?' (John 11:26). Did she have the faith to believe the truth of what Jesus had just said? Faced with the enormity of such a statement, Martha testified to her faith and belief in Jesus as the Messiah and the Son of God (v.27). Though she may not have understood all the ramifications of resurrection and eternal life, she did understand that Jesus was the Son of God, and that was enough. Her statement of faith was of great significance; and does not Jesus require exactly the same response from us? Making it is undoubtedly the pivotal moment in our lives.

Jesus then presumably asked after Mary, because Martha went back to fetch her (vv.28–30). Their Jewish visitors, who had come to mourn with them, accompanied Mary, assuming she was going to the tomb (v.31). When Mary met Jesus, we see again the contrast between the two sisters. Mary said exactly the same words as her sister had previously done (vv.21,32), which suggests they had discussed Jesus' lack of response to their message many times. But, whereas Martha had stood there and spoken to Jesus face to face, Mary was on her knees and couldn't stop weeping (vv.32–33). This same conviction that the sisters expressed was echoed by some of the mourners (v.37), who may well have been present when Jesus healed the man born blind (see Chapter 21).

Weeping together

Seeing not only Mary, but all the others around Him weeping, Jesus 'was deeply moved in spirit and troubled' (v.33), and asked where Lazarus had been laid (v.34). I imagine Martha and Mary on either side of Jesus, with tears in their eyes, each taking Him by the arm, and saying, 'Come and see, Lord' (v.34). On arrival there, tears filled His eyes too and streamed down His face: 'Jesus wept' (v.35).

What a wonderful picture this presents. Here we see a God who empathises with us and is deeply moved by our situation, who weeps with us and cares deeply about us. What an encouragement this is to us. God loves us so much that He is prepared to involve Himself with us in our daily lives. He understands our deepest emotions, because He has experienced them for Himself. So when we pray, we are not coming to a God who hasn't got a clue about how we're feeling. He knows, He cares, He understands, and His compassion never fails.

'Come out!'

In those days, tombs were usually caves cut into the limestone hillsides. You could walk into and around them standing upright, and several bodies were normally placed in one tomb. A large stone or rock was positioned across the entrance (v.38). Jesus gave the command for this to be removed (v.39). Martha, practical to the last, was concerned about the unpleasant consequences of such an action, in carefully chosen words (v.39). I can just imagine her raising her hand up to her nose as she spoke of the 'bad odour'!

With the stone removed, everything was ready, and Jesus prayed out loud for the benefit of the assembled crowd (vv.41–42). I try to picture the scene. Jesus, with Martha and Mary at His side, facing the tomb; the stone rolled away to one side, where the disciples were standing; the crowd of mourners, swollen by curious villagers, forming a semicircle behind Jesus. Then, a short, tense silence. Jesus praying to the Father. The tension building. Jesus then shouting loudly: 'Lazarus, come out!' (v.43).

All eyes fixed on the entrance to the tomb. Gasps of amazement and cries of disbelief suddenly filling the air as a figure, slowly and with some difficulty, emerged from the darkness of the tomb, 'his hands and feet wrapped with strips of linen, and a cloth around his face' (v.44).

Martha, for once, seemed lost for words. Along with her wide-eyed sister, she was rooted to the spot, probably with her mouth wide open, but with nothing coming out. They were both vaguely aware of Jesus saying: 'Take off the grave clothes and let him go' (v.44). To whom Jesus actually said this, we are not told. Was it the disciples who went to his assistance? Or was it Martha and

Mary who joyfully flew to his aid? Whoever it was, Lazarus was released, given new life and restored to his family.

What a poignant picture this is of each one of us. We were once sinful, making us dead to God. But, having responded to His personal call, we have now been released from the bondage of our sin, given new life in Christ, and had our family relationship with God our Father restored.

Jesus anointed (Mark 14:1–9)
A pint of perfume

On a later visit to Bethany, Jesus was invited to a dinner given in His honour by a man known as Simon the Leper (Mark 14:3; John 12:2). Presumably, Simon was one the many lepers healed by Jesus, who had been restored to society (see Chapter 6). Martha, Mary and Lazarus were all there. Typically, Martha was involved in preparing and serving the meal, even though it wasn't held in her house, while Lazarus was among the guests (John 12:2). Mary seemed to have disappeared from the scene temporarily, but she was about to make an entrance in an untypically dramatic way. Significantly, while events were unfolding at the dinner, two miles away in Jerusalem the chief priests and teachers of the law were plotting Jesus' death in the palace of Caiaphas, the high priest (Mark 14:1–2; Matt. 26:3). These two happenings were linked together.

Suddenly, during the dinner, Mary appeared 'with an alabaster jar of very expensive perfume, made of pure nard' (14:3). An alabaster jar was a beautiful and expensive vase, carved from a translucent gypsum, and it contained 'about a pint' (John 12:3). Pure nard was a fragrant liquid ointment imported from the mountains of India, where it was made from a plant which grew there. Consequently, it was a very expensive perfume, and a pint would have cost a whole year's wages.

When Mary appeared with this jar, I can imagine the conversation around the dinner table stuttering to a halt, and the eyes of all those present being fixed on Mary as she walked round the back of the reclining guests straight to Jesus. What she did next must have taken their breath away in astonishment: 'She broke the jar and poured the perfume on his head' (14:3). I imagine them gawping at the sight, then turning to one another and whispering, 'Whatever is Mary doing?'

Reaction

I wonder how long it took to pour a whole pint of perfume on Jesus?! The dinner guests must have watched in amazement as the ointment trickled down His robe and on to His feet. All those present were certainly affected by it: 'And the house was filled with the fragrance of the perfume' (John 12:3). They couldn't get the smell out of their nostrils.

And they were affected in more ways than one! The dinner table conversation had moved on from wondering what Mary was doing to indignant comments such as, '"Why this waste of perfume? It could have been sold for more than a year's wages and the money given to the poor." And they rebuked her harshly' (Mark 14:4–5). The Greek word used for 'rebuked' literally means 'snorted at her; glowered at her'. They were probably so hostile to Mary because they were shocked by what she had done, and embarrassed by her 'over-the-top' behaviour. If she wanted to make an extravagant gesture, they snorted, why hadn't she played Lady Bountiful to the poor?

I wonder how Mary felt at being on the end of all this snorting and glowering? Was she taken aback, or had she half expected it? Then Jesus stepped in, telling them to 'leave her alone', and to stop 'bothering her' (v.6). At which point, I imagine the murmuring and muttering stopped, as they listened to what Jesus had to say.

A beautiful act

The dinner guests didn't see anything significant or symbolic about what Mary had done, but Jesus certainly did. Not only did He appreciate the love behind it, which the others either couldn't or wouldn't see, but He also saw it as an act of great significance. Indeed, so significant was it that Jesus declared: 'wherever the gospel is preached throughout the world, what she has done will also be told, in memory of her' (v.9). Jesus made the point that, yes, it was important to help the poor (v.7), but He wanted them to understand that Mary had 'done a beautiful thing to me' (v.6), and why her action was beautiful in His eyes.

It was beautiful because Jesus recognised that this one-off, extravagant, sacrificial gesture was an act of devotion on Mary's part. Although it may seem rather bizarre to us, in those days it was polite to pour a little perfume on your guests when they arrived at your house. Perfume was precious, and it showed how much you welcomed them. The fact that Mary poured a whole jar of perfume over Jesus showed just how much she loved and valued Him.

It was also beautiful to Jesus because He saw it as prophetic of what was going to happen to Him. In those days, when people died, their families and friends anointed their bodies with perfume. The jars were never used again: they were broken, and the pieces were placed in the tomb with the corpse. Jesus was about to die, but there would be no time to give His body the normal care. So, perhaps without knowing it, Mary was preparing Jesus' body for burial while He was still alive. This was certainly how Jesus saw it: 'She poured perfume on my body beforehand to prepare for my burial' (v.8). While evil men were plotting His death, Mary was anointing Him for His death.

We can't pour jars of perfume over Jesus, but can we not express our devotion to Him by following His teachings faithfully, and by giving of ourselves sacrificially to the work of His kingdom? May our lives be 'poured out' for God, and result in the fragrance of Jesus being spread abroad.

Chapter 26

Political Expediency

Caiaphas and Pontius Pilate

(Other bit part players appearing: Judas, Pilate's wife)

Final straw

The news of the resurrection of Lazarus was the final straw for many of the Pharisees, who felt that something needed to be done about Jesus once and for all. They reported what they had heard to the chief priests, and a meeting of the Sanhedrin was called (John 11:47). The Sanhedrin was the Jewish Council, an assembly which the Romans allowed to administer strictly Jewish affairs. It was made up of Sadducees and Pharisees, who had very different political and religious views, which caused problems and tensions in their meetings.

The power lay in the hands of the chief priests, who were almost all Sadducees. They were the rich upper class of Jewish society, and were arrogant and boorish in their attitude to everyone else, including the Pharisees. The Sadducees ruled the Sanhedrin, and owed their power and influence to the fact that they cooperated fully with the Romans. Their leader was the high priest, Caiaphas

– the Romans' 'yes-man'. He held the office from AD 18–36, and was the son-in-law of Annas, who had been high priest from AD 6 until AD 15, when he had been deposed by the Romans. It seems that Annas still had a lot of influence in the Sanhedrin.

There was one issue, however, on which the Sadducees and the Pharisees were in complete agreement: they had to do something permanent about Jesus. His miracles were causing disturbances, and rumours that He was the Messiah were gathering in strength. They would have been aware that the Romans were getting increasingly concerned about the situation in Galilee and Judea: they didn't like disturbances, and they didn't like talk of messiahs. The chief priests knew that if they didn't act, the Romans would remove them, deal with the trouble brutally, and probably destroy the nation (vv.47–48) – and that would be an end of their power and cushy lifestyle, not to mention the end of the priesthood itself.

Obvious solution

Caiaphas must have been sitting there thinking: 'What's the problem? The solution is obvious!' He decided to take control of the meeting. Opening with the words, 'You know nothing at all!' (v.49), a typically arrogant Sadducee-like remark, he proceeded to persuade the assembly that all they had to do to bring this matter to an end was to get rid of the man who was causing all the trouble. His actual words were, 'You do not realise that it is better for you that one man die for the people than that the whole nation perish' (v.50). Caiaphas was proposing that the Sanhedrin sanctioned murder; and in their desperation for a final solution to the Jesus problem, they went along with him (v.53).

The fact that Jesus was innocent didn't come into it as far as Caiaphas was concerned. Political expediency was what mattered, not a person's guilt or innocence. Caiaphas operated on the principle that any threat to his power should be removed by any means necessary. He wasn't interested in justice – only in power. Jesus was a threat, so He had to be eliminated: it was simply a matter of how and when. The meeting did decide that during the Passover feast was not a good time, because 'there may be a riot among the people' (Matt. 26:5).

What Caiaphas didn't realise as he uttered those words of political expediency (John 11:50) was that, as high priest, God was speaking prophetically through him about Jesus' death. His sacrifice on the cross would be for the whole Jewish nation: but not just for them – for the whole world as well (vv.51–52).

Ironically, the scenario that Caiaphas and the Sanhedrin feared, and thought they were preventing by colluding in the death of Jesus, would take place about forty years later. In AD 70, Jerusalem would be sacked, the Jewish nation scattered and the Temple destroyed, along with the priesthood. A further irony can be seen in the fact that it was not the Romans who actually brought the priesthood to an end – it was the sacrifice of Jesus on the cross, which Caiaphas himself had engineered.

'Blood money'

The arrival of Judas offering to betray Jesus to them must have been a bonus to Caiaphas and his cronies. Caiaphas would have been delighted, because now he had a mole in Jesus' circle of disciples, and all for the modest sum of thirty pieces of silver (Matt. 26:14–16; Luke 22:4–6). Judas would be able to let him know the best time to arrest Jesus when there were no crowds around to cause a riot.

Little did Caiaphas realise that Judas would throw the money back into the Temple when he found out that Jesus was condemned to death, and go off and commit suicide (Matt. 27:5). This caused Caiaphas a problem, because such 'blood money' (v.6) could not be put back into the Temple treasury. In consultation with the other priests, Caiaphas decided to buy a field with it in which foreigners could be buried, thus fulfilling a prophecy of Jeremiah (vv.7–10).

Illegal

Judas must have returned to Caiaphas to let him know when to have his men ready to go with Judas and arrest Jesus. While that was happening, Caiaphas assembled the Sanhedrin, probably in his palace as before (Matt. 26:3,57). He must have been anticipating with some relish the prospect of interrogating this lowly carpenter from Nazareth. However, Caiaphas had a problem: although his men had found many people willing to testify against Jesus, presumably at a price, 'their statements did not agree' (Mark 14:56). No evidence that would stand up in court could be found. In the end, two witnesses were brought before Caiaphas who both testified that Jesus had said, 'I will destroy this man-made temple and in three days will build another, not made by man' (14:58). Yet even then, their evidence did not stand up to close scrutiny (v.59).

Caiaphas must have been getting extremely frustrated and annoyed at the way the trial was proceeding – or rather, wasn't proceeding. So he decided to take matters into his own hands in order to secure a conviction. Caiaphas stood up, and asked Jesus, 'Are you not going to answer? What is this testimony that these men are bringing against you?' (v.60). Caiaphas must have been hoping that Jesus would say something which he could then twist into an accusation. Imagine his rising anger when Jesus refused to say anything at all in reply.

Caiaphas must have been desperate by now. He knew there was only one thing left for him to do – to ask a direct, leading, incriminating question. Yes, it was illegal: but then, so was holding a trial at night, and not dismissing the accused when no evidence could be found against them, or when evidence contradicted. In a voice which I imagine rising in pitch to almost a scream, Caiaphas said to Jesus, 'I charge you under oath by the living God: Tell us if you are the Christ, the Son of God' (Matt. 26:63). The mouths of all those present must have dropped open at the audacity of Caiaphas to ask such a question. The atmosphere must have been electric as the assembled throng waited to see what Jesus would say – if He replied at all.

Triumphant

I wonder how long Jesus made them wait before He said, 'I am'. They were the first words He had spoken, and what dramatic words they were. At this point I imagine gasps all around the hall, and Caiaphas standing there with a self-satisfied smirk on his face that said, 'Gotcha!' But Jesus hadn't finished. Just in case there was any doubt left that He was claiming to be God, He continued, 'And you will see the Son of Man sitting at the right hand of the Mighty One and coming on the clouds of heaven' (Mark 14:62).

Caiaphas must have been triumphant. He tore his clothes, declaring, '"He has spoken blasphemy! Why do we need any more witnesses? Look, now you have heard the blasphemy. What do you think?" "He is worthy of death," they answered' (Matt. 26:65–66). And the physical abuse and mockery began, as Caiaphas looked on, undoubtedly enjoying his moment of triumph.

Tearing one's clothes was generally a sign of great grief or shock, and the high priest was usually forbidden to do this (Lev. 21:10). However, this was a highly unusual situation, and was a mark of the high priest's horror at the blasphemy he believed Jesus had spoken in both claiming to be God, and to have the majesty and power of God. Under Jewish law, the penalty for blasphemy was death by stoning (Lev. 24:16).

Changed charge

Yet, exultant as he was, Caiaphas knew he had a problem. It was all very well the Sanhedrin condemning Jesus to death, but only the Romans could carry out the death penalty; and they weren't going to be interested in executing Jesus on a religious charge such as blasphemy. Caiaphas knew that the only way he would be able to persuade the Romans that Jesus was worthy of death would be on a political charge.

In consultation with the Sanhedrin, Caiaphas changed the charge against Jesus to that of treason – claiming to be a king. After all, claiming to be the Messiah was the same as claiming to be the king of the Jews; and anyone claiming to be a king was setting himself up against the Roman emperor, and was therefore guilty of treason. The whole of the Sanhedrin agreed this decision, and took him to Pontius Pilate, the Roman governor of Judea, on this changed charge (Mark 15:1).

Antagonistic

Pilate can't have been too pleased to be aroused from sleep 'very early in the morning' (15:1) by a delegation from the Jewish Sanhedrin. His relationship with the Jews was tempestuous at the best of times, and Pilate showed little inclination to take any account of Jewish sensibilities during his time in power. The Jewish people, apart from the ruling class who toadied up to him, disliked him intensely, and showed him only grudging respect.

Pilate not only appointed the high priests, but also controlled the Temple and its funds. Caiaphas even had to come to Pilate to obtain the high priest's vestments, which were only released by the governor for festivals, when Pilate himself would come to Jerusalem, bringing extra troops with him to patrol the streets. As it was now the time of the Passover festival, Pilate was in residence in Jerusalem.

Since his appointment as governor of Judea in AD 26 by Emperor Tiberius, Pilate had managed to antagonise the Jews on several occasions. For example, he had brought standards bearing the image of the emperor into Jerusalem; his four predecessors had refrained from such an action out of respect for the Jewish religion. Pilate had also used money from the Temple treasury to build an aqueduct. Such actions had resulted in major disturbances and riots taking place, which were brutally quelled by the occupying Roman army under Pilate's command. The main force was stationed in Caesarea, but there was a detachment on garrison duty at Jerusalem in the fortress of Antonia.

Pilate seems to have been a rather nasty piece of work. The verdict of history is that he was stubborn, harsh, spiteful and easily angered. Bribery, corruption, murder, violence and brutality were hallmarks of his career. But, when it came to dealing with Jesus, Pilate seems to have been weak and vacillating.

Early one morning

Pilate must have wondered what on earth these Jews could be wanting at this early hour of the morning. Imagine his astonishment, then, to find that they had brought this Jesus character to him. Pilate would surely have been informed by his network of spies that Jesus was attracting large crowds, but wasn't the usual kind of self-proclaimed Jewish Messiah that they'd had to deal with on various occasions before. Pilate must have been asking himself why the Sanhedrin hadn't dealt with this man themselves; why did they need to involve him? He was soon to find out. When Pilate told them to 'Take him yourselves and judge him by your own law' (John 18:31), their reply, presumably from Caiaphas, revealed what they were after, and why they had brought Jesus to him: 'But we have no right to execute anyone' (v.31). So that was it! They wanted this Jesus dead.

Before Pilate had time to say anything, Caiaphas was laying out the charges against Jesus: 'We have found this man subverting our nation. He opposes payment of taxes to Caesar and claims to be Christ, a king' (Luke 23:2). I imagine Pilate suddenly becoming interested when Caiaphas got to the 'Christ, a king' bit of the charge, because he picked up on this immediately, asking Jesus, 'Are you the king of the Jews?' (23:3). When Jesus replied that He was, Pilate seems to have been intrigued, if not baffled. This man standing before him certainly didn't look like a king. Surely this harmless-looking teacher couldn't be guilty of treason? Or could He?

Pilate was also 'amazed' (Mark 15:5) that Jesus made no reply to any of the charges brought against Him. In fact, Pilate tried to persuade Jesus to do so (15:4), knowing that, according to Roman law, failure to make a defence would give Pilate no option but to find Him guilty.

Pilate decided to probe Jesus further on the subject of His claim to be a king in a private conversation (John 18:33–38). When

Pilate repeated the question, 'Are you the king of the Jews?' and asked Jesus, 'What is it you have done?', Jesus went on to explain that His kingdom was not an earthly one; at which point Pilate exclaimed, 'You are a king, then!' Jesus answered him: 'You are right in saying I am a king. In fact, for this reason I was born, and for this I came into the world, to testify to the truth.' At the mention of the word 'truth', I imagine a cynical smile crossing Pilate's face. All the political shenanigans this hardbitten career-politician had been involved in over the years were distilled and reflected in his reply: 'What is truth?'

Lifeline

Pilate didn't wait for a response to the question from Jesus, but went back outside to address the delegation and the crowd that was beginning to gather: 'I find no basis for a charge against this man' (Luke 23:4). It seems that Pilate had decided as a result of his conversation with Jesus to release Him. But Caiaphas and his cronies weren't going to allow that, so they continued, 'He stirs up the people all over Judea by his teaching. He started in Galilee and has come all the way here' (v.5).

Hearing that Jesus came from Galilee, Pilate must have felt that fate had thrown him a lifeline to rescue him from the trouble his instincts must have told him was brewing. He could palm this man off to Herod Antipas, the ruler of Galilee, who just happened to be in Jerusalem. Pilate didn't like Antipas anyway (v.12), so why not put him on the spot and let him decide what should happen to Jesus? That way, the Romans needn't be involved in what happened to Jesus, and that would stave off any repercussions from the Jews. So Pilate sent Jesus to Antipas (vv.6–7; see Chapter 17); but, having questioned Jesus, Antipas decided to defer to Pilate's judgment, and sent Jesus back to him. In a way, Pilate must have been pleasantly surprised by the deference shown to him by Herod Antipas, with the result that 'Herod and Pilate became friends – before this they had been enemies' (v.12).

Dilemma

But this didn't solve Pilate's dilemma. On the one hand, he was convinced that Jesus was innocent of the charges brought against Him: he knew full well that Caiaphas and the Jewish leaders were envious of Jesus' powers and His popularity with the people (Mark 15:10). But, on the other hand, Pilate must have had a bad feeling about where this was all heading. The mood of the swelling crowd seemed to be getting uglier by the moment. He knew he would have to do something.

Pilate must have been pondering this, when he was reminded that 'it was the custom at the Feast to release a prisoner whom the people requested' (Mark 15:6,8). And then it dawned on him: surely the people would want Jesus to be released; it was only the Jewish leaders who hated Him, wasn't it? Didn't the people hang on His every word, and marvel at what He did? Hadn't they welcomed Him uproariously as He had processed into the city only a few days ago?

Little did Pilate realise that the people had begun to turn against Jesus, because He had not proved to be the kind of Messiah the Jews were looking for: namely a king who would lead them to fight the Romans, set their country free, and set up a kingdom that would never end – a kingdom of this world that could be marked on a map. Indeed, during their private conversation, Jesus had already told Pilate that this was not the sort of kingdom He had come to establish.

When Pilate tried to steer the crowd to ask for the release of Jesus, Caiaphas and his cronies whipped them up to shout for the release of Barabbas (15:9,11). Barabbas was a notorious bandit, criminal and murderer, currently languishing in a prison cell for his part in leading a recent rebellion against the Romans (Luke 23:19).

Holy innocent

As Pilate sat 'on the judge's seat' (Matt. 27:19), presiding over this growing mayhem, a message came from his wife. He must have been fuming at this ill-timed interruption. I can imagine

Pilate thinking, 'What does she want that can't possibly wait till later? As if I haven't got enough on my mind at the moment!' Nevertheless, he decided to ask what the message was about. Imagine his astonishment when he found that it was about the very man on trial before him: 'Don't have anything to do with that innocent man, for I have suffered a great deal today in a dream because of him' (v.19).

Tradition says that Pilate's wife's name was Claudia Procula. It seems that she was a member of one of Rome's noblest families, and that her family had pulled rank in order to get permission for her to accompany her husband to his governorship, which was an unusual occurrence. She must have been watching what was going on from a nearby vantage point, and realised the urgency of getting her message to her husband. It seems highly likely that Claudia had heard reports about Jesus, maybe even seen Him for herself, and had come to believe that He was a holy man. She must have feared the consequences for them both should Pilate send a holy man to His death.

Claudia may well have overheard her husband's interview with Jesus, and could now hear the crowd shouting for the release of Barabbas. Knowing him to be the political animal that he was, Claudia must have realised that Pilate would never allow riots to break out in Jerusalem, as that would incur the wrath of Emperor Tiberius, and result in him being recalled to Rome in disgrace, with the distinct possibility of being put to death. Yet she couldn't stand by and see her husband sentence to death a man she was convinced was holy and wholly innocent. Nor could she live with herself if she said nothing about the dream she had experienced until she saw Pilate later, when it would be too late. In her eyes, she had no alternative but to send the message.

Innocent but guilty

Pilate must have felt that he was between a rock and a hard place. He knew himself that Jesus was innocent; he also knew that according to Roman law, an innocent man should not be put to death; and, to cap it all, now his wife was pleading with him not to convict this Jesus. So Pilate tried again to persuade the throng to ask for the release of Jesus, but once more the answer came back, 'Barabbas' (27:21). When he asked what he should do with Jesus, the crowd demanded that He be crucified (v.22). Pilate persisted, asking, 'Why? What crime has he committed?', to which the crowd screamed back, 'Crucify him!' (v.23). Then Caiaphas and his cronies really put the frighteners on him by shouting, 'If you let this man go, you are no friend of Caesar. Anyone who claims to be a king opposes Caesar' (John 19:12). Pilate knew that they would have no compunction about reporting his actions to Tiberius; and he knew what would happen as a result.

Pilate's mind must have been in turmoil by now. Pressurised by the Jewish leaders and getting nowhere with the crowd, who were on the point of rioting, it seems Pilate felt he had no choice but to hand Jesus over to be crucified. He *did*, of course, have a choice: but when it came to the crunch, his own career and survival mattered far more to Pilate than the fate of a Galilean preacher. To find Jesus innocent but guilty was the politically expedient thing to do. I wonder if there is anything in our lives that ultimately matters more to us than Jesus?

In a dramatic gesture, Pilate washed his hands in front of the crowd, proclaiming, 'I am innocent of this man's blood' (Matt. 27:24). I wonder if he really believed his own words? It seems that Pilate's guilty conscience was troubling him, because he sought to shift all the blame for Jesus' death on to the Jews with the words, 'It is your responsibility!' (v.24). The crowd's response was frightening, even blood-curdling: 'Let his blood be on us and on our children!' (v.25). Then, in order to satisfy and placate the crowd, Pilate released Barabbas and had Jesus flogged, handing Him over to the Roman soldiers to be crucified (Mark 15:15).

While Pilate went back into his palace with his misgivings to face his distraught wife, Caiaphas must have gone away grinning from ear to ear. For Pilate, it was a case of crisis averted; for Caiaphas, it was mission accomplished. And when Jesus was finally nailed to the cross which had originally been earmarked for Barabbas, I imagine that Caiaphas was among the Jewish leaders who went to Golgotha to indulge themselves in a spot of triumphalist gloating. It may well have been Caiaphas who led their mocking of Jesus: 'He saved others, but he can't save himself! Let this Christ, this King of Israel, come down now from the cross, that we may see and believe' (vv.31–32). We can almost taste the sarcasm dripping from those words.

Precautions

Having had their fun at the cross, Caiaphas and the others went back to speak to Pilate. Caiaphas was not best pleased about the wording on the board nailed to the cross above Jesus' head. Every crucified victim had such a board nailed above them describing their crime, as a deterrent to others. Caiaphas had noticed that the board above Jesus read 'The King of the Jews'. He protested to Pilate, 'Do not write "The King of the Jews", but that this man claimed to be king of the Jews' (John 19:21). But Pilate wasn't going to budge on that issue, and replied, 'What I have written, I have written' (v.22).

And there was something else niggling Caiaphas and his cronies, which they needed Pilate to act on. So they said to him, 'Sir, we remember that while he was still alive that deceiver said, "After three days I will rise again." So give the order for the tomb to be made secure until the third day. Otherwise, his disciples may come and steal the body and tell the people that he has been raised from the dead. This last deception will be worse than the first' (Matt. 27:63–64). As a Sadducee, Caiaphas didn't believe in the resurrection – unlike the Pharisees; but he wanted to make absolutely sure that the whole episode concerning Jesus would remain dead and buried: that there was no possibility of the people being hoodwinked into thinking that Jesus had risen from the dead, as this would cause even more trouble than had been the case when He was alive.

Pilate himself must have seen the wisdom of what Caiaphas was saying; and he certainly didn't want any more disturbances in Jerusalem. So Pilate put the required precautionary measures in place: 'Take a guard ... Go, make the tomb as secure as you know how' (v.65). So the tomb was sealed, and a guard was posted (v.66). I wonder what those guards thought of their orders to keep watch over a dead body. Were they in for a shock!

Bribery

When the angel appeared, 'rolled back the stone and sat on it', the guards were scared witless. They were so afraid of the angel that 'they shook and became like dead men' (Matt. 28:2,4). I would love to have seen the expression on Caiaphas's face when some of the guards appeared at his door and told him everything that had happened at the tomb (v.11)! Caiaphas would have known that decisive and immediate action was essential to deal with this unforeseen circumstance.

A hurried meeting was arranged to discuss how to counteract the rumours which were bound to spread about the resurrection of Jesus. The upshot of the meeting was that the soldiers were heavily bribed (v.12), and told to say, 'His disciples came during the night and stole him away while we were asleep' (v.13). Caiaphas also promised the guards that, 'If this report gets to the governor, we will satisfy him and keep you out of trouble' (v.14). The soldiers did exactly as they were told (v.15).

Caiaphas must have known that the governor would soon get to hear about what had occurred, so it seems likely that he would have gone to see him, and told Pilate that he had got everything under control. When Pilate realised what had happened, I wonder if he thought back to his conversation with Jesus, when he had asked Him, 'Where do you come from?' (John 19:9), and how Jesus had spoken about His kingdom not being of this world; and of the fear that he had felt (19:8)? Pilate must have been satisfied with what Caiaphas had done, because apparently he took no further action.

Postscript

Although Pilate disappears from the pages of Scripture at this point, history tells us that he continued his brutal acts. He was finally ordered back to Rome to appear before Emperor Tiberius for butchering large numbers of Samaritans. Tiberius died in AD 37 while Pilate was on his way to Rome. The outcome of his trial is not known, but it seems that he was forced to commit suicide at some point during the reign of Emperor Claudius (AD 37–41).

As for Caiaphas, he managed to survive this crisis, and continued to pursue and persecute the followers of Jesus with unabated vigour, putting many of them on trial (see Chapter 28). He was finally deposed from his position in AD 36.

Although Caiaphas and Pilate thought they were in control of the situation, they were mistaken. God was in control, and was working out His purposes through them, making it possible for each one of us to experience God's love and forgiveness through the sacrifice of Jesus on the cross. Let's make no mistake – God is still in control, although we may sometimes wonder what is happening in the world in which we live; God is working out His purposes, and His plans can never be thwarted by what man might seek to do.

Chapter 27

Burning Hearts

Cleopas and friend

Luke 24:13–35

Deep despair

Cleopas and his friend were walking to the village of Emmaus, which lay about seven miles to the north-west of Jerusalem (v.13). And, as they walked, they were in deep discussion about everything that had happened over the past few days (v.14). Presumably their discussion encompassed Jesus' triumphal entry into Jerusalem, His subsequent arrest, trial, crucifixion, and the rumours about His resurrection.

I imagine them walking along with their heads down in deep despair as together they chewed over the events that had occurred. They had fervently hoped that this Jesus was the promised Messiah: but how could He have been? He had allowed Himself to be arrested, tried and crucified – not what they and most other Jews were expecting to happen to their Messiah. Wasn't He supposed to be a great, powerful King who would conquer the Romans, set their country free, and establish the kingdom of God on earth, with the Jews in positions of power, restoring the 'golden age' experienced under His ancestor, King David (Acts 1:6)? Their dreams had all been shattered; their Messiah crucified and laid in a tomb. What a let-down this Jesus had proved to be; and they had been so sure about Him – look at all the miracles He had performed, and the way He had entered Jerusalem in triumph. And yet – nothing had come of it. No wonder they were disillusioned and 'downcast' (v.17). There was nothing for it but to return home, and carry on waiting for their Messiah to come.

Jesus hadn't done what they had expected Him to do. And isn't that way of thinking often the cause of many of our own discouragements? In my experience, it's so easy to focus on hopes and dreams we may have had which have not materialised, that we become disillusioned and find ourselves in despair. So much so, that we stop looking up at Jesus (Heb. 12:2), look down instead, and don't recognise His presence with us any more (v.16).

The stranger
Suddenly they were aware that a stranger had appeared out of nowhere: but they didn't realise that it was 'Jesus himself' (v.15) who was walking along with them. Jesus had not sent a messenger or an angel: He had come to them Himself in their despair. Isn't it wonderful to know that Jesus is always there when we need Him?

Why didn't they recognise Him (v.16)? Was it the clothing He was wearing? Was it the fading light? Or was it simply that He was the last person they were expecting to see? The stranger asked them what they were discussing (v.17); He undoubtedly knew full well, but wanted to hear it from their own lips.

'What things?'
His question brought them both to an immediate halt: 'They stood still, their faces downcast' (v.17). Then Cleopas piped up with words that were so full of irony, although I'm sure he didn't realise it, as he looked the stranger straight in the eye and

asked: 'Are you only a visitor to Jerusalem and do not know the things that have happened there in these days?' (v.18). I just love Jesus' reply to Cleopas's question: 'What things?' He asked, innocently (v.19). As if Jesus needed telling! But this was part of Jesus' technique in dealing with them: He wanted to draw the problem out from within them, and get them to express it in their own words.

Presumably it was Cleopas who spoke for both of them by telling the stranger what had happened to Jesus of Nazareth (vv.19–21). Then I imagine him pausing for a second before continuing with words which summed up their disillusionment: 'but we had hoped that he was the one who was going to redeem Israel' (v.21). They didn't understand that the Messiah had indeed come to redeem Israel – but to redeem them from sin, not to deliver them from their enemies as they had expected; so no wonder they couldn't comprehend why God had allowed the Messiah to die.

Clearly, they had heard what Jesus had said about the significance of 'the third day' (v.21; see Matt. 16:21). They were expecting something, but nothing had occurred that had satisfied their expectations. They had even heard the testimony of the women who had gone to the tomb that very morning and found it empty, later confirmed by others, and had brought back the message of the angels (vv.22–24). But for them, the negatives outweighed the positives – 'but didn't find his body'; 'but him they did not see' (vv.23–24). There was no proof. I can just hear the disillusionment and disappointment in their voices, sense the confusion in their minds, and see the sadness in the expressions on their faces.

Bible study

Cleopas and his friend must have been shocked when the stranger then said, 'How foolish you are' (v.25): 'foolish' in that they believed what they could see, rather than having faith in what God had said. Like many of us, they had found living 'by faith' a lot harder than living 'by sight' (2 Cor. 5:7). The stranger also said that they were 'slow of heart to believe all that the prophets have spoken!' (v.25). So He went on to explain it all to them, using the Scriptures to help them to understand (vv.26–27).

What an amazing Bible study that must have been! I wonder what scriptures Jesus used? Perhaps He began with the first promise of the Redeemer in Genesis 3:15; touched on the prophecies in Psalms 22, 69, 110; talked about the Suffering Servant in Isaiah 53, the promise of the new covenant in Jeremiah 31, and the one who was pierced in Zechariah 12:10. What we do know is that He explained to them 'what was said in all the Scriptures concerning himself' (v.27), showing them that Jesus really was the promised Messiah.

Praise God that everything we need to know is contained in the pages of Scripture; but how we need the Holy Spirit to teach us and to bring us 'into all truth' (John 16:13).

Opened eyes

By the time Jesus had completed His tour of the Scriptures, they had arrived at Emmaus. Interestingly, 'Jesus acted as if he were going further' (v.28), but they insisted that He stayed with them as the evening was approaching (v.29), and had something to eat. If they hadn't invited the stranger in, they wouldn't have experienced the Risen Lord. And isn't the same true for us? If we want to experience God ministering to us, do we not need to invite Him into our lives, and into that specific situation?

It was when the stranger broke the bread and began to give it to them (v.30) that 'their eyes were opened and they recognised him' (v.31). It seems likely that they saw the nail marks in His hands as He raised them in the air to give thanks for the bread, as the Jewish custom was – and even more so as He handed the bread to them. Their faces must have been an absolute picture as realisation and understanding dawned.

I imagine them staring, open-mouthed. No longer was this man a stranger: He was Jesus, the Messiah they had longed for, risen from the dead! The proof they had sought stood before them – and then disappeared from their sight (v.31). Suddenly, the meal didn't matter any more; all that mattered was Jesus. They asked each other, 'Were not our hearts burning within us while he talked with us on the road and opened the Scriptures to us?' (v.32). Knowing God in our heads is one thing; knowing Him in our hearts is quite another!

Their burning hearts fuelled their immediate return to Jerusalem in the growing darkness (v.33). They just couldn't stay at home and keep what they had experienced to themselves: they had to share it with the others (vv.33–35). Their priorities and attitudes were completely changed due to their encounter with Jesus. Their unbelief was gone, and they wanted to witness. Isn't that how we should be, having experienced Jesus in our lives? Are our hearts still burning within us?

Chapter 28

Drama at the Gate

A crippled beggar

Acts 3:1–10

'Beautiful'

As far as the crippled beggar was concerned, it was going to be just another day. He would be carried, presumably by family or friends, to a spot next to the 'temple gate called Beautiful' (v.2), just as he was every day of his life. There, he would 'beg from those going into the temple courts' (v.2), no doubt along with many other beggars. His helpers would bring him there just before three o'clock in the afternoon (v.1), one of the three daily hours of prayer. That would ensure a large number of people would pass by him and be inclined to give money to him as part of their duty of almsgiving.

There were in fact nine gates which led from the court of the Gentiles into the Temple itself. The gate described as 'Beautiful' was probably the Nicanor gate, the main eastern entrance, which was the most frequently used of the nine, and therefore the best place to sit and beg. It was certainly a very impressive gate. Made out of Corinthian brass, it was approximately twenty-three metres high, had gigantic double doors, and gleamed like gold. It was against this magnificent backdrop that a drama was about to unfold.

No coins

The beggar's arrival at the gate seems to have coincided with that of Peter and John, who were on their way to the Temple (v.1). 'When he saw Peter and John about to enter, he asked them for money' (v.3), probably holding up his open hands in their direction as he did so, without looking at them at all. But he felt no coins drop into his palms; instead, he heard one of the men saying, 'Look at us!' (v.4).

The cripple must have thought that was an unusual thing to say. In all his years of begging there, and he was now in his forties (4:22), this was probably the first time he had looked any giver in the eye. But he did as he was told, 'expecting to get something from them' (v.5). What he was about to receive would certainly far exceed his expectations!

Imagine the disappointment that the cripple must have felt when Peter said, 'Silver or gold I do not have' (v.6). He didn't know that Peter and John had sold all they had, and 'had everything in common' with the rest of the believers (2:44–45). I imagine him being rather annoyed and thinking, 'Well, if you haven't got any money for me, why are you wasting my time? Get out of the way, so someone who has got some can give it to me!' And when the cripple heard Peter say, 'but what I have I give you' (v.6), he must have thought, 'What can you possibly have to give me? You've said you've got no money; what else could you give me that's going to help me?' Was he in for a surprise!

Far greater

I wonder how the crippled beggar reacted when Peter commanded him, 'In the name of Jesus Christ of Nazareth, walk' (v.6)? He would surely have known about Jesus and His miracles. He may well have even seen Jesus in person during His visits to the

Temple courts; indeed, he may have actually been there when Jesus drove the merchants and money-lenders out of the court of the Gentiles (Mark 11:15–17). But it wasn't Jesus who was giving him this command; so could he, dare he, act upon it? Perhaps he sat there thinking, 'I've been crippled since birth (v.2); how can I possibly walk?' Or did he respond immediately and try to get up, but found it difficult?

Whatever the case, the cripple was suddenly aware that Peter had grasped his right hand, and was helping him up on to his feet (v.7). He must have felt the power of God flowing through his legs as his 'feet and ankles became strong', with the result that he 'jumped to his feet and began to walk' (vv.7–8). Here he was doing something which he had seen others do, but had never ever been able to do himself. What an amazing feeling that must have been! No longer crippled, but walking.

The crippled beggar expected money, but he received something far greater and more wonderful. And isn't it true that sometimes God answers our prayers in unexpected ways – ways which are far greater and more far-reaching than we could ever have imagined?

Praising

What a wonderful picture this conjures up of the man walking, maybe even running, and certainly jumping for joy! He must have been so excited that he wanted to go and tell all his family and friends the good news. But he didn't go home, 'he went with them into the temple courts, walking and jumping, and praising God' (v.8). His priority was praise. And when the people saw him, they recognised him; they realised that this was none other than the crippled beggar who had sat at the gate begging for as many years as most of them could remember; and now he was walking and praising God (vv.9–10)! No wonder they were 'filled with wonder and amazement at what had happened to him' (v.10).

What an example this man is to all of us! His first thought was to thank and praise God, and to give Him the glory for what He had done, in front of everybody. How often do we forget to do that simple thing? And the result of him getting his priorities right was to create a fantastic opportunity for Peter to preach the gospel to all the people who 'were astonished and came running to them in the place called Solomon's Colonnade' (v.11), a place where Jesus Himself had taught (John 10:23). We never know how God might use our witness to His grace in our lives, as we bring praise to His name in the congregation of the people.

Holding on

We are told that 'the beggar held on to Peter and John' (v.11). What a lovely picture that presents! It's almost as though the man can't believe what's happened, and he doesn't want to let go of the men who brought this great joy into his life. He wasn't holding on to them so they would bless him, but rather because they had brought blessing *to* him. Why do we hold on to God? Do we just hold on to Him to beseech Him, or do we also hold on to Him to praise Him?

I like to think that the man was still holding on to Peter as the apostle addressed the crowd with these opening words, which clearly referred to the once-crippled beggar: 'Men of Israel, why does this surprise you? Why do you stare at us as if by our own power or godliness we had made this man walk?' (v.12). And, as a result of this second sermon given by Peter calling on them to repent, 'many who heard the message believed, and the number of men grew to about five thousand' (4:4).

Standing alongside

The content of Peter's sermon didn't go down well with the Jewish authorities. Peter and John were seized and were forced to appear before the Sanhedrin, led by Caiaphas (4:6; see Chapter 26). As always, Peter, under the anointing of the Spirit, used the opportunity to preach to the Council about the Jesus they had crucified, saying that 'Salvation is found in no-one else, for there is no other name under heaven given to men by which we must be saved' (4:12).

Amazingly, the once-crippled man didn't flee when Peter

and John were arrested; he went to the court and stood there in solidarity with them. And his very presence there had consequences for both the apostles and the Sanhedrin: 'But since they could see the man who had been healed standing there with them, there was nothing they could say' (4:14). His presence as a living witness added weight and power to what Peter had said.

In my experience, there are times when just being present and standing alongside others can be a powerful witness for God. We may not feel that we can take an 'upfront' role, but we can always be there, supporting the witness for God by our presence and by our prayers. We can also stand alongside Christian brothers and sisters whom we don't know, who are persecuted for their faith around the world.

We don't know what happened to this man, but it seems likely that he would have joined the group of believers, and witnessed many of the exciting things that took place in the Early Church in those days.

Chapter 29

Deceit and Death

Ananias and Sapphira

Acts 5:1–11

Praise and prestige

Ananias and his wife, Sapphira, were among the rapidly increasing group of believers in Jerusalem. Some of the believers 'who owned lands or houses sold them, brought the money from the sales and put it at the apostles' feet, and it was distributed to anyone as he had need' (Acts 4:34–35). The latest person to make such a generous gift was Barnabas (see Chapter 33), who had 'sold a field he owned' (4:37).

When such donations were made, there would undoubtedly have been much thanksgiving and praise given to God by the believers. It seems likely that the donors would also have been thanked publicly and by the congregation, even though they had given the money to the glory of God. Ananias and Sapphira would have noticed the prestige this brought to the donors, and I imagine them discussing the matter when they got home. The result was that they hatched a plan which would bring them the maximum amount of praise for their generosity, and the prestige that went with it, without having to give sacrificially. Satan had spotted a 'chink in their armour' (see v.3), and was determined to exploit it to the full. Can we identify weaknesses in our own lives which the devil can use to bring us down? Are we still wearing the 'full armour of God' so we can take our stand 'against the devil's schemes' (Eph. 6:11)? Paul also warns us, 'do not give the devil a foothold' (Eph. 4:27). Unfortunately, Ananias and Sapphira did – with drastic consequences.

Their plan was brilliant in its simplicity. They connived together to sell a piece of property they owned, but to keep back part of the money for themselves, while pretending that they had given the whole amount to the apostles (vv.1–2). Thus they would gain the prestige and reputation that they seemingly craved for being just as spiritual as Barnabas and the others, and still have money in hand. Who would ever know? What could possibly go wrong? Like Ananias and Sapphira, are we foolish and arrogant enough to think that we can fool God as well as fooling the people around us (Gal. 6:7)?

They must have felt very pleased with themselves as they looked forward to basking in the glory that would surely come their way. Are we seeking praise and glory for ourselves in the church, or praise and glory for God alone? Is it time to re-examine our motives?

Dishonesty

At last, the day they must have been anticipating with such relish had arrived. The land had been sold, the amount to be given to the apostles agreed between them, and the rest stashed away somewhere safe. For some reason they must have decided that Ananias would go to the meeting of believers on his own, because Sapphira wasn't there when her husband 'brought the rest and put it at the apostles' feet' (v.2). It was an act brimming over with dishonesty and deceit.

Ananias must have been anticipating words of thanks for his generosity from Peter, and glowing with pride at the very thought of it. But instead, he heard Peter say, 'Ananias, how is it that Satan has so filled your heart that you have lied to the Holy Spirit and have kept for yourself some of the money you received for the land?' (v.3). Ananias's face must have dropped a mile with shock and horror. 'How could Peter possibly know?' he must have wondered as he stood there, no doubt feeling flustered and fearful as he realised that they hadn't got away with their deception.

Ananias then heard Peter reminding him that there had been no obligation on him to sell the land at all; and even when he had decided to, there was no expectation that he would bring any, let alone all, of the money to the apostles (v.4).

Hypocrisy

But it was what Peter said next that must have chilled Ananias to the core: 'What made you think of doing such a thing? You have not lied to men but to God' (v.4). It wasn't the fact that he had kept some of the money back that was the issue. It was the fact that he had been hypocritical: bringing only a part of the money, while pretending to give it all. The hypocrisy of Ananias had been unmasked. He was shown up for what he was: a downright liar, who was not giving the money to help the needy, but rather to enhance his own reputation among the believers. Not only had he lied to the people, which was bad enough; but foolishly, and more importantly, he had lied to God, thus placing himself under His awesome judgment: 'When Ananias heard this, he fell down and died' (v.5).

About three hours later (v.7), the scenario was replayed. Sapphira arrived, not knowing that her husband lay dead and buried (vv.6–7). Had she come looking for him, wondering why he hadn't returned home? Presumably Peter showed her the bag of money brought to him by Ananias and looked her straight in the eye as he said, 'Tell me, is this the price you and Ananias got for the land?' (v.8). Sapphira must have wondered why Peter was asking her that question, not realising that he was probing to find out whether this deceit had just been Ananias's idea, or whether she had connived with him. I imagine Sapphira looking at Peter unflinchingly as she said unequivocally, 'Yes, that is the price' (v.8).

Now knowing that this hypocrisy had been a joint effort, Peter condemned them both for having sought 'to test the Spirit of the Lord' (v.9) to see if they could get away with such a deception. Like Ananias before her, Sapphira must have been shocked and horrified as Peter told her what had befallen her husband, and announced that the same fate awaited her (v.9). 'At that moment' Sapphira too experienced the awesomeness of God's judgment, and 'she fell down at his feet and died'. She was carried out and 'buried ... beside her husband' (v.10). No wonder 'Great fear seized the whole church and all who heard about these events' (v.11)!

This incident leaves us in no doubt that God hates hypocrisy. Are there ways in which we are being hypocritical before God? Are we living lives of integrity before Him, or does what we say and what we do not quite match up? Could we be counted among the people whom Jesus described as those that 'honour me with their lips, but their hearts are far from me' (Matt. 15:8)?

Chapter 30

How much?

Simon the sorcerer

Acts 8:5–24

(Other bit part player appearing: Philip the Evangelist)

Boldness

In the wake of the martyrdom of Stephen and the persecution of the Christians which followed, led by Saul of Tarsus (7:59–8:3), Philip went to a city in Samaria and 'proclaimed the Christ there' (v.5). In view of the hostility that existed between the Jews and the Samaritans (see Chapter 9), this was a very bold move by Philip. But God was with him in a mighty way: 'When the crowds heard Philip and saw the miraculous signs he did, they all paid close attention to what he said. With shrieks, evil spirits came out of many, and many paralytics and cripples were healed. So there was great joy in that city' (vv.6–8).

Philip the Evangelist, as he became known so as not to confuse him with Philip the apostle, was a Greek-speaking Jew 'full of the Spirit and wisdom' (Acts 6:3). He was originally chosen along with Stephen as one of the seven deacons, whose responsibility it was to oversee the food distribution project undertaken by the church (6:1–6). The ministry of Stephen and Philip developed, and they both became involved in preaching and performing miracles (6:8,10; 8:5–6). And the result of Philip's boldness in preaching the good news of Jesus to the Samaritans was that many became followers of Christ, and were reunited with the Jews who had also become believers, making them 'all one in Christ Jesus' (Gal. 3:28). The message of the gospel had broken down the barriers between them; and by the time Paul wrote those words in Galatians, the Gentiles would be included as well. This restored unity between the Jews and Samaritans who had become followers of Jesus was cemented by the arrival of Peter and John from Jerusalem, by the laying on of whose hands the Samaritans received the Holy Spirit (8:17).

Do we take the gospel to everybody or just to certain groups of people? Is it time to revisit the Great Commission (Matt. 28:19; Mark 16:15), and to evaluate our outreach ministry in the light of it?

Out of the limelight

But there was someone in that Samaritan city who must have been extremely angry about what was happening. His name was Simon, and he 'practised sorcery in the city and amazed all the people of Samaria' (Acts 8:9). He revelled in the limelight that his satanic powers afforded him, and had become conceited and arrogant: 'He boasted that he was someone great' (v.9). It must have been heady stuff for Simon, being fêted and receiving adulation from rich and poor alike, to the point where they all 'gave him their attention and exclaimed, "This man is the divine power known as the Great Power." They followed him because he had amazed them for a long time with his magic' (vv.10–11). I imagine him strutting round the city, enjoying every minute of the recognition and prominence that his magic had brought him, to the point where he was virtually worshipped as some sort of messiah or god. The city was at his feet, and he could have anything he wanted.

But then, out of the blue, something happened that changed

everything completely. Simon must have begun to notice that suddenly the number of people fawning all over him was decreasing by the day, and it wouldn't have taken him long to realise why. He would have heard of the arrival in the city of somebody called Philip, and that this man was performing even greater miracles than he could. There was nothing for it but to go and see what was happening for himself. And when he saw what Philip was doing, Simon couldn't believe his eyes. He was so impressed that, along with hundreds of others, he 'believed and was baptised', and continued to follow Philip everywhere, 'astonished by the great signs and miracles he saw' (v.13).

No change

The trouble was, it seems that Simon's belief was based on what he had seen rather than on what he had heard: on the signs and wonders rather than on the gospel message that Philip was preaching. There doesn't appear to have been the fundamental change in Simon's life that occurs when a person truly repents and gives their life to God, owning him as Lord. Simon still hankered after power and prestige, and all the trappings that went with it. If there was a power greater than he had experienced so far, he wanted it desperately so he could use it for his own ends.

So when Peter and John arrived, and began laying their hands on people to receive the Holy Spirit, Simon was so amazed by what he saw that he wanted the power to be able do that himself, for his own honour and glory. As money was no object, he went to Peter and John and asked them how much they wanted (v.18); how much would it cost for him to be given this same ability they had 'so that everyone on whom I lay my hands may receive the Holy Spirit' (v.19)? He was prepared to pay any price to refocus the city's attention on him, so he could bask once again in the limelight and adulation of the people. There had been no change in his heart.

In my experience, it is possible for people to profess belief, even be baptised, without true repentance having taken place. The test is, can people see the 'fruit' of repentance in our lives (Matt. 3:8)?

And when we have truly repented, are we caught up with signs and wonders rather than God's Word? Do signs and wonders follow us as Christians (Mark 16:17–18), or do we follow them?

Exposure

As far as Simon was concerned, everything had a price and could be bought. So he must have been astonished when Peter rounded on him with such strong words: 'May your money perish with you, because you thought you could buy the gift of God with money!' (Acts 8:20). Interestingly, ever since then, as the Oxford English Dictionary explains, the word used for 'the buying or selling of pardons, benefices, and other ecclesiastical privileges' has been 'simony'.

Peter went on to confirm what Simon's problem was: no change had taken place in his heart, and he needed to repent (vv.21–22). He then exposed Simon's innermost thoughts and motives by saying, 'I see that you are full of bitterness and captive to sin' (v.23). Undoubtedly, Simon would have been deeply resentful at having his status in the city usurped by Philip, this intruder from Jerusalem; and his own selfish desires still made him a slave to Satan, who remained lord of his life.

Simon's reaction to Peter's rebuke is interesting and indicative of the man; 'Pray to the Lord for me so that nothing you have said may happen to me' (v.24). He didn't repent and ask God's forgiveness; rather, he was more concerned about avoiding God's judgment. It is cautionary to realise that, if Peter hadn't exposed Simon's wickedness publicly, he would have become a member of the Samaritan church, and no doubt caused it a lot of problems.

When we receive a rebuke from God, how do we react? Do we carry on regardless, arrogantly maintaining that we have done nothing wrong? Or, unlike Simon, do we fall to our knees in repentance and ask God's forgiveness?

Chapter 31

The Desert Road

The Ethiopian eunuch

Acts 8:26–39

(Other bit part player appearing: Philip the Evangelist)

Out of Africa

The Ethiopian eunuch, who was presumably a black African, set out on his long journey of approximately 200 miles from Jerusalem back to his native country, which lay to the south of Egypt. This important official, who was 'in charge of all the treasury of Candace' (v.27), this being a title for the Queen Mother, had gone to Jerusalem to worship. This suggests that he was either a Jew or a convert to Judaism, and that he had probably gone to the city to celebrate one of the Jewish festivals.

The fact that he made such a long journey by chariot indicates that this Ethiopian must have been a very devout and God-fearing man: a seeker after God, who wanted to learn more. Indeed, as he sat in his chariot on the journey home, he was reading from the Jewish Scriptures: from Isaiah 53:7–8 to be precise. The trouble was, he couldn't make sense of what he was reading; but God was preparing his heart to receive His Word.

The official must have been wondering who he could get to explain this passage to him now that he had left Jerusalem. He was so engrossed in reading the passage out loud, as was the custom, that he was oblivious to the fact that a man had come up to his chariot and was running alongside it. Little did he know that the man concerned was acting on God's instructions (vv.29–30).

Leave behind

That man was Philip, who must have been astonished when God sent an angel to tell him to leave behind the God-anointed and hugely successful work he was doing in Samaria (see Chapter 30), and 'Go south to the road – the desert road – that goes down from Jerusalem to Gaza' (v.26). Philip must have wondered why God wanted him to go out there; after all, there weren't many people to preach to in the desert! But Philip was obedient; and because he was obedient, God's purposes would come to pass with the conversion of the Ethiopian.

Are we prepared to leave behind the anointed and successful ministry that God has given us in obedience to His command, and do something else that we find much less appealing, even though we can't see any possible reason why we are being led down that road? It must have been hard for Philip to obey; but, as he discovered, God always has a purpose in what He commands us to do, and prepares the way before us.

Personal evangelism

Suddenly, the Ethiopian heard a voice speaking to him, and asking, 'Do you understand what you are reading?' (v.30). He must have been both shocked and surprised by the sudden appearance of this man, apparently from nowhere. But he soon recovered his poise and, in what I imagine to have been a despairing rather than a disparaging voice, replied, 'How can I, unless someone explains it to me?' (v.31). Did Philip then offer to help the Ethiopian, who promptly commanded the chariot to stop? What we do know is that 'he invited Philip to come up and sit with him' (v.31). Even though he was a highly important official, he wasn't too arrogant or pompous to ask for help with his understanding of the Scriptures (v.34). But what about us? Are we too proud to do the same?

The official's humility was rewarded, as Philip explained the gospel to him, starting 'with that very passage of Scripture' (v.35). What a wonderful picture of personal evangelism this conjures up: the Ethiopian sitting with the scroll spread out in front of him, possibly held by a slave, and Philip sitting beside him, pointing to various words and phrases as he explained the gospel, while the chariot continued its bumpy progress south.

In my experience, that's always the best place to start when witnessing: right where the person is at that moment in their lives, addressing their concerns and their questions, and bringing them from that point step by step to the cross. And isn't it encouraging to know that, like Philip, we too can experience God's leading as we ask Him to direct us to the right person, whose heart He has already prepared to receive what we have to say?

Into Africa

The Ethiopian's heart had been so well prepared, that he not only responded immediately to the gospel message, but wanted to be baptised as well, saying, 'Look, here is water. Why shouldn't I be baptised?' (v.36). When Philip raised no objection, the Ethiopian commanded the chariot to stop (v.38). In front of the no doubt startled eyes of his entourage, this high and mighty government official then subjected himself to the humiliating ritual of baptism (v.38).

As soon as it was completed, 'the Spirit of the Lord suddenly took Philip away, and the eunuch did not see him again, but went on his way rejoicing' (v.39). It seems that, even though his mentor had been whisked away, the Ethiopian was so sure of his salvation that he praised God all the way home. And I can't imagine him keeping the good news to himself when he got there, either! Africa was about to hear the gospel message for the first time.

Chapter 32

He's my Brother?

Ananias

Acts 9:10–25

Visions

Ananias was a pious Jew who had become a Christian, and yet had retained the respect of the Jewish community in Damascus, because he lived an upright life according to the Law of Moses. In the words of Paul, 'He was a devout observer of the law and highly respected by all the Jews living there' (Acts 22:12). No doubt Ananias would have begun every day with prayer. That could well have been the time when, one day, he had a vision, the content of which I'm sure he would never forget.

The fact that Ananias was not at all fazed by having a vision in which the Lord spoke to him (9:10) suggests to me that he may well have had such an experience before. When God called to him by name, he replied in a very matter-of-fact way, 'Yes, Lord' (v.10), whereas most of us would probably be shaking in our shoes and trembling with fear at such an occurrence! Is that, I wonder, because we have lost the sense of the nearness and consciousness of God's presence which so characterised the Early Church?

But if the vision itself didn't cause Ananias to tremble, what God said to him through it certainly would have! It seems that the news of what had happened to Saul on the road to Damascus had spread around the city, and that Ananias had heard all about it (v.17). Now, here was God giving Ananias Saul of Tarsus's current address, and telling him to go round there posthaste and visit him (v.11)! But this was not just to be a social call; there was a distinct purpose to this visit. Ananias was to 'place his hands on him to restore his sight' (v.12), in accordance with what Saul had been shown happening to him in a vision.

Not keen

Not surprisingly, Ananias wasn't too keen on racing round to the 'house of Judas on Straight Street' (v.11). With the arch-persecutor of the Church in town, lying low would have been the order of the day! So much so, that Ananias had the temerity to tell God exactly what he thought about the situation: 'Lord, I have heard many reports about this man and all the harm he has done to your saints in Jerusalem. And he has come here with authority from the chief priests to arrest all who call on your name' (vv.13–14). He might well have felt like adding, 'And that includes me!'

Clearly, Ananias had heard all about Saul and what he was doing from Christians who had come from Jerusalem to warn their brothers and sisters in Damascus that the fearsome persecutor had been given permission to carry out his search-and-destroy mission in their city too. Although Ananias was available to God, he wasn't keen to obey Him in this instance. The idea that this man, who 'was still breathing out murderous threats against the Lord's disciples' (9:1), could become a brother in Christ must have seemed impossible to Ananias.

Do we ever find ourselves thinking that a certain person could never come to faith in Christ, so we are not keen to witness to them? Yet God could be preparing their heart to receive His Word, as He was Saul's; and who knows what this person might accomplish for God? Dare we limit what God can and wants to do?

Obedience

In response to his concerns, God graciously revealed His purpose for Saul's life to Ananias: 'This man is my chosen instrument to carry my name before the Gentiles and their kings and before the people of Israel. I will show him how much he must suffer for my name' (vv.15–16). Once again, God told Ananias to 'Go' (vv.11,15). His obedience was urgently required. It was the first step in the process of bringing God's plan to fruition.

In view of what he had heard, Ananias must have realised that Saul was going to need all the support he could get. Nevertheless, as he walked down the main east-west thoroughfare of Damascus that was Straight Street, Ananias must still have felt a certain amount of trepidation at the thought of meeting this man Saul face to face for the first time. The fact that God had told Ananias that not only was Saul praying, but that Saul also knew the name of the man who was coming to lay hands on him (vv.11–12), must have encouraged Ananias and stilled his beating heart.

What conflicting emotions must have flooded through Ananias as Judas brought him into the room where Saul was sitting. I imagine that all the way there, Ananias had been praying that God would give him the right words to say. Yet the first word that came out of his mouth may well have surprised him, but it was very significant. As he placed his hands on Saul in obedience to God's command, he called this persecutor of the Church 'Brother' (v.17)! In his heart, Ananias had accepted Saul as a brother in Christ, and welcomed him into the brotherhood of believers.

What joy that word, which signified acceptance and welcome, must have brought to Saul's heart! Saul must have been wondering what this man Ananias would have to say to him when he came; yet instead of the words of censure and expressions of anger that Saul may well have been expecting, Ananias brought nothing but love in his words, and gentleness in his touch. It can be hard to love those whom we may fear or whose motives we may be suspicious of. May God help us to follow the example of Ananias and show loving acceptance of new believers, no matter what their background or track record.

But, after his sight had been restored, Ananias also brought words that must have stunned Saul to the core. Later in his life Saul, now called Paul, recalled those words, which could only have been spoken to him by a fellow Jew like Ananias: 'The God of our fathers has chosen you to know his will and to see the Righteous One and to hear words from his mouth. You will be his witness to all men of what you have seen and heard' (22:14–15).

Because Ananias was obedient, Saul the persecutor would become Paul the apostle. Let us never underestimate the importance of one person brought to Christ. Are we obedient when God directs us to make contact with someone, no matter how sceptical we may be about the outcome? Like Ananias, we may be God's 'man for the job' because of our background, or personal experience, or some other quality that we possess, which makes us uniquely qualified to bring that person to Christ.

Baptism and basket

Paul also gives us a glimpse into the more forthright, even outspoken side of Ananias, when he recalls how Ananias then turned to him and said, 'And now what are you waiting for? Get up, be baptised and wash your sins away, calling on his name' (22:16)! I wonder where they took Saul to be baptised; perhaps to the local river, in full view of everyone, including the Jews of the city, who must have been extremely angry that their champion had turned traitor (9:21).

Indeed, eventually these Jews got so fed up of Saul preaching 'that Jesus is the Son of God' (v.20) and outarguing them by 'proving that Jesus is the Christ' (v.22) that they 'conspired to kill him' (v.23). Fortunately, Saul heard of their plan (v.24), and planned his secret escape from the city with the help of the local Christians. I imagine Ananias being one of those who 'took him by night and lowered him in a basket through an opening in the wall' (v.25).

I wonder how Ananias felt as he waved goodbye to Saul from the city wall. As far as we know, they never met again. Indeed, Ananias is never heard of again. I imagine him becoming a pillar of the church in Damascus, faithfully serving his Lord, and being an example to all by means of his lifestyle, and through his willingness to be open and obedient to God.

Chapter 33

Master Encourager

Barnabas

Acts 4:36–37; 9:26–30; 11:22–26,30;
13:1–14:28; 15:36–39
(Other bit part players appearing: Stephen; Agabus;
James, the brother of Jesus; John Mark)

Joseph the Levite

According to Galatians 1:17–18, three years elapsed between Saul's experience on the road to Damascus and his arrival in Jerusalem. During that time, news of Saul's conversion, his baptism, and his subsequent preaching campaign in Damascus must have reached the ears of the believers in Jerusalem. Surely such tidings would have brought great joy to them all? Not a bit of it! Bad reputations die hard; particularly when the person concerned has caused widespread fear and carnage, as was the case with Saul. The upshot was that the believers in Jerusalem were still afraid and suspicious of him, and he was shunned by them all (Acts 9:26). All, that is, except one.

That one exception was a man called Barnabas. In fact, Barnabas was not his actual name. His real name was Joseph, and he was a Levite who came originally from Cyprus (4:36). It seems likely that Joseph had come to Jerusalem to live with his aunt Mary and his cousin, John Mark (Col. 4:10). Presumably he became a believer while in Jerusalem, and he joined the church there. Perhaps he was one of the many thousands converted under the ministry of Peter, or maybe it was through the witness of his Jewish family, who had become followers of Jesus.

Contribution

Joseph had certainly made a huge impact on the community of believers in Jerusalem. Not only had he 'sold a field he owned' (presumably in Cyprus) 'and brought the money and put it at the apostles' feet' (Acts 4:37), but he had done something else, which could be said to be an even more valuable contribution than his financial one. Joseph had gained a reputation among the believers for being an encourager. If anyone needed supporting, helping or uplifting, Joseph was the man with the vision to see the need, and the will to respond to it immediately. It seems that the apostles, no less, were so impressed by the effectiveness of Joseph's ministry of encouragement, that they decided to give him the name Barnabas, which means 'Son of Encouragement' (v.37) – and from then on, that was the name he was known by.

In my experience, encouragement remains one of the most important ministries to the Church. And, unlike some other ministries, it is one in which we can all be involved. When was the last time we encouraged anybody? Why not pick up the phone, send a card, write a letter, send an email, or visit somebody today?

While the other believers kept their distance, Barnabas welcomed Saul with open arms. He introduced Saul to the leadership, notably Peter and James, during Saul's short stay in Jerusalem (Gal. 1:18). Barnabas made sure they were aware of what had happened to Saul on the Damascus road, and how 'in Damascus he had preached fearlessly in the name of Jesus' (Acts 9:27). The discipling work begun in Saul's heart and life by Ananias in Damascus was carried on by Barnabas in Jerusalem, and its value cannot be overestimated.

The apostles obviously accepted Saul, because he began to

preach in Jerusalem, and debated with Grecian Jews, 'but they tried to kill him' (9:29). I imagine that Barnabas was one of 'the brothers' who, on hearing of this, advised Saul to leave the city, and went with him to the coastal port of Caesarea, so he could return by boat to the safety of his hometown of Tarsus (9:30). I wonder how Barnabas felt as he watched his new-found friend sail away? Saul may have been out of sight, but he was certainly never out of Barnabas's mind, as events were to show.

Antioch

When the apostles decided they needed to send someone to check out the burgeoning church in Antioch, the capital of Syria, they chose Barnabas (11:22), and he proved to be the ideal man for the job. In fact, Barnabas was so impressed with what was happening in Antioch that he decided to stay there, and became one of the leaders of the church (13:1). Perhaps he preferred the radicalism of Antioch to the conservatism of Jerusalem.

Barnabas knew how to nurture new Christians, discipling them, supporting them and encouraging them (11:23). Barnabas was an exemplary leader: he was morally upright, full of the Holy Spirit and full of faith (v.24). Barnabas also had the vision to see what was required, and he realised very quickly that all these new Christians (vv.21,24) needed a solid grounding in their faith. Being the self-effacing, modest man that he was, Barnabas realised that, although he could teach these converts himself, he needed someone whose primary gifting was teaching – and he knew just the man! So Barnabas 'went to Tarsus to look for Saul, and when he found him, he brought him to Antioch' (vv.25–26). For a whole year, Barnabas and Saul held in-depth Bible studies in the church, and 'great numbers of people' benefited from them (v.26). Now that's a course I wouldn't have minded going on!

What an example Barnabas is to all of us, and especially to those who are in leadership in any capacity. May God help us to emulate Barnabas's many qualities as we seek to serve Him in our churches.

Stephen

Interestingly, many of the founder members of the church in Antioch were friends of Stephen who had fled up the coast to that city following his martyrdom under the supervision of Saul (Acts 11:19–20; 7:58; 8:1). Originally, Stephen had been elected as one of seven deacons, who were 'known to be full of the Spirit and wisdom' (6:3). They were given the task of organising the distribution of food to the poor, so that the apostles could focus on praying and preaching (6:1–4).

But it soon became clear that God had marked Stephen out for a much greater role than that of a deacon. God anointed Stephen with His 'grace and power', with the result that he 'did great wonders and miraculous signs among the people' (6:8). Stephen can't have been surprised to find himself experiencing sustained opposition from certain Jews: specifically 'from members of the Synagogue of the Freedmen' (v.9). They began to argue with Stephen, but found that he was a skilled debater. So much so, that 'they could not stand up against his wisdom or the Spirit by whom he spoke' (v.10).

It wasn't long before Stephen found himself arrested and brought before the Sanhedrin on trumped-up charges supported by false witnesses (vv.12–14). Stephen must have known what the outcome would be, but he was determined to speak the truth. Not only did he show his eruditeness by giving a brief account of the history of the Jews, but he really got under the skin of the members of the Sanhedrin by what he said about them. In a display of the most amazing courage, Stephen accused them of being 'stiff-necked ... with uncircumcised hearts'; of being no better than their fathers, who had resisted the Holy Spirit and persecuted the prophets, culminating in them murdering 'the Righteous One'; of receiving God's law, but not obeying it (7:51–53).

Their furious reaction confirmed to Stephen that he had signed his own death warrant. But at that moment, Stephen had an amazing experience – he 'looked up to heaven and saw the glory of God, and Jesus standing at the right hand of God' (v.55).

When he told the Sanhedrin this, they couldn't bear to hear it: 'they covered their ears and, yelling at the top of their voices, they all rushed at him, dragged him out of the city and began to stone him' (vv.57–58). Like his Lord before him, Stephen commended his spirit into God's hands, and prayed for the forgiveness of his persecutors (vv.59–60).

I wonder how Stephen's friends in the church at Antioch must have felt when they heard that Barnabas was off to fetch the very man who had approved of Stephen's death, and had masterminded the persecution that followed, which had caused them to flee for their lives to Antioch. Whatever their feelings, there is no suggestion that any of them shunned Saul when he arrived, as the believers had done in Jerusalem. I wonder if that was because Barnabas had done such a brilliant job of preparing their hearts to receive Saul before he went to Tarsus to find him.

Agabus

During that time, some prophets from Jerusalem arrived in Antioch (11:27). One of them was Agabus. Under the anointing of the Spirit, he prophesied that 'a severe famine would spread over the entire Roman world', which 'happened during the reign of Claudius' (v.28).

The church in Antioch responded magnificently to the need. Each person gave as much as they could to provide help for their brothers and sisters in the area of Judea, which included Jerusalem (v.29). This was a mark of how much the church in Antioch had grown, to the extent that it was now in a position to assist the church in Jerusalem. Barnabas and Saul took their gift to the elders in Jerusalem (v.30).

This would not be the last time that Saul would come across Agabus. He would meet him again in Caesarea when he was on his way to Jerusalem many years later, and Agabus would prophesy his forthcoming imprisonment in rather dramatic fashion: 'he took Paul's belt, tied his own hands and feet with it and said, "The Holy Spirit says, 'In this way the Jews of Jerusalem will bind the owner of this belt and will hand him over to the Gentiles'"'

(Acts 21:11). Shortly afterwards, Agabus's prophecy would come to pass, and Paul's series of trials would begin, resulting in his journey to Rome (21:17–26:32).

Missionary journey

There is no doubt that the church in Antioch played a formative role in the developing ministries of Barnabas and Saul. It was during one of the church leadership's worship, prayer and fasting sessions that God spoke: 'Set apart for me Barnabas and Saul for the work to which I have called them' (13:2). Although it was a great loss for them, the Antioch church was obedient to God's call, and 'placed their hands on them and sent them off' (v.3).

Barnabas and Saul sailed to Cyprus, which was familiar ground for Barnabas, being his homeland. In recording their time on the island, Luke mentions that Saul was now also called Paul (v.9), and from that point on, Paul is usually mentioned first, indicating that he had taken over the main leadership role from Barnabas. The man who had been Barnabas's protégé had now eclipsed him and become his leader. That can't have been easy for Barnabas to handle, but he clearly accepted what was happening graciously, and was content to continue with Paul on their journey in the supportive role.

From what we know of Barnabas, I wouldn't be surprised to learn that he was actually delighted to see what God was doing in Paul's life, praised God for it, and considered it a privilege to have played some part in Paul's development. Is this how we react when we find ourselves in a similar situation, or are we consumed with jealousy and resentment that this has happened?

And because Barnabas showed such an exemplary humble attitude, he proved God in new ways, and had experiences that he would have missed had he taken the hump and stormed off back to Antioch. For example, there was the incident with a sorcerer named Bar-Jesus in Paphos (vv.6–12; see Chapter 36); the healing of the crippled man in Lystra, which led to them being fêted as gods, and then the whole atmosphere changing with Paul being stoned and left for dead, but surviving (14:8–20); the joy of establishing fledgling churches and appointing elders in many towns of Asia Minor: Derbe, Lystra, Iconium, Antioch in Pisidia and Perga (vv.20–25); and the suffering caused by persecution which followed the preaching of the gospel, mainly due to the opposition of the local Jews (13:45,50; 14:2–5,19).

Like Barnabas, are we prepared to be humble before God, and accept the new challenges He presents us with, thus giving us the opportunity to prove Him in new ways?

Witness for the Gentiles

On their return to Antioch, Barnabas further showed his commitment to the acceptance of Gentiles into the kingdom of God by going with Paul to give evidence before the Council in Jerusalem. There he bore witness to 'the miraculous signs and wonders God had done among the Gentiles' (15:12).

Barnabas must have been overjoyed at the outcome of the meeting. A letter was prepared stating that Gentile converts were not expected to follow Jewish customs, such as circumcision, in order to become Christians (vv.19–29). This refuted the teaching being given by some Jewish converts that Gentiles had to do this in order to be saved (15:1). This lobby had been so strong in the church that even Barnabas appears to have been influenced by them temporarily (Gal. 2:13). I like to think that it was Barnabas who had the joy of reading this letter to the Antioch church (15:30–31).

James, the brother of Jesus

It was James who had presided over the Council meeting in Jerusalem. He was one of the brothers of Jesus, mentioned along with Joseph, Simon and Judas (Matt. 13:55; Mark 6:3). It seems that, along with the rest of the family, he did not accept that his brother Jesus was the Messiah, believing Him to be 'out of his mind' (Mark 3:21). Perhaps he was not surprised that his brother ended up on a cross. But then his brother certainly would have surprised him by appearing to him personally, risen from the dead (1 Cor. 15:7)!

I would love to have seen the look on James's face when he realised who it was standing in front of him. It must have been then that he realised that his brother was truly the Messiah, the Son of God. I wonder if this made him feel very guilty about not believing in Him during Jesus' lifetime. Was it at this moment that James determined to make up for his failure to believe by doing his utmost to support the apostles in any way he could?

James became a leader of the community of believers in Jerusalem (Gal. 2:9; Acts 12:17). In his letter to the Early Church, he described himself as 'a servant of God and of the Lord Jesus Christ' (James 1:1). If this letter is anything to go by, James was a very practical, down-to-earth man, who could be blunt and to the point, not mincing his words. Yet he also possessed great wisdom, as shown at the Council meeting attended by Paul and Barnabas (Acts 15:13–21). It was James who made the judgment about how the Gentiles should be treated, and suggested the writing of the letter that was taken to Antioch. Indeed, James probably drafted it himself.

Apparently, in later years he became known as 'James the Just', because he adhered faithfully to the Jewish law and lived in an austere manner. According to contemporary sources, he was martyred around AD 61, being condemned to death by stoning at the behest of Ananus, the high priest.

John Mark

When Paul suggested to Barnabas that they should 'go back and visit the brothers in all the towns where we preached the word of the Lord and see how they are doing' (15:36), it seems that Barnabas was very keen on the idea, but wanted to take his cousin John Mark with them again (v.37).

John Mark was a member of the Jerusalem church, which often met in the house where he lived with his mother, Mary. He was almost certainly there when their servant girl, Rhoda, went to answer the door, and found the apostle Peter standing there. Unbeknown to the believers gathered in the house to pray, Peter had been miraculously released from prison in answer to their prayers. In her excitement to tell everyone, Rhoda had left Peter waiting outside (12:12–16). I shouldn't think John Mark believed Rhoda's announcement any more than the others did!

John Mark had accompanied Paul and Barnabas on the Cyprus leg of their missionary journey, but had left them abruptly when they arrived at the port of Perga in Pamphylia, and gone back home to Jerusalem (13:13; 15:38). We are not told why John Mark left them in this way. He could have been homesick; after all, he had been with them in Antioch for quite a while before embarking on the journey to Cyprus as their assistant (12:25). Perhaps he wasn't happy about Paul becoming the leader of the expedition rather than his cousin Barnabas, with whom he probably got on much better. Maybe it was just the fact that he found the experience all too much to cope with, so he ran away when the going got tough. It's easy to criticise John Mark for behaving like this, but aren't we all inclined to 'run away' from difficult situations rather than face up to them and deal with them through God's strength and grace?

Barnabas was all for giving John Mark a second chance, but Paul was strongly opposed to the idea, given what had happened on the previous occasion. This caused a 'sharp disagreement' between them (15:39). Paul and Barnabas remained friends, but Paul took Silas with him instead (see Chapter 37). They divided the itinerary between them, with Barnabas and John Mark going back to Cyprus, while Paul and Silas made their way through Syria and Cilicia and into Asia Minor (vv.39–41). So two new missionary journeys took place instead of one, reminding us that God is well able to work out His purposes, even through our disagreements and differences of opinion.

Are we prepared to give people who have let us down a second chance? If Barnabas hadn't been patient with John Mark, encouraging and supporting him, then his cousin may never have had the chance to repay Barnabas's loyalty and faith in him like he did. John Mark clearly learnt from his mistakes, because he became not only a help to Barnabas, but also in time to Peter, and even to Paul himself, who clearly forgave him (Col. 4:10).

Peter speaks of him tenderly as 'my son Mark' (1 Pet. 5:13), while Paul commends him as being 'helpful to me in my ministry' (2 Tim. 4:11).

John Mark overcame his failure, and became such a valuable servant of God that he was entrusted with the writing of the first Gospel record, although it is placed second in the canon of the New Testament. If Barnabas had not encouraged him, the vibrant account of the ministry of Jesus that is Mark's Gospel, most of the information for which seems to have come from his close relationship with Peter, may well never have been written.

Interestingly, in his Gospel, John Mark referred to a 'young man, wearing nothing but a linen garment' who was there in the Garden of Gethsemane when Jesus was arrested. And, 'When they seized him, he fled naked, leaving his garment behind' (Mark 14:51–52). This 'young man' was probably John Mark himself.

How do we react to the failures in the service of God which we all experience? Do we allow them to shackle us, and prevent us from serving God as we should? Or, like John Mark, do we learn from those times, then let go of them and serve the Lord again? And who knows in what mighty ways He will use us when we do!

Chapter 34

Just a Needle and Thread

Dorcas

Acts 9:36–42

Stirred by the needs

Tabitha was a member of the community of believers in Joppa, nowadays called Jaffa. It is a coastal town which served as the seaport for Jerusalem, which lay about thirty-five miles to the south-east. Tabitha was more commonly known by the Greek form of her name, Dorcas.

We know only two things about Dorcas: she 'was always doing good and helping the poor' (v.36); and she was absolutely brilliant with a needle and thread and a pair of scissors. As far as we know, this was her one and only talent: the ability to make clothes (v.39). And how effectively Dorcas used it in God's service to minister to so many people around her! I imagine her sitting there by a window in her home day after day, sewing away, surrounded by large piles of materials of different colours, with a range of needles of varying types close to hand, praising the Lord as she worked. From what happened later, it seems that she didn't just use her talent for the benefit of the believers. Anyone in the town who was in need could expect to receive a gift of love, hand-made personally by Dorcas.

Her kind heart was stirred by the needs of others around her to the point where she didn't just feel sorry for them, but did what she could in a practical way to help them. Like Dorcas, is our concern for the plight of others translated into action to bring practical help to them, or does it just remain a matter of words?

Tragedy strikes

And then, suddenly, tragedy struck the poor people of Joppa. Dorcas 'became sick and died' (v.37). She was so highly regarded in the community that the believers, knowing the apostle Peter was in the nearby town of Lydda, sent two men to persuade him to 'come at once!' (v.38). The immediate arrival of this esteemed leader from Jerusalem was a further indication of how much Dorcas was valued among the believers.

Peter must have been swamped by the widows of the town, as they all brought the clothes that Dorcas had made for them and showed them to him, sobbing as they did so (v.39). It seems that many of them were not members of the church (v.41), yet Dorcas had touched their hearts and shown them the compassion of Christ by her actions. Talk about effective personal evangelism!

Alive!

What a moving scene that must have been: the body of Dorcas prepared for burial, with all the widows encircling it, weeping, clutching the fruits of her labours. It must have been too much for Peter, who 'sent them all out of the room' (v.40) so that he could concentrate on his praying. As he knelt there, I imagine his mind racing back to that occasion when he, along with James and John, was present in another room when Jesus brought Jairus's daughter back to life (Mark 5:37–42; see Chapter 16). On that occasion, Jesus spoke to the girl in Aramaic. Is that, I wonder, why Peter addressed Dorcas by the Aramaic form of her name, Tabitha? And, just as Jesus had done, Peter told her to 'get up' (v.40), to which she also responded immediately. What unconfined joy there must have been as Peter 'called the believers and the widows and presented her to them alive' (v.41)!

In this spectacular way, God was showing His approval of not only what Dorcas was doing, but also of her attitude. She is a fine example of the ideal 'one-talent' person, and stands in complete contrast to the third servant in the Parable of the Talents (Matt. 25:14–30). Like him, she could have hidden her talent away, deeming it to be insignificant when compared to the talents of others, such as the apostle Peter and all the miracles that God was doing through him. She could have sulked in a corner, being jealous of the talents of others in the church at Joppa. But she didn't. Dorcas reacted in exactly the right way, faithfully serving God by using her one talent for His glory. Dorcas took the initiative in using her gift, and took seriously her responsibility for making the most of it.

Do we react in the same way as Dorcas, or are we more like the disgruntled servant in the parable? Do we use the talent God has given us with enthusiasm in His service, or are we so busy looking at others, and being jealous of the giftings God has given them, that we sulkily bury ours 'in the ground' (Matt. 25:18), considering it to be of no importance? Dorcas stands as a lovely example of how God will honour and bless the ministry of any person who is willing to use whatever gift they have received from God in His service.

Dorcas being brought back to life quickly became the talk of the town, with the result that 'many people believed in the Lord' (v.42). Interestingly, it was Dorcas, not any of the apostles, whom God brought back to life. Now, I wonder what conclusions we can draw from that?

Chapter 35

Eager to Hear

Cornelius

Acts 10:1–8,19–48

'God-fearing'

Cornelius lived in the garrison city of Caesarea, which lay thirty miles up the coast to the north of Joppa. The city had been named after Augustus Caesar, and was the administrative capital of the district of Judea. This area included Jerusalem, which was situated sixty-five miles to the south-east. One of the features of Caesarea was its magnificent harbour, which had been constructed by Herod the Great (see Chapter 2).

Like the Roman officer who lived in Capernaum, and whose servant Jesus had healed (see Chapter 11), Cornelius was a centurion. Although they lived in different places and belonged to different regiments, they had both turned to Judaism in their search for God, and they both experienced God working in their lives in a remarkable way. Both of them would have experienced the hostility vented upon their Roman conquerors by the Jews; yet, at the same time, both of them had gained the respect of the local people due to their devotion to God and upright lives.

Cornelius certainly observed the Jewish religious duties of almsgiving and prayer – 'he gave generously to those in need and prayed to God regularly' (v.2). Added to which, 'He and all his family' had the reputation of being 'devout and God-fearing' (v.2). Here was a man whose heart was ready to receive the gospel.

Vision

One day, Cornelius went to pray at the appointed hour of three o'clock in the afternoon (v.3), unaware that he was about to have a rather startling experience. Interestingly, it was at the same appointed time for prayer that Peter and John had encountered the crippled man at the Beautiful Gate (3:1; see Chapter 28). As he was at prayer, Cornelius had a vision in which an angel appeared to him, and called him by name (v.3). Unlike Ananias (see Chapter 32), Cornelius was scared out of his wits by this vision, and 'stared at him in fear' (v.4). I'm sure most of us can understand that reaction! I imagine that when he asked the angel, 'What is it, Lord?' (v.4), it would have been in a rather trembling, shaky voice.

Cornelius probably thought that God had sent the angel to reprimand him about something, but nothing could have been further from the truth. What the angel said in reply must have comforted and reassured Cornelius that God was not angry with him at all. Indeed, according to the angel, God had noticed the centurion's faithful praying and generosity to the poor, which He had found to be a very pleasing sacrifice (v.4). Such proven sincerity and dedication to God meant that Cornelius was ready to be taken on to the next stage in his spiritual experience, so the angel instructed him to 'send men to Joppa to bring back a man named Simon who is called Peter' (v.5), and even told him in whose house Peter was staying (v.6).

In my experience, it is when we have proved ourselves faithful in what God has already given us to do, that He deems us ready to move on to new challenges in the work of His kingdom, where we will experience Him in a deeper way.

Sharing

I imagine Cornelius sitting quietly for a while as he tried to pull himself together after what he had seen and heard. What Cornelius did next is interesting. He didn't just summon a couple of trusty servants, but also one of his attendants who was 'a devout soldier' (v.7). Perhaps he and this devout attendant had prayed and studied the Scriptures together – a lovely picture of how faith in God brings people together, irrespective of race, gender, status or background.

But that's not all. Cornelius didn't just send the servants and the soldier off to Joppa to get Peter. Before he did so, 'He told them everything that had happened' (v.8) – presumably all about the vision, and what the angel had said. Cornelius could well have kept his experience to himself, but he shared it with these men, even though they were well beneath him, socially speaking. Do we share what God is doing in our lives with others, so that they might be encouraged, and give glory to God along with us? Don't let's keep God's goodness to ourselves!

It is also interesting that God didn't tell Cornelius to send for Philip the Evangelist (see Chapters 30–31), who may well have been in Caesarea at the time (8:40), but rather told him to send for Peter, who was in Joppa, over thirty miles away! Philip would seem to have been the ideal person for the job, because he had previous experience of sharing the gospel with people who were not Jews, whereas Peter hadn't. Indeed, God knew that Peter had severe misgivings about the whole issue of Gentiles becoming believers, and wanted to confront him with it (10:9–16). Telling Cornelius to send for Peter rather than Philip was all part of God's plan to deal with Peter's deeply rooted racial intolerance problem. It could be said that it wasn't just Cornelius who needed converting: Peter did as well!

Preparation

Little did Cornelius's servants and soldier know that, while they were on their way to Joppa, God was preparing Peter's heart to receive them, by means of a dramatic vision (vv.9–16). Indeed,

'Peter was wondering about the meaning of the vision' (v.17) while the men sent by Cornelius were getting directions, arriving at the house of Simon the tanner, and asking if Peter was there (vv.17–18).

Meanwhile, Peter was still up on the roof thinking about what he'd seen, when he heard the Spirit of God saying to him, 'Simon, three men are looking for you. So get up and go downstairs. Do not hesitate to go with them, for I have sent them' (vv.19–20). The next thing Cornelius's men knew was that Peter had appeared at the door. He told them that he was the man they were seeking, and asked them why they had come (v.21). They in reply told Peter about Cornelius, and his vision of an angel telling the centurion to send for him, 'so that he could hear what you have to say' (v.22).

Taboo broken

Having stayed overnight with Peter at Simon the tanner's house, they set off for Caesarea the next day, accompanied by some Jewish believers from Joppa (v.23). Meanwhile, Cornelius had been busy getting his family and close friends together at his house (v.24), ready to hear what Peter had to say when he came. Presumably Cornelius had told them all what had happened to him.

I imagine Cornelius eagerly looking out of the window to see if they were arriving yet, and the excitement that must have risen within him when he saw them approaching. I picture him rushing to the door to meet the man the angel himself had spoken of. No wonder Cornelius 'fell at his feet in reverence' (v.25). But Peter was having none of it, even though it must have been very flattering for him, a humble Jewish fisherman, to have a powerful Roman centurion bowing before him. Peter said to Cornelius, 'Stand up, I am only a man myself' (v.26). All the glory for anything that happened was to go to God.

Cornelius did as he was told, and a conversation took place between them as he ushered Peter into the room where the 'large gathering of people' (v.27) was assembled. When he invited Peter to visit him, Cornelius must have realised the enormity of what he was actually asking him to do; and this was reflected by Peter's opening words to the gathering: 'You are well aware that it is against our law for a Jew to associate with a Gentile or visit him' (v.28). The people gathered there must have been wondering why, then, Peter had indeed decided to break this centuries-old taboo. His next words must have thrilled them all: 'But God has shown me that I should not call any man impure or unclean' (v.28). No longer did he regard people like Cornelius as 'dogs' (see Chapter 18), so he had willingly come when called (v.29).

Peter had allowed God to melt his heart and change his thinking. Are we prepared to respond in a similar way to God's correction over wrong attitudes that we may hold, which are barriers to God's work progressing in our own churches?

Shock waves

Although he had no doubt heard what had happened to Cornelius from the men he had sent, clearly Peter wanted to hear it from Cornelius's own lips (v.29). Cornelius replied to Peter's question by going over what had occurred – though, interestingly, he missed out the bit about being terrified! Cornelius realised that this was no ordinary meeting. As he said to Peter, they were all there 'in the presence of God to listen to everything the Lord has commanded you to tell us' (v.33).

What a wonderful opportunity that opened up for Peter! And he took full advantage. He began by testifying to what God had been showing him personally: 'I now realise how true it is that God does not show favouritism but accepts men from every nation who fear him and do what is right' (vv.34–35). These words would send shock waves through the community of Jewish believers, and must have stunned those who had come with Peter from Joppa, and were sitting right there in the room when he said it. I would love to have seen their faces!

Peter surely realised that there would be consequences to face back in Jerusalem for what he was saying. But so fundamental had been the change in his thinking that he didn't seem to care about that. Peter went on to give them a summary of Jesus' life, death and resurrection, bringing them to the point of repentance: 'everyone who believes in him receives forgiveness of sins through his name' (v.43). It seems that there was a mass response to this in the hearts of all present, because 'While Peter was still speaking these words, the Holy Spirit came on all who heard the message' (v.44), with the result that they could be heard 'speaking in tongues and praising God' (v.46). This was God's confirmation that these Gentiles were truly born again, and that Gentiles and Jews were in fact equal in His sight. Yet another shock for the Jewish believers from Joppa (v.45)! The events that had occurred in the house of Cornelius that day would prove to be very significant in the development of the Early Church.

In view of these dramatic events, Peter realised that there was nothing to prevent these Gentile believers from being baptised in water; and they duly were (vv.47–48). Aware that they needed to be taught more about the faith they had embraced, they persuaded Peter to stay with them for a few days (v.48). Perhaps Peter got Philip to help him disciple these new converts, who must surely have been a wonderful addition to the fellowship of believers in Caesarea. Are we just as keen to be taught more about God, and to learn from those who are more mature in the faith?

Aftermath

Peter would indeed be hauled over the coals by those at headquarters in Jerusalem for what he had said and done in Caesarea (11:2–3). But his account of what God had done among these Gentiles would be instrumental in bringing about a sea change in the thinking of the Jews in the Early Church (11:18), with the result that Gentiles would eventually be accepted as believers in their own right, without having to become Jews first (15:1–29; see Chapter 33). Jews, Samaritans (see Chapter 30) and Gentiles had now all experienced God's salvation, and been filled with the Holy Spirit. Now they were all united in the Body of Christ (1 Cor. 12:13; Gal. 3:27–28).

As for Cornelius, it seems likely that he would have been

posted back to Rome sooner or later, given that he was in the Italian Regiment (10:1). So his conversion, and everything that went with it, could well have been a major factor in the spread of the gospel to Rome itself.

Chapter 36

Occult Involvement

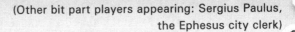

Bar-Jesus, the fortune-telling slave girl, the seven sons of Sceva, Demetrius

(Other bit part players appearing: Sergius Paulus, the Ephesus city clerk)

Introduction

From time to time during his missionary journeys, Paul encountered people involved in occult practices or worship of other deities. These included Bar-Jesus, a fortune-telling slave girl and her owners, the seven sons of Sceva, and Demetrius.

Bar-Jesus (Acts 13:6–12)
'Son of salvation'

Bar-Jesus was a Jew who lived in the town of Paphos on the west coast of Cyprus. He was a 'sorcerer and false prophet' (v.6), who was employed as 'an attendant of the proconsul, Sergius Paulus' (v.7), presumably for his occult abilities. It was unusual to find a Jew involved in such activities, given that such practices as divination and sorcery were forbidden under the Jewish law (Lev. 19:26; Deut. 18:10–11).

The name Bar-Jesus means 'son of Joshua', or 'son of salvation'. He was also known as Elymas (Acts 13:8–9), which means 'sorcerer' or 'wise man'. He was 'wise' in the sense of being able to supposedly predict the future (see Chapter 2), which is why many leaders in those times had such people in their entourage.

Dismay

Everything was going so well for Bar-Jesus, until Paul and Barnabas appeared. He would have been a man of importance, whose advice and opinions were sought by the proconsul, and undoubtedly he would have had a nice, cushy lifestyle to match his status. Bar-Jesus may well have heard that Paul and Barnabas had been preaching in Salamis, a city on the east coast of the island, about ninety miles away. And then they arrived in Paphos.

Bar-Jesus probably went to see Paul and Barnabas in action. I'm sure it didn't take him long to realise that the message of salvation and faith in God that they were preaching was a threat to everything he stood for and believed in. Imagine his dismay, then, when his boss, Sergius Paulus, decided that he would like to hear what Paul and Barnabas had to say, and invited them round 'because he wanted to hear the word of God' (v.7). The proconsul, fascinated as he seems to have been by the occult, was obviously searching for the truth. He is described as 'an intelligent man' (v.7), who seemingly enjoyed debating and listening to the latest ideas.

Bar-Jesus feared for his livelihood, should Sergius Paulus be persuaded by Paul and Barnabas to accept this new teaching. He made sure he was present when the proconsul was listening to them, and 'opposed them and tried to turn the proconsul from the faith' (v.8). I imagine him arguing vehemently against Paul and Barnabas, and using all his guile to persuade the proconsul to continue down the path of the occult, which had served him so well in the past.

Confrontation

Bar-Jesus surely cannot have anticipated what would happen next. He probably couldn't believe that Paul would have the effrontery to speak to him in such a manner in front of the proconsul, and with such boldness and power as well. I'm sure that the look in Paul's eyes as he turned on him, and the unequivocal language Paul used, would have stayed in Bar-Jesus' memory for a long time: 'You are a child of the devil and an enemy of everything that is right! You are full of all kinds of deceit and trickery. Will you never stop perverting the right ways of the Lord?' (v.10).

Paul condemned Bar-Jesus because he belied his name, being a son of the devil rather than a son of salvation. He identified him as an enemy of all that was good and true, and pronounced him guilty of perversion, deceit, and all kinds of wickedness. But then, to what must have been Bar-Jesus' growing horror, Paul announced the punishment God was inflicting upon him because of his evil deeds: 'Now the hand of the Lord is against you. You are going to be blind, and for a time you will be unable to see the light of the sun' (v.11).

No sooner were the words out of Paul's mouth than Bar-Jesus found himself going blind: 'Immediately mist and darkness came over him, and he groped about, seeking someone to lead him by the hand' (v.11). Bar-Jesus had come under the awesome judgment of God. Sergius Paulus was 'amazed' (v.12) at what he had seen. Before his very eyes, Bar-Jesus had been defeated by a power clearly greater than that which empowered his sorcerer. The gospel had triumphed over the occult. No wonder 'he believed' (v.12)!

Seeking to engage in rational debate with Bar-Jesus would not have worked. He needed to be confronted. In my experience, there are times when a calm and amiable conversation is the best way to deal with a situation in the church; but there are other times when directly confronting the problem is the only way to resolve it. May God give those of us in leadership the wisdom to know when to adopt which approach.

The fortune-telling slave girl (Acts 16:16–24)
'Pythoness'

Although she was a slave, this anonymous girl was possessed by an evil spirit which gave her the ability to tell fortunes, and even to supposedly predict the future. Being able to do this meant that she made a lot of money for her owners (v.16). Apparently, it would have been believed that she was possessed by what was known as 'a python spirit'. This was a reference to the snake which in mythology guarded Apollo's temple. Apollo was thought to be embodied in the snake and to bestow the powers of clairvoyance on his female devotees, known as 'pythonesses'.

It seems that this slave girl felt drawn to Paul and his companions; so much so that she followed them round the streets of Philippi shouting, 'These men are servants of the Most High God, who are telling you the way to be saved' (v.17). This went on day after day. They ignored her for a while, but eventually Paul 'became so troubled' (v.18) about the situation that he decided to take decisive action. I imagine him stopping abruptly, turning round, and looking the girl straight in the eye. She was probably startled by this turn of events, and stopped dead in her tracks, her words choking in her throat.

Exorcism

She may not have realised it, but it was the spirit within her that Paul was angry with, not her personally. He proceeded to address the spirit with authority: 'In the name of Jesus Christ I command you to come out of her!' (v.18). And the effect was immediate. Whether it shrieked, or threw her on the ground, we are not told.

Why did Paul do this, when the spirit was telling the truth about them? It may have been because he didn't want a demon doing a PR job for him, as that would have linked the gospel message with the occult, which clearly he would not want.

When the girl's owners realised that their rich source of income was no longer operational, 'they seized Paul and Silas and dragged them into the market-place to face the authorities' (v.19).

They kept the real reason for their anger to themselves, and instead stirred up racial and religious hatred against Paul and Silas by emphasising the fact that not only were they Jews, but they were teaching religious beliefs not approved by Rome (v.21). The result was that Paul and Silas were 'severely flogged' and 'thrown into prison' (vv.22–24; see Chapter 37).

On his release, did Paul subsequently spend some time with the girl, explaining the gospel to her, with the result that she became a member of the church in Philippi? It is quite possible that she did, given the fact that Luke records this incident between the conversions of Lydia and the jailer.

The seven sons of Sceva (Acts 19:11–20)
Ephesus

During his third missionary journey, Paul arrived back at Ephesus in Asia Minor (present-day Turkey). Not only was Ephesus a large commercial centre and the capital of the Roman province of Asia Minor, it was also one of the main religious centres of the Empire. There were temples dedicated to the worship of the emperor, but its main claim to fame was the huge temple of Artemis, the goddess of fertility.

Apparently, this temple was four times the size of the Parthenon in Athens, with over one hundred pillars, each around twenty metres high, topped with a white marble roof. It was one of the seven wonders of the ancient world. The temple contained an enormous and rather grotesque statue of Artemis, which was carved in the shape of a woman with many breasts, symbolising fertility. This image was said to have fallen from heaven (19:35), and could well have originally been a meteorite. Festivals in celebration of Artemis were characterised by wildness and immorality; and occult practices, many stemming from the worship of Artemis, were widespread in the city.

There in that place steeped in the black arts and magic, 'God did extraordinary miracles through Paul' (v.11) which topped anything that the people had seen before. So it wasn't long before Paul began attracting the attention of the occult elements of the city. Ephesus was full of people performing occult practices and exorcisms for money, and among them were the seven sons of Sceva. They were among various itinerant groups who went from place to place carrying out exorcisms and other practices (v.13). Some of these groups, including Sceva's sons, were Jews. Like Bar-Jesus, they seemed to have no qualms about disobeying the Jewish law which forbade such practices. Even though the sons of Sceva came from a priestly family (v.14), they were clearly serving money rather than God (Matt. 6:24). Which prompts the question: Which of the two is my master?

Copying

These Jews, including the sons of Sceva, were totally amazed by what Paul was doing, so they decided to copy him. Often, those performing exorcisms would include in their incantation a list of the names of various gods and goddesses, just to make sure they were calling on the name of the right one for that particular situation. Hearing Paul just using the one name, the name of Jesus, clearly impressed them no end. Obviously, there was greater power in that name than the ones they were calling upon; so they decided to tap into that power by invoking the name of Jesus in their exorcisms (vv.13–14).

What the sons of Sceva and the other Jews failed to realise is that the name of Jesus is not a magic formula that can be used by anyone willy-nilly. God's power cannot be manipulated by man, as they were about to find out. We have to know God personally before we are able to call upon the power that is in the name of Jesus.

One day, the sons of Sceva were performing an exorcism in a man's house and said, 'In the name of Jesus, whom Paul preaches, I command you to come out' (v.13). But this time, the evil spirit answered back and said, 'Jesus I know, and I know about Paul, but who are you?' (v.15). I can only imagine the look of horror that must have formed on their faces. I picture them standing there, rooted to the spot, mouths wide open, terrified. And with good reason, because 'the man who had the evil spirit jumped

on them and overpowered them all. He gave them such a beating
that they ran out of the house naked and bleeding' (v.16).

Bonfire

Not surprisingly, this incident had quite an impact on the
citizens of Ephesus! When they heard about what had happened,
'they were all seized with fear, and the name of the Lord Jesus
was held in high honour' (v.17). The result was that many people
became believers (v.18). So genuine was their repentance that 'A
number who had practised sorcery brought their scrolls together
and burned them publicly. When they calculated the value of
the scrolls, the total came to fifty thousand drachmas' (v.19);
a drachma was the equivalent of a day's wage. These converts
threw anything to do with their occult past on this huge bonfire,
including written magic formulas and spells, which they could
have sold for a lot of money.

I have found that, when people come to Christ, it is essential
they renounce any occult involvement and receive appropriate
ministry. This renunciation includes getting rid of any occult
literature, artefacts, symbols, clothing and anything at all
that is connected with such activities. To follow the example
of the people of Ephesus may seem a little extreme, but in my
experience it is very effective and helpful to the person as they
turn their back on their old way of life and make a new start in
life following Christ.

I have noticed that failure to renounce occult involvement
often results in deep spiritual problems, with the consequent lack
of spiritual progress and growth in God. And having emptied
themselves of all that is evil and connected with the occult,
it is vital that a person allows God to fill them with His Holy
Spirit, otherwise they may well find themselves in an even worse
predicament, such as Jesus Himself described (Matt. 12:43–45).

Demetrius (Acts 19:23–41)

(Other bit part player appearing: the Ephesus city clerk)

Rhetoric

Another interesting episode took place while Paul was in Ephesus. The great temple of Artemis was understandably a huge tourist attraction. Men like the silversmith, Demetrius, would obviously have taken full advantage of that, and made themselves a fat profit. Demetrius, who was probably the master of the guild of silversmiths at the time, 'made silver shrines of Artemis', and 'brought in no little business for the craftsmen' (v.24). However, it wasn't long before Demetrius noticed a worrying decline in sales, which coincided with Paul's presence in the city. It didn't take a genius to work out that due to Paul's preaching, the sale of goods associated with Artemis had fallen rapidly as people stopped worshipping the goddess and followed this new teaching called 'the Way' (v.23).

I'm sure Demetrius gave serious thought as to the best course of action to reverse this trend. In the end, he decided to stage a riot. He called a union meeting of all the silversmiths and 'workmen in related trades' (v.25). I imagine Demetrius delivering his speech with great passion, as he stirred the meeting into a fury.

It was a carefully constructed speech. Demetrius started by playing on their fear that they would lose their 'good income from this business' (v.25). Then he stirred up their racial and religious prejudice, placing the blame squarely on the shoulders of Paul, well known to be a Jew, for this state of affairs: 'you see and hear how this fellow Paul has convinced and led astray large numbers of people here in Ephesus and in practically the whole province of Asia' (v.26). He followed this up by pouring scorn on what Paul was teaching: 'He says that man-made gods are no gods at all' (v.26).

Then finally he whipped the throng into a frenzy by stirring up their patriotism and religious fervour for all that their city stood for: 'There is a danger not only that our trade will lose its good name, but also that the temple of the great goddess Artemis will be discredited, and the goddess herself, who is worshipped throughout the province of Asia and the world, will be robbed of her divine majesty' (v.27). I can hear his voice rising in pitch and volume as he spoke about their beloved goddess. Stirring rhetoric indeed!

Riot

And it had the desired effect. The silversmiths and tradesmen were beside themselves with anger and fervour, and began shouting, 'Great is Artemis of the Ephesians!' (v.28). It seems that they spilled out into the streets, presumably still shouting this refrain, because 'Soon the whole city was in an uproar' (v.29). The mob seized Paul's companions, Gaius and Aristarchus (see Chapter 42), who found themselves being propelled through the streets in the direction of the city's huge amphitheatre (v.29), which could apparently hold 25,000 people.

When Paul heard about what had happened, he was desperate to go to the amphitheatre and speak to the crowd, presumably to rescue his two companions; but wiser counsels prevailed (vv.30–31). It seems that large numbers of citizens had got caught up with the baying mob, because confusion reigned in the amphitheatre, and 'Most of the people did not even know why they were there' (v.32).

Alexander, a Jew, was pushed to the front by his fellow Jews, who shouted instructions to him as he tried to address the crowd. If he had been given the chance, he would presumably have told the mob that the Jewish community had nothing whatsoever to do with what this Jew Paul was saying, and shouldn't be held accountable with him for the nosedive in their trade (v.33). But when the crowd realised that Alexander was a Jew, they all began to shout again in unison 'Great is Artemis of the Ephesians!' – and didn't let up for two whole hours (v.34)!

Peace restored

The news of what was happening in the amphitheatre must have reached the ears of the council, because the city clerk eventually appeared on the scene. His speech was just as skilful as that of

Demetrius. He denied that the cult of Artemis was in any danger, so they were getting in a state about nothing (vv.35–36); he pronounced that Gaius and Aristarchus were innocent of saying or doing anything against the goddess (v.37); he reminded Demetrius that if they had a legitimate grievance, there were procedures in place for dealing with it (vv.38–39); and he warned all present that the Romans would not take kindly to reports of riots in their city, and there could well be repercussions if they didn't disperse peacefully (v.40). And, with that, 'he dismissed the assembly' (v.41). Once again, a Satan-inspired attack on Paul's ministry had been thwarted. Isn't it wonderful to be reminded that Satan is a defeated foe, and has no power over us?

I wonder how Demetrius reacted? Did he go home with his tail between his legs? Or did he smoulder about the situation, and look for another opportunity to make trouble for Paul and the believers? Whatever the case, Demetrius the silversmith is not heard of again, while the church in Ephesus became firmly rooted and grounded in the faith.

Chapter 37

Surprising Choice

Silas

Acts 15:22,27,32,34; 15:40–17:15; 18:5
(Other bit part players appearing: Timothy, Luke, Lydia,
the Philippian jailer, Jason)

Chosen

It seems that Silas was a prominent member of the church in Jerusalem. There, he had demonstrated prophetic gifts (15:32), and was chosen by the church to accompany Paul and Barnabas back to Antioch, along with Judas Barsabbas (vv.22,27; see Chapter 33). It isn't clear whether Silas stayed in Antioch, or went back to Jerusalem (v.34). But something about him must have impressed Paul, because he chose Silas to accompany him on his second missionary journey, following his disagreement with Barnabas (vv.39–40; see Chapter 33). Paul's selection of Silas may have had something to do with the fact that, like himself, Silas was a Roman citizen (16:38). However, it could be said to be rather a surprising choice because, as we shall see, it seems that Silas was more of a literary man than an 'upfront' person. Perhaps Paul wanted Silas along to keep a record of what happened, and maybe Silas passed his notes on to Luke.

Silas must have been absolutely thrilled to be asked by Paul to go with him, having heard what had happened in the places Paul and Barnabas had visited. This would certainly be a completely new experience for him. However, it seems that Silas had a more subservient role than Barnabas, because nowhere is Silas referred to in general terms as an apostle, as Barnabas was (14:14).

Hindrance (Acts 16:1-3)

Paul's plan was to encourage the churches established during his first journey, and having visited Derbe, where Gaius was one of the believers (20:4), he and Silas arrived in Lystra (16:1). It was there that they met and got to know a young man called Timothy, who had become a highly regarded disciple (v.2). Perhaps Paul and Silas stayed in his family home with his mother Eunice and grandmother Lois (2 Tim. 1:5). Timothy could well have been among those present when Paul had been stoned and left for dead during his previous visit to Lystra (14:19-20; 2 Tim. 3:11).

Paul was so taken with Timothy, and saw such potential in him, that he 'wanted to take him along on the journey' (v.3). It seems that when the leaders at Lystra laid hands on Timothy, a prophetic message was given about him receiving a certain ministry gift from God (1 Tim. 1:18; 4:14), which would have endorsed Paul's choice of him.

Timothy must have been really excited about the prospect of going with Paul; but there was a potential problem. Timothy was of mixed race parentage: his mother was a Jewess who had become a believer; his father was a Greek (v.1). In the eyes of the Jews, this made Timothy a half-breed, like a Samaritan. Paul asked Timothy to be circumcised to avoid any problems with Jews 'in that area' (v.3) who still thought that believers had to become Jews before they could be saved. The Council of Jerusalem had made it quite clear that this was not required (15:1-29; see Chapter 33), so Timothy did not have to undergo this. The fact that he was prepared to be circumcised shows how keen Timothy was not to be a hindrance to the spread of the gospel in any way; and how desperate he was to go with Paul. What are we prepared to do – or maybe stop doing – that affects us personally, so that we might be more effective witnesses for Christ?

Into Europe (Acts 16:6–10)

I wonder what Silas thought about Paul inviting this young man to accompany them, albeit in the role of an assistant? As they travelled on, the Spirit of God clearly led them, allowing them to preach in some areas but not others, and finally guiding them to the port of Troas (vv.6–8). It was there that they met up with the man who was to become the author of the third Gospel and 'The Acts of the Apostles' – Doctor Luke, a Greek, who may have been originally from Antioch, and therefore known to Paul. Clearly Luke accepted Paul's invitation to join them, because from this point on (v.10) the pronoun 'we' is used in the narrative, indicating that Luke was now an eyewitness to all that occurred.

I imagine Silas, Timothy and Luke sitting there having breakfast one morning, wondering where they might be going next, when Paul came bursting in, talking excitedly about a vision he had experienced during the night. He had seen 'a man of Macedonia standing and begging him, "Come over to Macedonia and help us"' (v.9). Clearly, God was guiding them into Europe, so 'we got ready at once to leave for Macedonia, concluding that God had called us to preach the gospel to them' (v.10).

In my experience, there are times when God does not open the doors we expect but leads us into places we might not have anticipated, or even wanted to go. These are often places of great challenge and difficulty, as Paul and his companions would soon discover, but also bring great rewards for the kingdom of God.

Lydia (Acts 16:11–15)

Having crossed the sea and arrived in Macedonia, they headed for the main city of the area, Philippi (vv.11–12). The ruler known as Philip of Macedon had so named it in the fourth century BC. It seems that a woman called Lydia, 'a dealer in purple cloth from the city of Thyatira, who was a worshipper of God' (v.14), and some like-minded women used to gather by the river outside the city to pray. Imagine their surprise and curiosity, then, when one Sabbath day they saw four men approaching, who sat down close by them, obviously with the intention of speaking to them (v.13).

Lydia was a businesswoman, and was probably quite wealthy due to the fact that purple cloth was by no means the cheapest on the market, and was often worn as a sign of royalty or nobility. Lydia would probably have been the agent in Macedonia for a manufacturer in Thyatira, a city renowned for its dyes. But it seems that Lydia realised that there was more to life than a successful business. She and her friends were clearly seeking God, and had apparently failed to find Him in any of the religions practised in Philippi.

Perhaps it was Lydia herself who invited the men to speak to them. As Paul spoke, something must have stirred within her as 'The Lord opened her heart to respond to Paul's message' (v.14), and she became a believer. She was baptised soon after, presumably in that river, along with all her household (v.15). Then she invited Paul, Silas, Timothy and Luke to stay at her home, which I imagine would have been rather large and opulent. Apparently Lydia was a very persuasive lady (v.15). After all, she was in the business of selling and marketing! Her house became the base for the work of Paul and Silas, and the place where the growing number of believers would gather (v.40).

The jailer (Acts 16:16–40)
Songs in the night

It wasn't long before Paul and Silas found themselves languishing in the local jail. Following Paul's exorcism of a fortune-telling slave girl (see Chapter 36), her furious owners had grabbed hold of Silas as well as Paul, and dragged them before the magistrates, accusing them of 'throwing our city into an uproar by advocating customs unlawful for us Romans to accept or practise' (vv.20–21). At that point, the crowd joined in, and Silas found himself being stripped and subjected to the excruciating pain of being beaten, along with Paul, on the order of the magistrates (v.22).

After this severe flogging, he and Paul were thrown into the prison. The jailer was given strict instructions to guard these men carefully (v.23), so he clamped them in the stocks reserved for the most dangerous prisoners, 'in the inner cell' (v.24) of the prison. Little did the jailer know it, but he was about to have a night to remember!

I wonder if at that point Silas began to wish that Paul had never asked him to accompany him? Clamped in stocks, his body wracked with pain, Silas would not have experienced anything like this before. The most discomfort this literary man had probably suffered until now was writer's cramp! Paul had been warned that he would 'suffer for my [Christ's] name' (9:16); but when he set out from Antioch, did Silas have any idea that he would be called upon to suffer in such a way?

Does it ever occur to us in the cocoon of the Western world that we may be called upon to suffer for the sake of the gospel in the future? Not an appealing thought, I know; but one that may spur us on to pray more fervently for our brothers and sisters in other lands, for whom suffering for the sake of the gospel is an everyday occurrence.

Rather than feeling sorry for themselves and questioning God as to why He had let this happen to them, as we so often do, Paul and Silas not only began to pray, but began to sing hymns of praise to God, even though it was midnight (v.25). Do we look at God rather than at the circumstances we find ourselves in? Do we praise God, even in our darkest 'midnight' times, acknowledging that He is still worthy of our praise, or does our worship depend on our circumstances?

The result was that 'the other prisoners were listening to them' (v.25). No doubt they were amazed at Paul and Silas's response to their situation, and wondered how they could react like that when their own reactions were so different. People are watching us, too; and who knows how many of them will be affected by the way we conduct ourselves in difficult times, with the result that they will come to Christ – as was about to happen in this prison.

A quaking awakening

The jailer had probably just dropped off to sleep, when he was rudely awakened by an earthquake. It was so violent that 'the foundations of the prison were shaken. At once all the prison doors flew open, and everybody's chains came loose' (v.26). Talk about the power of praise!

When he saw the prison doors flung wide open, fear must have gripped the jailer's whole being. He would have assumed that all the prisoners had escaped, and that he would be held accountable by the authorities. The jailer knew that meant only one thing: he would be put to death (see Acts 12:19). To save himself and his family the indignity of public humiliation, he decided to end his life then and there, and drew his sword to commit suicide (v.27).

But then the jailer heard a voice coming from the inner cell. One of those high-risk prisoners he had clamped in the stocks was shouting at him. His ears couldn't believe what they heard: 'Don't harm yourself! We are all here!' (v.28). The jailer's mouth must have dropped open for a moment. Could it possibly be true? There was only one way to find out! So he called for lights to be brought, and checked out the situation. When he realised that no one had indeed escaped, he 'rushed in and fell trembling before Paul and Silas' (v.29). He obviously thought that somehow they were responsible for the fact that the prisoners were all still there, despite them not being chained up any more.

Salvation

The jailer was so grateful that he brought them out of the prison and took them to his house. But before he ministered to them physically, he realised that he had a greater need – he needed them to minister to him spiritually. So he asked them, 'Sirs, what must I do to be saved?' (v.30). Paul finished up telling not only the jailer but his whole household the answer: 'Believe in the Lord Jesus, and you will be saved' (vv.31–32). They all responded immediately, and were baptised, having first tended to Paul and Silas's wounds (v.33) – which must have taken some time, considering all that they had been through. Finally, they all sat down for a meal together. The jailer could scarcely contain his joy: not because none of the prisoners had escaped – although he must have been mightily relieved about that – but rather 'because he had come to believe in God – he and his whole family' (v.34).

The next morning, the jailer received an order from the magistrates telling him to 'Release those men' (v.35). So the jailer told Paul, 'The magistrates have ordered that you and Silas be released. Now you can leave. Go in peace' (v.36). But Paul was having none of it, and said to the officers, 'They beat us publicly without a trial, even though we are Roman citizens, and threw us into prison. And now do they want to get rid of us quietly? No! Let them come themselves and escort us out' (v.37).

Paul wanted it demonstrated to the whole of Philippi that he and Silas were innocent, and had been freed by the magistrates themselves. This climb down by the authorities would send the clear message that the gospel was no longer to be regarded as 'unlawful ... to accept or practise' (v.21), which would help to protect any converts in Philippi from persecution in the future. The magistrates were all sweetness and light when they arrived at the prison (vv.38–39), mainly due to the fact that Paul and Silas were Roman citizens, who shouldn't have been treated in this way, and could complain about it to higher authorities.

Answered prayer

Paul and Silas complied with their request to leave the city, taking Timothy with them. But it seems that Luke stayed behind, as the pronoun 'they' replaces 'we' in the narrative (v.40). However, Paul and Silas didn't leave before they had gone to Lydia's house and encouraged the believers (v.40). Surely they must have been praying there for Paul and Silas; and their prayers had been answered. What a fillip that must have been for the Philippians! Not to mention the growth that was happening, with people from all strata of society and backgrounds – like Lydia, the jailer and maybe even the slave girl – joining the ranks of believers. Now that must have made for some interesting discussion groups!

Included in their number was Clement, and two women called Euodia and Syntyche, who seem to have been at each other's throats all the time (Phil. 4:2–3). Paul in his letter pleaded with them to sort out their differences and be reconciled to each other for the sake of the gospel. Is there anyone in our church with whom we need to be reconciled?

Thessalonica (Acts 17:1–9)

From Philippi, Silas and Timothy went with Paul to Thessalonica, a journey of one hundred miles south-west along the Via Egnatia. There, they stayed in the house of a man named Jason (v.5). Once again, Silas would have listened as Paul explained to the Jews in the local synagogue how Jesus was the Christ (vv.2–3), and had the joy of seeing some of them being persuaded by Paul's cogent argument, and becoming believers, 'as did a large number of God-fearing Greeks and not a few prominent women' (v.4). It seems likely that among them would have been Aristarchus and Secundus (20:4).

Fuelled by jealousy at the success of Paul's ministry, the rest of the Jews 'rounded up some bad characters from the market-place, formed a mob and started a riot in the city' (v.5). The Jews obviously told 'rent-a-mob' to go and get Paul and Silas, and bring them before the citizens' council, giving them the address of their host. But when the mob charged into Jason's house, the two they were after weren't there, so they 'dragged Jason and some other brothers before the city officials' (v.6). They had obviously been well primed by the Jews as to what to say, which they proceeded to do at a very loud volume: 'These men who have caused trouble all over the world have now come here, and Jason has welcomed them into his house. They are all defying Caesar's decrees, saying that there is another king, one called Jesus' (vv.6–7). These accusations of treason against the Roman Emperor threw the court into a state of total confusion (v.8). The decision was made to allow the accused out on bail (v.9).

It was probably Jason who stumped up the money and gave the necessary assurances that there would be no further trouble.

Jason was obviously a very courageous man to host Paul, Silas and Timothy in the first place, and to take the flak for them. Because of him, they were more able to be effective during their time in the city. Do we continue to faithfully play our part in the work of the kingdom, even though, like Jason, it may cause us some grief at times?

Berea (Acts 17:10–15)

The believers knew that the Jews wouldn't let the matter rest there. So they insisted that Paul and Silas (and Timothy) should move on to Berea, fifty miles to the south-west, as soon as it got dark (v.10). When they arrived in Berea, Silas again accompanied Paul to the local synagogue. The response there was even better than it had been in Thessalonica (v.12), and among the converts would probably have been Sopater (20:4). The gospel message was received 'with great eagerness', and the Bereans 'examined the Scriptures every day to see if what Paul said was true' (v.11).

Would that all Christians today did the same! In my experience, many are still deceived by honeyed words, a handsome appearance, an appealing style, or a charismatic personality. Do we test everything we hear against what the Bible says, irrespective of where the words are coming from?

It wasn't long before the Jews in Thessalonica heard what Paul was doing in Berea, so 'they went there too, agitating the crowds and stirring them up' (v.13). Silas and Timothy stayed behind for the moment but the believers sent Paul to the coast out of harm's way (v.14). From there, Paul was escorted to Athens (vv.16–34), where Dionysius and Damaris, among others, became believers.

What happened to Silas?

By the time Silas and Timothy caught up with Paul, he had moved on from Athens to Corinth (18:1; see Chapter 38). It is at this point (18:5) that Silas disappears from the narrative. It seems likely that Silas stayed in Corinth, because Paul makes mention of his work there (2 Cor. 1:19), and names him in his introduction to the two letters to the Thessalonians, which were both written when Paul was in Corinth.

It seems that, at some point in his life, Silas met up with Peter, and that he assisted the apostle in the writing of his pastoral letter to the church (1 Pet. 5:12). Silas may well have been Peter's scribe, or it could be that he helped Peter to actually construct the letter. This would be further evidence that Silas was a literary man. He could well have even been Paul's scribe for the letters to the Thessalonians, which he almost certainly delivered. Similarities in style between Thessalonians, 1 Peter and the letter sent to Antioch by the Council of Jerusalem (15:23–29) indicate that Silas may have penned the Council's letter as well.

From his adventures in the company of Paul, it is evident that Silas proved to be a strong and determined character, who was prepared to take every opportunity and means to communicate his faith. He was not put off by the rigours and suffering involved in preaching the gospel, but just kept on going. Silas was a team player, who was flexible and willing to serve God in whatever capacity He chose, even if that meant being hidden away writing rather than out in the spotlight. It seems to me that Silas is an excellent example for us all to follow.

What happened to Luke?

Having apparently stayed on in Philippi for a while, Luke met Paul again when the apostle returned to that city. They sailed to Troas together, and joined the rest of the group who were to accompany Paul to Jerusalem (20:6). They stayed in Troas for a week, during which time Luke witnessed Paul raise from the dead a man named Eutychus, who had dropped off to sleep during one of Paul's lengthy sermons and fallen out of a third-storey window (vv.7–12).

When Luke, Paul and the others arrived in Jerusalem, 'the brothers received us warmly' (21:17). It isn't clear whether Luke was still in Jerusalem when Paul was arrested following trouble stirred up by visiting Jews. But he was certainly with Paul on the journey to Rome (27:1–28:16; see Chapter 39), because the pronoun 'we' reappears in the narrative. It seems that Luke stayed in Rome, because Paul refers to him in the greetings list of two of his letters written during his period under house arrest there, speaking of him as 'Our dear friend Luke, the doctor' (Col. 4:14), and naming him as one of his fellow-workers in Philemon verse 24. No doubt Luke's professional skills as a doctor were of great help to Paul during the experiences they shared together over the years. Like Luke, are we prepared to use our professional abilities in God's service, and to go wherever He sends us?

Some years later, during his second term of imprisonment in Rome, Paul wrote that 'Only Luke is with me' (2 Tim. 4:11). So it seems that Luke was with Paul to the end. What happened to Luke after the martyrdom of his friend Paul is not clear. He may well have stayed in Rome to write his Gospel and The Acts of the Apostles during the years AD 63–70.

In writing these accounts, Luke showed himself to be a meticulous chronicler, who claimed to 'have carefully investigated everything from the beginning' (Luke 1:3), and to have produced 'an orderly account' of all that occurred pertaining to the life of Jesus Christ, the ministry of the apostles, particularly Paul, and the growth of the Church. His close personal contact with many of the apostles and leaders of the Church, and his visits to Jerusalem and other places connected with the ministry of Jesus, meant that he had excellent opportunities to gather first-hand material to use in his writings. Luke was a well-educated Greek, and the style of his writing reflects this, showing an extensive and rich vocabulary. His main theme was the good news that Jesus was the Saviour of the world, and how this gospel of great joy was proclaimed throughout the then known world. Some sources say that Luke died in Greece at the age of eighty-four.

What happened to Timothy?
As for Timothy, he also stayed in Corinth for a while (2 Cor. 1:19), but then joined Paul in Athens. Paul showed great confidence in the youthful Timothy by sending him from Athens to Thessalonica to hearten the Christians there who were being persecuted; and he brought back an encouraging report to the

apostle (1 Thess. 3:1–7). Paul subsequently included Timothy's name as well as that of Silas in his letters to the Thessalonians.

It seems that Timothy was with Paul during his time in Ephesus, from whence he was sent with Erastus to Macedonia (Acts 19:22), and then on to Corinth. It is clear that, by this time, a very close relationship had developed between Timothy and Paul, to the extent that Paul referred to him as 'my son whom I love, who is faithful in the Lord' (1 Cor. 4:17). It seems that Timothy was of a timid disposition (2 Tim. 1:7), because Paul made a point of urging the believers in Corinth to accept him kindly (1 Cor. 16:10–11), especially since he would have been regarded as rather young for such responsibilities.

Even though it appears that Timothy's mission did not achieve the desired results (see 2 Corinthians), Paul did not lose confidence in him, but continued to take Timothy with him. Paul even took him along when he next visited Corinth, because Timothy was with him when he wrote his letter to the Romans from that city (Rom. 16:21).

Timothy was also among the group of men who accompanied Paul to Jerusalem (Acts 20:4), and is warmly commended by Paul in his letters to the Colossians (1:1) and to Philemon (v.1). Paul also speaks highly of him in his letter to the Philippians, and expresses his intention of sending Timothy to visit them to see how they are getting on (Phil. 1:1; 2:19–23).

Timothy had become one of Paul's closest friends. They had been through a lot together, and no doubt had experienced the whole gamut of emotions together in the work of God. By now, Paul was confident enough in his youthful companion to leave him in charge of overseeing the infant church in Ephesus, while he went to Macedonia (1 Tim. 1:3–4). When Paul realised that he might not be returning to Ephesus, he wrote the first of two personal letters to Timothy, giving him advice, instructions, warnings, comfort and help. The second of these epistles was written from Paul's prison cell in Rome. Timothy himself seems to have been a prisoner too at some point in his life, but no one knows where; and although he was released (Heb. 13:23), there is no record of what happened to him.

The letters which Paul wrote to Timothy have proved to be a source of help and inspiration for many people down the years. Towards the end of his second epistle to Timothy, Paul wrote these triumphant words, which inspire us to have the same kind of confidence in God that he had: 'The Lord will rescue me from every evil attack and will bring me safely to his heavenly kingdom. To him be glory for ever and ever. Amen' (2 Tim. 4:18).

Chapter 38

Equally Yoked

Priscilla and Aquila

**Acts 18:2–3,18–19,24–26; Romans 16:3–5;
1 Corinthians 16:19; 2 Timothy 4:19**
(Other bit part player appearing: Apollos)

Expelled

If ever there was a couple who exemplified togetherness in both their marriage and their work for God, it was Priscilla and Aquila. Not only do their names rhyme, but they seem to have lived together harmoniously, and to have complemented each other perfectly. I'm sure their relationship had some ups and downs, like all marriages do, but it doesn't seem to have affected their unity and devotion to one another.

Interestingly and unusually, Priscilla is always named first. This possibly suggests that she was a Roman lady of higher rank than her husband, or it may be that she was the more prominent of the two in the church. Nothing is actually known about Priscilla's background, but Aquila was a Jew who came from Pontus (18:2), a town on the northern Black Sea coast of Asia Minor (Turkey). Whether he married Priscilla there, or met her after he migrated to Rome isn't clear, but they were among the Jews expelled from Rome in AD 49 by Emperor Claudius (v.2). The writings of the historian Suetonius suggest that this expulsion of all the Jews in Rome occurred because of prolonged disturbances in the Jewish community caused by the preaching of the gospel of Jesus Christ. It seems likely then that Priscilla and Aquila had become Christians while in Rome. I wonder if Cornelius on his return to Rome had anything to do with their conversion (see Chapter 35)?

They must have been devastated to have to leave their home in Rome, and the business that they would undoubtedly have established. What discussions Priscilla and Aquila must have had about where to seek refuge can only be imagined; but, in the end, they decided to leave Italy altogether, and make their home in Achaia (southern Greece) in the city of Corinth. They arrived there, homeless and destitute.

Tentmakers united

In those days, Corinth was more important than Athens in many ways. It was the commercial centre of Greece, a fact which may have attracted Priscilla and Aquila as business people. The downside was that it was a city renowned for its sexual immorality, largely due to the worship of Aphrodite, the goddess of love, which flourished there. No wonder sexual immorality was a subject high on the agenda when Paul wrote his letters to the believers there in future years.

Aquila was a tentmaker by trade (v.3), and no doubt Priscilla pitched in to help. It was hard work sewing the coarse camel hair or goat hair cloth into tents, and the remuneration wasn't great. They probably sold the tents they made to the Roman army, where they were used to house troops on the move.

One day, Priscilla and Aquila were working away when a man stopped to talk to them (v.2). As they got into conversation with this visitor to the city, they learnt that he was a tentmaker like them. But what must have delighted them far more was the fact that he was also a Jew who had become a believer. Priscilla and Aquila must have been enthralled as the man told them about the amazing circumstances of his conversion. Whether they had heard about Paul before isn't clear, but they invited him to stay with them; and, in return, he offered to work alongside them, helping them to make the tents (v.3).

We can only imagine the discussions that took place between them as they worked together and relaxed together. Priscilla and Aquila must have learnt so much about God from Paul during that time, causing their faith to grow enormously. Not only were the three of them united in their profession of tentmaking, but also in their profession of faith in Christ.

It's great to get together with others who are of the same profession and work as ourselves – people who really understand what the job entails, and truly empathise with what we are going through. Such times can be very mutually supportive. But isn't it even more wonderful to be able to share fellowship with those of like mind in Christ: to learn about God together; to grow in faith together; to pray, praise and worship together; to support each other and bear one another's burdens; to grow in love for one another in 'the unity of the Spirit through the bond of peace' (Eph. 4:3)?

In Corinth

I'm sure Priscilla and Aquila went with Paul to the synagogue every Sabbath and sat there fascinated, listening intently as he 'reasoned in the synagogue, trying to persuade Jews and Greeks' (18:4), and found their understanding of the gospel growing all the time.

One day, Paul's companions, Silas and Timothy (see Chapter 37) arrived from Macedonia (v.5). I imagine that Priscilla and Aquila put them up as well! Now that Silas and Timothy had arrived, Priscilla and Aquila must have agreed that Paul should spend his time concentrating on his preaching (v.5), while they continued to support them all through their tentmaking and hospitality. The result was that many people came to faith in Christ in Corinth and nearby Cenchrea. They included Titius Justus, also known as Gaius, in whose house Paul held meetings, and who also provided Paul with hospitality (v.7, Rom. 16:23); Crispus, the synagogue ruler, and his family (v.8); Chloe, Stephanas and his family, Fortunatus and Achaicus (1 Cor. 1:11,14–16; 16:15,17); Phoebe, Tertius, Erastus, who was 'the city's director of public works', and Quartus (Rom. 16:1,22–24).

Paul stayed in Corinth for eighteen months, 'teaching them the word of God' (18:11). As well as continuing to learn such a lot during this time, Priscilla and Aquila would have supported Paul as he experienced abusive opposition from some Jews (v.6), presumably led by Sosthenes, the successor to Crispus, who had become a believer (v.8). It ended up in a court case (vv.12–17), where Paul was virtually accused of treason for preaching the gospel. The case was summarily dismissed by Gallio, the proconsul, thus allowing the gospel to be preached freely.

Priscilla and Aquila must have been thrilled at this verdict, and at all that God was doing in Corinth. They come across to me as an amazingly staunch and effective 'back room' team. Priscilla and Aquila were not 'upfront' people; but without them, I don't think Paul would have been able to carry on his ministry in Corinth with such success.

Shock

Priscilla and Aquila must have realised that Paul wouldn't be staying in Corinth for ever. So, it can't have come as a surprise to them when Paul announced that he was leaving and returning to Syria (v.18). However, Priscilla and Aquila must have been completely shocked when Paul told them that he wanted them to go with him. How unsettling that must have been for them! They were now well established in Corinth with a home and business; they had put down roots, and must have been feeling comfortable at last. And here was Paul asking them to leave it all behind. It was the Rome experience all over again: except, this time, it was their decision whether to leave.

Did they agonise about it for hours, days or weeks, or did they respond immediately to the call? We can only imagine; all we know is that they did go with Paul (v.18). They may even have funded his trip. How do we react when God asks us to move out of our comfort zone into the unknown? Do we cling on to the safety of what we know, or do we revel in the excitement of what God has in store for us in this new opportunity?

In Ephesus

On their way by boat to Syria, Paul, Priscilla and Aquila stopped off at the port of Ephesus in Asia Minor. While there, Paul went to the synagogue, where the people were very responsive, and wanted him to stay longer (vv.19–20). Was this why Paul decided to leave Priscilla and Aquila there in Ephesus, so they could follow up on what Paul had begun? Did this mark a change of plan, or had God already told Paul to leave Priscilla and Aquila in Ephesus rather than take them on to Syria with him?

It seems that this remarkable couple were so submitted and committed to God's will that they were quite prepared to stay in Ephesus, even though when they left Corinth they probably thought they were going to be accompanying Paul to Syria and beyond. How open are we to what God wants us to do?

How must they have felt when they had to say goodbye to Paul, and watched him sail away? Paul did promise to return, if that was God's will (v.21); and indeed he did (19:1–41). But Priscilla and Aquila weren't to know that. All they knew was that for the foreseeable future, the responsibility for the nurturing of the new believers in Ephesus now lay squarely on their shoulders. And the obvious place for them all to meet would be in Priscilla and Aquila's home. These believers may well have included Trophimus (20:4; 21:29), Tychicus (20:4; Eph. 6:21) who would become Paul's personal representative in the years to come (see Chapter 42), and Onesiphorus (2 Tim. 4:19). Priscilla and Aquila would need to draw on all the teaching and wisdom they had received from Paul during his time with them in Corinth. Do we take full advantage of the opportunities we have to feed on and digest God's Word, so that when the call comes, we are ready to minister?

Apollos

During the time Priscilla and Aquila were in Ephesus, a Jew named Apollos arrived in the city (18:24). Apollos came from Alexandria in Egypt, where there was a large Jewish community. There, he had been thoroughly grounded in the Jewish Scriptures, and had become very knowledgeable and erudite (v.24). Apollos was also a naturally gifted public speaker, as he showed when he visited the city's synagogue, and spoke there 'boldly' (v.26). Although he 'had been instructed in the way of the Lord, and he spoke with great fervour and taught about Jesus accurately', there was a problem – 'he knew only the baptism of John' (v.25).

Priscilla and Aquila got to hear about Apollos, and went to listen to him. They soon realised that here was a man with great potential for the work of God; but he clearly only knew part of the truth. How much Apollos knew and didn't know is open to debate. Perhaps he was unaware of the significance of Jesus' life, death and resurrection. He would have known about repentance from what John had said, but he may not have known the need to believe in Jesus Christ as Son of God and Saviour. And it is unlikely he knew anything about the coming of the Holy Spirit.

Surely it can't have been coincidence that Apollos arrived in Ephesus while Priscilla and Aquila were there, because they were ideally suited to take him into their home and gently school him in the fullness of the Christian faith (v.26). And to Apollos's great credit, he showed a humble attitude, being willing to be taught and to learn, when he could have reacted arrogantly and ignored Priscilla and Aquila. Are we teachable and willing to learn from others, no matter what we may have accomplished for God already?

Priscilla and Aquila did such an excellent job that when Apollos wanted to go and preach in Achaia, the believers in Ephesus had no hesitation in encouraging him. They even took the trouble to write a letter of introduction to the disciples there (v.27). Apollos's skills as an orator and debater were mightily used by God, as he 'vigorously refuted the Jews in public debate, proving from the Scriptures that Jesus was the Christ' (v.28).

Indeed, 'he was a great help to those who by grace had believed' (v.27). What a wonderful testimony Apollos was to the unseen work and dedication of Priscilla and Aquila!

Apollos finished up in Corinth (19:1), and proved to be just the shot in the arm the church there needed. However, his popularity did cause a problem. Divisions in the church resulted, and there were quarrels among the various factions which emerged under the names of Paul, Apollos, Cephas (Peter), and even Christ (1 Cor. 1:12). When Paul got to hear about this from Chloe's family (1:11), he wrote his first letter to the church in Corinth, the first four chapters of which tackled this issue. While expressing appreciation of Apollos's ministry, saying they were 'fellow-workers' (3:9), Paul pointed out to the Corinthians that the growth in the church was not down to him or Apollos, or anyone else; it was all God's doing, and they were only servants working together for God: 'What, after all, is Apollos? And what is Paul? Only servants, through whom you came to believe – as the Lord has assigned to each his task. I planted the seed, Apollos watered it, but God made it grow' (3:5–6).

At some point, Apollos must have left Corinth. Perhaps he realised what was happening was splitting the church apart, and felt that if he wasn't there, it might help. This shows that Apollos had a sensitive, analytical and thoughtful side to his character. Later in his letter, Paul told the Corinthians that he had 'strongly urged' Apollos to return to Corinth; however, 'He was quite unwilling to go now, but he will go when he has the opportunity' (16:12). Whether Apollos did eventually go back to Corinth isn't known, although he did make some kind of journey somewhere (Titus 3:13).

Interestingly, there is a very strong possibility that Apollos was the author of the letter to the Hebrews, which was clearly written by a highly intellectual, learned Jewish Christian, who was steeped in the history and religious practices of the Jews.

Back to Rome

How long Priscilla and Aquila stayed in Ephesus is not clear. No mention is made of them on Paul's return to the city during his third missionary journey (Acts 19:1–41). However, in his first letter to the Corinthians, written from Ephesus around AD 55 during that second visit to the city, Paul sent greetings to the church in Corinth from their old friends Priscilla and Aquila and the church that met in their house (1 Cor. 16:19). This suggests that they were indeed still in Ephesus when Paul returned, and therefore would have experienced the riot led by Demetrius (see Chapter 36). It could be that they were two of the restraining voices stopping Paul getting involved (Acts 19:30–31).

Priscilla and Aquila certainly went back to Rome at some point, presumably after Emperor Claudius died in AD 54, and Jews had become acceptable citizens once again. Their lives had come full circle as they finished up in the place they had been forced to flee from all those years ago. When Paul wrote his letter to the believers in Rome in AD 57, Priscilla and Aquila were at the top of his greetings list – which to me shows just how important they had become to him. Paul called them 'fellow-workers in Christ Jesus' (Rom. 16:3), which must have really warmed their hearts. Priscilla and Aquila were still showing their characteristic hospitality by allowing the believers to meet in their house (v.5).

But, in his greeting to Priscilla and Aquila, Paul mentioned something else that he wanted everyone to know: 'They risked their lives for me. Not only I but all the churches of the Gentiles are grateful to them' (v.4). Whether this happened in Corinth, or Ephesus, or somewhere else, Paul didn't say; nor did he mention in what way this 'back room' team were actually prepared to put their lives on the line when necessary. Tantalisingly, we are left wondering what they actually did!

It seems that Priscilla and Aquila left Rome yet again, and returned to Ephesus to support Timothy. Was this in response to a personal request from Paul, made when they visited him during his time under house arrest in Rome? In his second letter to Timothy, who was now pastoring the church in that city (see Chapter 37), Paul sent his greetings to Priscilla and Aquila (2 Tim. 4:19). Somehow, I doubt that was their last move!

Priscilla and Aquila remain an example of the effectiveness for God of a couple who are devoted to one another and to Him. Nothing seemed to be too much trouble for them in the work of God. They were prepared to go were God sent them, offer hospitality to both individuals and churches, sensitively mentor believers, while at the same time working hard at their trade to provide for themselves. Doesn't every church need couples like Priscilla and Aquila: mature, solid, modest, dependable stalwarts; 'back room' people, whom I see supporting and praying for others, and who work tirelessly for the sake of the gospel? How do we measure up to the standard they have set?

Chapter 39

The Shipwrecked Centurion

Julius

Acts 27:1–28:16

Embarkation

Julius was a Roman centurion in the Imperial Regiment (v.1). On this particular day, he would have been standing at one of the quays of Caesarea harbour, having been put in charge of transporting a group of prisoners to Rome. It seems likely that Julius would have supervised the embarkation of the straggling line of prisoners on to the 'ship from Adramyttium about to sail for ports along the coast of the province of Asia' (v.2), which would take them on the first stage of their voyage to Rome. Julius must have been rather annoyed that he couldn't find a ship that was going straight to Italy, which would have made his task that much more straightforward.

As he watched his soldiers getting the prisoners on board, Julius may even have felt a moment of pity for them. He would have known that those prisoners who had already been sentenced to death, which was the majority, were being transported to

Rome to face the likelihood of a horrible death in the arena of the capital city.

Kindness

Amongst this motley collection of felons, however, there was one prisoner whose fate had not yet been sealed: a man named Paul. Undoubtedly, Julius would have known that Paul was going to Rome to face trial before Caesar at his own request (25:11–12) – a right extended to all who were Roman citizens. It seems likely that the authorities in Caesarea would have told Julius to keep a close eye on this man Paul, and make sure he arrived safely for his trial in Rome.

The fact that Paul was a Roman citizen would undoubtedly have influenced Julius's treatment of him, such as allowing two friends, Aristarchus and Luke, to accompany Paul on the journey (27:2) – a courtesy not normally extended to prisoners. But it seems that there was more to their relationship than this. It appears that Julius was favourably impressed by Paul's attitude and demeanour, and immediately became kindly disposed towards him. So, when the ship stopped off at the port of Sidon the next day, 'Julius, in kindness to Paul, allowed him to go to his friends so they might provide for his needs' (v.3). Do other people find our disposition attractive? Do we draw people to Christ, or do we put them off?

Warning unheeded

They eventually arrived at the port of Myra (v.5), after what would probably have been a fortnight's sailing. Julius must have been delighted to find that there was a ship from Alexandria in the harbour there, which was 'sailing for Italy' (v.6). So he had all the prisoners transferred to this ship, and they set sail. Not surprisingly, the ship's cargo was grain (v.38), since Alexandria in Egypt was the chief grain supplier to Rome.

The going was slow due to adverse wind conditions, but eventually the ship made it to the port of Fair Havens on the southern coast of Crete. It was now 'after the Fast' (v.9), the Day of Atonement, which apparently in the year in question, AD 59, occurred on 5 October. Sailing was difficult enough in September, and by November it was out of the question. So everybody knew that they were going to have to winter somewhere: the only question was where exactly. Julius was the one to make the decision (v.11): whether to stay in Fair Havens, or to sail on the forty miles to Phoenix, which lay towards the western end of Crete, and was considered by the pilot and the owner of the ship to be a far better harbour to winter in (v.12).

Paul spoke up, warning everybody that such a voyage would be 'disastrous and bring great loss to ship and cargo, and to our own lives also' (v.10). In the end, Julius ignored Paul's advice to stay put, preferring to go with the preference of the nautical men – a choice backed up by the majority (vv.11–12). So they set sail for Phoenix.

Storm

For a while, it seemed that Julius had made the right decision, as the ship made good progress due to the 'gentle south wind' (v.13). But then, disaster struck. The wind changed direction to the north-east, and became 'hurricane force' as it 'swept down' (v.14) from the mountains of Crete. Luke describes what happened next: 'The ship was caught by the storm and could not head into the wind; so we gave way to it and were driven along' (v.15). Luke then logs all the measures the crew took to try to save the ship (vv.16–19).

I try to imagine what panic, chaos and confusion there must have been on board as the winds raged, the thunder crashed and the huge waves buffeted the fragile ship, with its sails, torn by the storm, flapping wildly; and all against a backcloth of blackness, illuminated only by shafts of lightning. It can't have been long before everybody began to accept the inevitable, and fear gripped their hearts as they 'finally gave up all hope of being saved' (v.20).

They were at the mercy of this storm for a fortnight (v.27). At some point during this time, Paul had a vision of an angel, assuring him that none of them would die (vv.23–24), although they would 'run aground on some island' (v.26) and the ship would be 'destroyed' (v.22). I wonder what went through Julius's mind as Paul went on to say, 'So keep up your courage, men, for I have faith in God that it will happen just as he told me' (v.25). He could have thought that Paul's words were mere wishful thinking, and they had no chance of survival, or that he hoped to goodness Paul was right! But, in view of what happened later, it seems that Julius believed with all his heart that events would unfold as Paul had predicted.

I'm sure Julius would have noticed that Paul couldn't resist reminding them all that they were only in this predicament because his warning had gone unheeded (v.21). Julius knew that the ultimate responsibility for this impending disaster lay with him alone, which must have made him feel very guilty indeed; but believing what Paul had said must have given Julius hope that everything would turn out well for him.

Escape attempt

About midnight on the fourteenth night, the sailors 'sensed they were approaching land' (v.27); so they 'took soundings' (v.28) which confirmed that they were right. In spite of Paul's assurance, the sailors were afraid that the ship would be wrecked on the rocks, so they 'dropped four anchors from the stern' (v.29). But they knew very well that this action would probably not hold it back from the rocks; so they made an attempt to escape from the ship. Under the pretence of dropping anchors from the bow of the ship, the sailors actually began lowering the lifeboat (v.30).

But they were spotted, and Paul said to Julius, 'Unless these men stay with the ship, you cannot be saved' (v.31). Clearly, Julius now trusted Paul completely, because he ordered his soldiers to cut the ropes that held the lifeboat, and let it fall into the sea (v.32). Had he not trusted Paul, Julius would surely have kept the lifeboat on board in case it was needed, since he would have been guaranteed a place in it.

Momentous decision

Just before dawn, Paul spoke to all 276 of them on board again, urging them to eat something, and reassuring them of their survival (vv.33–38). What joy must have been theirs when they could actually see land; and not only that, but 'a bay with a sandy beach, where they decided to run the ship aground if they could' (v.39). Unfortunately, the bow of the ship got stuck fast on a sandbar, and the powerful waves began to smash up the stern (v.41).

At that moment, Julius made a momentous decision which would affect the future spread and development of Christianity: he decided to spare Paul's life (v.43). This is also further evidence of the esteem in which Julius had come to hold Paul, and his belief that Paul's prediction about all 276 of them being saved would be fulfilled.

The soldiers knew that under Roman law their lives would be forfeit if any prisoners escaped; so they 'planned to kill the prisoners to prevent any of them from swimming away and escaping' (v.42). To their undoubted astonishment, Julius stopped them from doing this (v.43): surely further evidence that he believed Paul's prediction that everyone would be saved, including all the prisoners. Instead, Julius 'ordered those who could swim to jump overboard first and get to land. The rest were to get there on planks or on pieces of the ship' (vv.43–44). And so it was, no doubt to Julius's great relief when the count was taken, that 'everyone reached land in safety' (v.44).

Miracles on Malta

They had in fact come ashore on the island of Malta (28:1). The islanders, who must have watched the ship being wrecked from the safety of the shore, put themselves out to help the survivors, despite the rain and cold (v.2). They built a fire, and Julius probably supervised the collection of wood to keep it burning. Paul did his bit to help; but when he put the 'pile of brushwood' he had collected on to the fire, 'a viper, driven out by the heat, fastened itself on his hand' (v.3).

Seeing the snake hanging from Paul's hand, the islanders jumped to the conclusion that he must be a murderer, who may have escaped the storm, but justice had caught up with him (v.4). They probably even believed that this poisonous snake had been sent by Dikē, the goddess of justice and revenge. But when Paul shook the viper off his arm and suffered no ill effects, they changed their minds, saying that he must be a god rather than a murderer (vv.5–6). This was not the only miracle involving Paul that Julius would witness while they were on the island.

The local landowner just happened to be Publius, 'the chief official of the island' (v.7). Some of the survivors were welcomed into his house and entertained there for three days (v.7). Paul and Luke were certainly among that number, so it seems very likely that Aristarchus and Julius would have been too. While there, Paul healed Publius's father of 'fever and dysentery' (v.8). News of this spread rapidly all over the island, and Julius would have witnessed the crowds of people coming, and going home cured (v.9). The popularity of Paul was probably the main reason why, when they were ready to sail after three months' stay on Malta, the islanders 'furnished us with the supplies we needed' (v.10).

Rome at last

Meanwhile, Julius had found a ship that had wintered at the island and was sailing for Italy. It was the third vessel they had travelled in since leaving Caesarea. Like the ship that had been wrecked, this one also came from Alexandria. It had a carved figurehead of the twin gods Castor and Pollux (v.11), the gods of navigation and the patrons of seagoers.

They sailed to the Italian port of Puteoli, having called at Syracuse and Rhegium on the way (vv.12–13). Having disembarked the prisoners, Julius would have needed to wait in Puteoli for further instructions regarding them. After about a week (v.14), during which Julius allowed Paul to stay with some believers there, he was ready to move the prisoners to Rome on foot. As they proceeded along the route, Julius must have been amazed to see so many people coming to meet and welcome Paul (v.15), and mystified by the atmosphere of joy and happiness which undoubtedly prevailed, even though Paul was a prisoner. On arrival in Rome, Paul was put under house arrest, guarded by a soldier (v.16).

I wonder if Julius visited Paul during the years he spent there? Maybe Julius was still in overall charge of Paul, or perhaps he was sent on another assignment shipping prisoners around the Empire. It would be nice to think that Julius became a believer as a result of all that he had experienced while in charge of Paul. However, I'm quite sure that Julius never forgot about all the events that had occurred, or about Paul himself. The question is: Do people remember us because we are different, and live our lives for God?

Chapter 40

The Runaway Returned

Philemon and Onesimus

Philemon vv.1–22

Runaway slave

Onesimus was on the run with a bag of money he had stolen from his master, Philemon (v.18). As a runaway slave, Onesimus knew the awful punishments which could be visited upon him were he ever caught and returned to his master. So he needed a place to hide where he could easily lose himself among the populace. The obvious place was Rome; but that city was a long way away from Colosse in Asia Minor (Turkey) where he lived. However, Onesimus eventually made it to Rome, no doubt using some of the money he had stolen.

Then, one day, something happened which would change Onesimus's life for ever: he met the apostle Paul. The circumstances of this meeting are not known, but the outcome was that Paul brought him to repentance and faith in Christ, and Onesimus became a believer, which is what Paul meant by saying that he 'became my son' (v.10). It seems that Paul took

Onesimus under his wing, and he became very 'useful' to Paul (v.11). So much so, that Paul didn't want to send Onesimus back to Philemon at all (v.13). It seems that Onesimus had become more than useful, growing very dear to Paul's heart too (v.12).

Heartbreaking conversation

At some point, I imagine there must have been a heartbreaking conversation between Paul and Onesimus over the matter of the runaway slave's return to his master in Colosse. It seems that Paul knew he was obliged to return Onesimus to his owner, but decided to ask Philemon to send his slave back to him in Rome, so Onesimus could continue to be of use to him.

How Onesimus reacted to Paul's decision to send him back, we can only imagine. Philemon had the right to crucify him; slaves were regarded as possessions, even as tools, and had no rights at all. The least Onesimus could expect was to have the letter 'F' (standing for *fugitivus*, meaning 'runaway') branded with a red-hot iron on to his forehead. The thought of having to go back, face Philemon, and take his punishment must have caused Onesimus great and understandable distress, to the point where he probably felt like running away again. However, Paul must have persuaded Onesimus that now he was a believer, going back to Colosse was the right thing to do. To calm the trepidation that Onesimus must still have been feeling, Paul decided that he would write a letter to Philemon, pleading Onesimus's case, and explaining the great change that had taken place in this runaway slave since coming to faith in Christ. Onesimus must have been greatly comforted by this, and agreed to go back to Colosse. But Paul wouldn't be sending him back alone.

Two letters

Just when Epaphras had appeared on the scene isn't clear. Epaphras was the founder of the church in Colosse (Col. 1:7–8; see Chapter 42), and had brought news to Paul of the heresy which was infiltrating the church there. This had prompted Paul to write a letter to the Colossians tackling this subject. It seems likely that when he arrived, Epaphras recognised Onesimus, and this may have brought matters to a head.

It seems that Tychicus (see Chapter 42) was entrusted with the letter Paul wrote to the Colossians (Col. 4:7), and also with the responsibility of taking Onesimus with him to Colosse. Were both letters given to Tychicus, or did Paul place Philemon's letter into the hands of Onesimus? Did Paul read the letter to Onesimus before he sent them off with it, or was Onesimus left wondering what Paul had written?

I wonder how Onesimus must have felt as he mulled things over in his mind during that long journey back to Colosse. Even if he did know the content of the letter, Onesimus must still have wondered what sort of reception he would get from Philemon, and whether Philemon would pay the slightest attention to what Paul had written. His apprehension must have intensified as he and Tychicus drew ever nearer to Colosse.

The return

On arrival in Colosse, I can't imagine that Tychicus would have left Onesimus to face the music on his own. I'm sure he would have accompanied Onesimus to Philemon's house.

It seems more than likely that Philemon was a wealthy Greek landowner, and that he had become a believer through Paul's preaching, which is implied in verse 19. The Colossian church apparently met in his home (vv.1–2). One day, Philemon was informed that he had two visitors: one of them was a man named Tychicus and, to the undoubted amazement of all the slaves in the establishment – not to mention that of Philemon himself – the other one was Onesimus. I imagine Philemon greeting Tychicus, but just staring at Onesimus in disbelief. Onesimus probably fell to his knees before his master, not daring to look him in the face, holding the letter from Paul up above his head, his heart pounding. Philemon must have been puzzled by the fact that Onesimus had returned at all, and intrigued to know why. I imagine him taking the letter out of the hands of the fearful Onesimus, and sitting down to read it.

Carefully constructed

Paul had constructed his letter to Philemon with the utmost care, in an attempt to ensure that he would willingly accept Onesimus. Paul had written the letter very tactfully and in a light-hearted manner. Unusually, Paul did not start the letter by identifying himself as 'an apostle'; this letter was written from one friend to another. Paul addressed Philemon as 'our dear friend and fellow-worker' (v.1), and also included in his greetings Apphia, who was probably his wife, and Archippus (see Chapter 42), who may well have been his son, as well as the church as a whole (v.2). But this letter was in essence a personal appeal from Paul to Philemon.

In his appeal on behalf of Onesimus, Paul had followed the method prescribed by ancient Greek and Roman teachers: to build rapport (vv.4–10); to persuade the mind (vv.11–19); to move the emotions (vv.20–21). Paul didn't even mention Onesimus until the end of the 'rapport' section (v.10), with the appeal coming towards the end of the 'mind' section (v.17).

Philemon's heart must have been warmed as he read what Paul had written about him personally (vv.4–7). Paul commended Philemon for his faith in Jesus and his love for the believers (v.5), and how hearing about this had brought Paul 'great joy and encouragement' (v.7). Not only was Philemon a man of faith and love, but he had opened his house, which had become a place of refreshment for the believers (v.7).

Philemon must have been impressed by Paul's humility as he went on to explain that he was not writing with the authority of an apostle and telling Philemon what to do; but was rather appealing to him 'on the basis of love' (v.9): the love Philemon had for God and for him. It is at this point that Paul introduced the name of Onesimus, saying, 'I appeal to you for my son Onesimus, who became my son while I was in chains' (v.10).

Useful and equal

Having now mentioned Onesimus by name, Philemon would have appreciated Paul's play on the word 'Onesimus', which actually meant 'profitable' or 'useful'. Paul wrote that Onesimus was formerly 'useless' to Philemon; but such a great change had taken place within this slave that now he had 'become useful both to you and to me' (v.11). In other words, he was no longer just Onesimus by name, but had now become Onesimus by nature. Philemon must have been intrigued to read of such a transformation in his slave.

Philemon was probably taken aback as Paul went on to explain how Onesimus had become so useful and dear to him that he wanted to keep him; such a description may not have fitted the Onesimus that Philemon remembered! Philemon may well have been wondering why Paul had sent Onesimus back to him at all, considering how useful his slave had become to him. As he read on, Philemon found that Paul had answered that point: he did not want to do this without Philemon's consent. Paul explained that he was returning Onesimus to him so that Philemon could come to a decision that would be 'spontaneous' about what to do with his slave, and not have his hand 'forced' by Paul (vv.12–14).

Philemon must have found the next part of Paul's letter difficult to handle. Paul was asking him to go beyond forgiveness, and accept Onesimus back, not as the runaway heathen slave that he once was, but as the 'dear brother' in Christ that he had now become (vv.15–16); albeit he was still Philemon's slave to do with as he pleased. Onesimus had come back – but he had come back different. Paul appealed directly to the partnership in Christ that existed between them personally, and asked Philemon to welcome Onesimus in just the same way as he would welcome Paul himself (v.17). It must have been hard for Philemon to even contemplate doing what Paul was asking of him, and to accept that he and his slave were brothers in God's family (v.16), and equals in Christ Jesus (Gal. 3:28).

Personal guarantee

Philemon must have realised the depth of Paul's affection for his runaway slave when he read the next part of the letter. Here, Paul gave Philemon a personal guarantee that he would reimburse him for any inconvenience or financial loss that he had suffered due to the actions of Onesimus (v.18). To emphasise this point, Paul had taken the pen from his scribe at this point in the letter, and written the words 'I will pay it back' (v.19) himself: probably in large letters and underlined!

Paul then gently reminded Philemon of something that probably brought a lump to his throat and tears to his eyes: 'not to mention that you owe me your very self' (v.19). As he read those words, Philemon must have recalled the time when Paul had tenderly and lovingly brought him to Christ; and then gone on in his thinking to weigh what Paul owed him due to the wrong done by Onesimus, against the debt of gratitude he owed Paul for showing him the way of salvation. So when Philemon read Paul's next words, 'I do wish, brother, that I may have some benefit from you in the Lord; refresh my heart in Christ' (v.20), he would have known exactly what the apostle was asking him to do: to repay that debt of gratitude by forgiving Onesimus, being reconciled to his slave, and accepting him as a brother in Christ. Paul went on to tell Philemon that he had every confidence in him to do as he had requested, 'knowing that you will do even more than I ask' (v.21), and that he hoped to be able to come and stay with Philemon soon (v.22).

Barriers

Spare a thought for poor Onesimus, who more than likely stayed on his knees the whole time Philemon was reading Paul's letter, wondering what would become of him. Did Onesimus manage to sneak some glances in the direction of his master, and see the emotions on Philemon's face as he read down the scroll – emotions that gave him hope?

Scripture does not tell us what happened to Onesimus, but it seems more than likely that Philemon would have been swayed by such a powerful letter from his friend, and allowed him to return to Paul. This event would surely have had an enormous impact on the church in Colosse: that Philemon had accepted Onesimus back, had forgiven and been reconciled to him, and had accepted him as a dear brother in Christ. What a splendid example this would have been at that time of the difference between the kingdom of this world, where slaves were regarded as subhuman, and the kingdom of God, where slaves were accepted as equal brothers in Christ!

Today, slavery is no longer a barrier between people in most countries of the world; but are there not other barriers, which are just as pernicious? And shouldn't we, as Christians, be seeking to break these barriers down, and show people the love and compassion of Christ, irrespective of who they are? And what about barriers that exist between us as Christians? What are we doing to tackle those situations? Surely nothing should be allowed to separate us from fellowship with one another. Whom do we need to forgive? To whom do we need to be reconciled? Whom do we need to embrace once again as a dear brother or sister in Christ?

Bishop

According to the writings of Ignatius, a Christian martyr, about fifty years later, a man named Onesimus was appointed Bishop of Ephesus. Could it possibly have been the same person, who had once been a runaway slave?

Chapter 41

What a Contrast!

Gaius and Diotrephes

3 John:1–12

Lifestyle

Gaius was the sort of person of whom John heartily approved, and he was about to receive a letter from the apostle. Gaius had become a 'dear friend' (vv. 1,2,5) to John, and it seems likely that the apostle had stayed with him from time to time during his travels. According to tradition, John eventually appointed Gaius as Bishop of Pergamum: an indication of how highly the apostle rated him.

Gaius was a man whose life radiated his 'faithfulness to the truth' (v.3). He was a shining example of someone who not only believed the truth of the gospel of Jesus Christ, but who was walking in that truth day by day. His belief was more than just intellectual knowledge: it determined his lifestyle. I imagine Gaius reading and meditating on God's Word daily. But he did more than that; he allowed it to permeate his being and change his behaviour. So much so, that 'some brothers' (v.3) had made a point of telling John how impressed they had been with Gaius. These 'brothers' were travelling missionaries, who had visited the church where Gaius was possibly a leader. John rejoiced to hear this report (v.4), which confirmed what he had seen for himself.

Do we allow God's Word to change our hearts, or does it just stay in our heads? Do our lifestyles give testimony to the fact that we are true disciples of Jesus Christ? Does God rejoice when He sees the way we are living our lives?

Hospitality

Gaius was also a man given to hospitality. John commended him for this by saying, 'Dear friend, you are faithful in what you are doing for the brothers, even though they are strangers to you. They have told the church about your love. You will do well to send them on their way in a manner worthy of God' (vv.5–6). Gaius had shown generous hospitality and support to itinerant missionaries in the past, and John was writing to ask him to do the same again, this time for a group led by Demetrius (v.12). Gaius's reputation for friendship and generosity had spread, to the extent that his name had become a byword for hospitality. He was now recognised by no less a person than the apostle John as having a significant ministry in the church.

It is important to realise that these itinerant teachers, evangelists and missionaries accepted nothing from the local churches other than their hospitality, so that their motives for preaching could not be called into question. They gave up the comfortable life to take the Word of God far and wide across the Roman Empire, which made them worthy of receiving the hospitality of the local church (vv.7–8).

How hospitable are we? Do we 'Offer hospitality to one another without grumbling' (1 Pet. 4:9)? I believe hospitality to be a very important ministry in the Church for many reasons. For example, it draws people who are lonely or in need to God by showing them the compassion of Christ in a practical way; it helps people who are new to the church to feel welcomed and accepted; it enables us to show our support for visiting preachers or missionaries, and in so doing become co-workers with them (3 John 1:8). Should we not therefore view hospitality as a joy rather than a burden?

Control freak

Gaius must have been thrilled to receive a personal letter from the apostle John, and delighted to provide the hospitality requested. It seems likely that Demetrius brought the letter with him when he came. In the letter, John commended Demetrius to Gaius by giving him a glowing recommendation (v.12). But John knew that the arrival of Demetrius and his band was going to cause trouble in Gaius's church; and all because of a man named Diotrephes (vv.9–10), who would certainly refuse to have anything to do with them, and would undoubtedly try to remove anyone from the church who did welcome them.

Gaius comes across as a humble, generous, hospitable and teachable man. In complete contrast, Diotrephes displayed an attitude which the apostle John certainly did not appreciate. The apostle portrays Diotrephes as being a strong, dictatorial, arrogant church leader, who wanted to dominate the congregation. Diotrephes' position was clear: he didn't want any outside influence being brought to bear on the local church, to the point that he was quite prepared to defy the authority of the apostles over this issue. It appears that Diotrephes may well have intercepted a letter sent by John to the church (v.9) and even gone so far as to keep the contents to himself! He had become a complete control freak.

Tension

Diotrephes' attitude reflected a growing tension in the Church towards the end of the first century. A twofold ministry had developed over the years. On the one hand, there were the apostles and the itinerant missionaries (whom John calls 'the brothers'), whose ministry was not confined to one particular congregation; on the other hand, there were the elders, whose ministry was focused solely on the local church, which they sought to build up and establish in the faith. To some extent, a similar tension still exists in the Church today, with the impact of certain preachers, evangelists, 'prophets' and 'healers'.

In the early days of the Church, there was no problem; the newly-formed local churches needed support from the apostles and 'the brothers' to help them get established and begin to grow. However, towards the end of the century when this letter was written, the local congregations were beginning to see themselves as churches in their own right, who no longer needed so much input from outside the local church. Diotrephes was strongly of this opinion; indeed, he didn't want any such input at all!

Drastic measures

Certainly this growing tension in the church would have to be resolved, but the way Diotrephes was approaching the problem would only make matters worse, and he couldn't be allowed to get away with it. John told Gaius, 'So if I come, I will call attention to what he is doing, gossiping maliciously about us. Not satisfied with that, he refuses to welcome the brothers. He also stops those who want to do so and puts them out of the church' (v.10). A confrontation between Diotrephes and John was looming; but whether it actually ever took place is not known.

Diotrephes was clearly not a man of half measures! Besides the possible business with the letter, he refused even to have fellowship with the apostles (v.9). He also slandered them, refused to allow anyone associated with them into the church, and took drastic measures against any members who expressed an interest in hearing what 'the brothers' had to say.

It seems to me that it wasn't so much that the point of view held by Diotrephes was wrong – after all, in the coming years it would be accepted as the way forward in the development and running of the church; it was his total lack of love, wisdom, sensitivity, humility and servanthood that was the problem. Diotrephes remains an example of how not to be a leader, and provides salutary lessons for those of us in leadership positions. Do we heed them, or ignore them?

Chapter 42

Paul's People

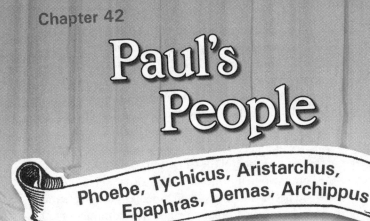

Phoebe, Tychicus, Aristarchus, Epaphras, Demas, Archippus

At the end of some of his letters, most notably to the Romans and the Colossians, Paul mentioned a whole string of names. Clearly, these were people he felt deserved a mention, for one reason or another. Unfortunately, in the majority of cases, Paul gave us no further information about them; but, there were some he talked about, albeit briefly. This chapter will be focusing on some of those particular individuals.

Phoebe (Romans 16:1-2)

In Romans 16, Paul sent greetings to twenty-six people by name. But before he embarked on that list, Paul commended to the Roman church a woman called Phoebe (v.1). She lived in Cenchrea, the port city which served Corinth (v.1), and it was while he was in Corinth that Paul wrote this letter to the believers in Rome. More accurately, Paul dictated the letter, and Tertius wrote it down (v.22).

It seems that Phoebe was entrusted with taking the letter to Rome, which was presumably why Paul mentioned her first, and asked the believers 'to receive her in the Lord in a way worthy of the saints and to give her any help she may need from you' (v.2). Clearly, Phoebe had impressed Paul as being a responsible person through her work in the church at Corinth as a deaconess – an alternative rendering of the Greek word translated 'servant' (v.1). Phoebe's ministry in that role would have focused on helping the poorer and weaker members of the Christian community, and on assisting the young women. Indeed, it seems that her service to the believers had become highly valued, because Paul wrote that 'she has been a great help to many people, including me' (v.2). That 'help' for Paul may well have included financial support. Like Phoebe, do we faithfully minister to the poor and needy, and take our responsibilities in church life seriously?

The example of Phoebe shows that women were involved in important ways in the Early Church. Interestingly, Paul greeted a number of women in this section of the letter. Six of them – Priscilla, Mary, Junias, Tryphena, Tryphosa and Persis – Paul described as fellow-workers, or made reference to their hard work in the church and for the Lord (vv.3,6–7,12). Apart from Priscilla and Aquila (see Chapter 38) and Phoebe, little is known about the others listed here, or those mentioned elsewhere in Paul's other letters. However, that doesn't mean to say that they weren't important people in the church. Like most of us, what they did in the service of the Lord may not have been widely known but, most importantly, it was known to God.

Tychicus (Colossians 4:7–8)

Tychicus was a believer from Asia (Acts 20:4), who probably lived in Ephesus. Paul used three lovely phrases to describe him: 'a dear brother'; 'a faithful minister'; a 'fellow-servant'.

Tychicus was 'a dear brother' because he was willing to stay with Paul during the period when the apostle was under house arrest in Rome. Tychicus could have just left Paul to get on with it, but he didn't. He saw that Paul was in need, and he was determined to do what he could to support him. Like Tychicus, do we stand alongside those in difficulty and encourage them? Are we 'dear' brothers and sisters to them? When we see people in need, do we support them, or just let them get on with it?

Interestingly, it was during that time that Paul not only wrote the letter to the Colossians, but also the letters to Philemon (see Chapter 40), to the Ephesians and to the Philippians. Who knows what our support during someone's time of difficulty might enable them to accomplish for God?

Tychicus was 'a faithful minister' by not only ministering *to* Paul in his need, but also ministering *for* Paul, carrying out various jobs and duties on his behalf. One of those tasks was to take this letter from Rome to Colosse, which shows how confident Paul was in Tychicus, knowing that he could be relied upon, was trustworthy, and would complete the job of delivering this precious document safely to its destination. Further evidence of Paul's confidence in Tychicus was the fact that he entrusted him to give a full and accurate report about his current situation to the Colossians (Col. 4:8). Tychicus was more than just 'a dear brother'; he was Paul's personal representative, not only to the Colossians, but also to the Ephesians (Eph. 6:21–22). Like Tychicus, are we trustworthy and dependable? When we are asked to carry out a particular task in the church, can we be relied upon to do it without having to be chased all the time? After all, isn't reliability a mark of maturity in our walk with God?

Tychicus was also a 'fellow-servant'. He was not an apostle himself, but he was a co-worker with Paul. Later, Tychicus was sent to Crete (Titus 3:12), and to Ephesus (2 Tim. 4:12). Paul must have really rejoiced to have this 'dear brother', whom he could send to these places on his behalf, knowing that Tychicus could be trusted to do whatever he had asked him to.

It can't have been easy for Tychicus to have been an associate of Paul. The apostle wasn't the most popular person in certain quarters, mainly Jewish ones, and had many enemies besides. By standing alongside Paul, Tychicus was putting himself in danger. Tychicus chose the right way rather than the easy way, even though there were consequences for him. When we have decisions to make, do we choose the right thing to do, or the easy thing to do?

What a splendid chap Tychicus must have been! What a great person to have as a member of your church! What a terrific example he is to us all of maturity in God! May God help each one of us to be 'a dear brother', 'a faithful minister', and a 'fellow-servant'.

Aristarchus (Colossians 4:10-11)

Aristarchus was a Jew who had become a believer. He was originally from Thessalonica (Acts 20:4), and became one of Paul's travelling companions. Aristarchus must have feared for his life at least twice during his travels with Paul. On the first occasion, he was in Ephesus when the riot led by Demetrius took place (Acts 19:23–41; see Chapter 36). He and Gaius, another of Paul's companions at the time, were seized by the angry mob and dragged into the amphitheatre (19:29) – presumably because the rioters couldn't find Paul himself. Fortunately for Aristarchus and Gaius, who must have thought they were about to be lynched, the clerk of the city arrived and quietened things down.

On the second occasion, he was on the ship with Paul and Luke sailing to Rome, when it was wrecked on the coast of Malta (Acts 27:1–44; see Chapter 39). It seems that he accompanied Paul all the way to Rome, and lived voluntarily with him during his time of house arrest, because Paul calls him 'My fellow-prisoner' (Col. 4:10).

Epaphras (Colossians 4:12-13)

Epaphras was the founder of the church in Colosse (Col. 1:7–8), but he was probably actually converted in Ephesus during Paul's time there. Epaphras eventually returned home and preached the gospel in Colosse. Such was the response that a church was founded there. He may well have also founded the churches at nearby Laodicea and Hierapolis (v.13). However, as time went on, the Colossian church began to experience a number of difficulties, but Epaphras managed to keep the people together. Like Epaphras, do we cement people together in the church, or do we split them apart?

The main problem in the Colossian church was heresy. Epaphras was so concerned about this that he journeyed to Rome to speak to Paul and give him a full report. The result was that Paul wrote the letter to the Colossians to tackle head-on the false teaching that was infiltrating the church there. In the letter, Paul described Epaphras as not just a 'servant' (v.12), but a 'fellow-servant' (1:7). In other words, the apostle was paying tribute to the fact that Epaphras was very much a part of his team in the service of the gospel. In my experience, it is so important that we are all team players in our churches, pulling together in the same direction for the sake of the gospel, rather than having our own personal agendas and pulling the church apart.

One of the reasons that Epaphras was so successful in his ministry was his prayer life. It was so amazing that it had even made an impact on Paul! The apostle told the church in Colosse, 'He is always wrestling in prayer for you' (v.12). This tells us four things about Epaphras's prayer life. Firstly, he prayed constantly – 'always'; although he wasn't there in Colosse with them, they were never out of his mind. Secondly, he prayed fervently – the Greek word translated 'wrestling' conveys the idea of 'agonising' about something; this was serious business as far as Epaphras was concerned. Thirdly, he prayed personally – 'for you'. Fourthly, he prayed definitely – he knew what he was praying for: 'that you may stand firm in all the will of God, mature and fully assured' (v.12). In other words, Epaphras was praying that they would have the strength to resist the false teaching of the Gnostics (and those like them) that was creeping into the church and would become mature and confident in God, as they grew in their understanding of Him and His ways.

Epaphras had a real prayer ministry; and who knows what would have happened in the church at Colosse had Epaphras not prayed? We never know what is accomplished because of our prayers. Even though we may not have a great prayer life like

Epaphras, we are still contributing to the reservoir of prayer that is being offered to God about a particular situation. But I also believe that God is looking for people like Epaphras in the Church today, whom He can call into a ministry of intercessory prayer. Will we respond to God's call to such prayer? It is a ministry that is desperately needed.

Demas

Demas is mentioned three times in Paul's letters. Paul described him as a fellow-worker in Philemon verse 24. In Colossians 4:14, he is just mentioned by name in passing, and we sense that all may not be well. It is in 2 Timothy 4:10 that we learn what became of him: 'Demas, because he loved this world, has deserted me and has gone to Thessalonica.' Here we have the profound sadness of a man who strayed from God's ways and fell again into the ways of the world. I'm sure we can all think of people in our experience like Demas; but let's never kid ourselves that it can't happen to us as well (1 Cor. 10:12). If we allow ourselves to slip back into the ways of this world, there can be only one outcome: the outcome of Demas.

Archippus (Colossians 4:17)

Paul described Archippus as a 'fellow-soldier' (Philem. v.2), so obviously he was a man who was prepared to do battle in the cause of the gospel. He was possibly the son of Philemon, since Paul mentions him in the same sentence as the slave owner (Philem. vv.1–2). It seems that Archippus may well have taken over from Epaphras as pastor of the church at Colosse.

It appears that Archippus had become discouraged in his work as leader of the church, possibly due to the problems caused by the infiltration of false teachings, and may well have been on the point of giving up. Paul reminded him that his ministry was a gift from God, and encouraged him to persevere, implying that God would help him to do so.

The situation with Archippus serves to remind us how much we need to pray for our leaders. In my experience, leaders do become discouraged, and need us to support them and to encourage them. Indeed, there are times when we all feel discouraged, frustrated, exhausted and unable to cope with the work God has given us to do. But let's be encouraged by the reassurance that the God who entrusted us with that work in the first place will empower us to see it through; that we, as bit part players, will be given the strength to play our parts to the full on the stage where God has placed us.

National Distributors

UK: (and countries not listed below)
CWR, Waverley Abbey House, Waverley Lane, Farnham, Surrey GU9 8EP.
Tel: (01252) 784700 Outside UK (44) 1252 784700 Email: mail@cwr.org.uk

AUSTRALIA: KI Entertainment, Unit 21 317-321 Woodpark Road, Smithfield, New South Wales 2164. Tel: 02 9604 3600 Fax: 02 9604 3699 Email: sales@kientertainment.com.au

CANADA: David C Cook Distribution Canada, PO Box 98, 55 Woodslee Avenue, Paris, Ontario N3L 3E5. Tel: 1800 263 2664 Email: swansons@cook.ca

GHANA: Challenge Enterprises of Ghana, PO Box 5723, Accra. Tel: (021) 222437/223249 Fax: (021) 226227 Email: ceg@africaonline.com.gh

HONG KONG: Cross Communications Ltd, 1/F, 562A Nathan Road, Kowloon.
Tel: 2780 1188 Fax: 2770 6229 Email: cross@crosshk.com

INDIA: Crystal Communications, 10-3-18/4/1, East Marredpalli, Secunderabad – 500026, Andhra Pradesh. Tel/Fax: (040) 27737145 Email: crystal_edwj@rediffmail.com

KENYA: Keswick Books and Gifts Ltd, PO Box 10242-00400, Nairobi.
Tel: (254) 20 312639/3870125 Email: keswick@swiftkenya.com

MALAYSIA: Salvation Book Centre (M) Sdn Bhd, 23 Jalan SS 2/64, 47300 Petaling Jaya, Selangor. Tel: (03) 78766411/78766797 Fax: (03) 78757066/78756360
Email: info@salvationbookcentre.com

Canaanland, No. 25 Jalan PJU 1A/41B, NZX Commercial Centre, Ara Jaya, 47301 Petaling Jaya, Selangor. Tel: (03) 7885 0540/1/2 Fax: (03) 7885 0545 Email: info@canaanland.com.my

NEW ZEALAND: KI Entertainment, Unit 21 317-321 Woodpark Road, Smithfield, New South Wales 2164, Australia. Tel: 02 9604 3600 Fax: 02 9604 3699
Email: sales@kientertainment.com.au

NIGERIA: FBFM, Helen Baugh House, 96 St Finbarr's College Road, Akoka, Lagos.
Tel: (01) 7747429/4700218/825775/827264 Email: fbfm@hyperia.com

PHILIPPINES: OMF Literature Inc, 776 Boni Avenue, Mandaluyong City.
Tel: (02) 531 2183 Fax: (02) 531 1960 Email: gloadlaon@omflit.com

SINGAPORE: Alby Commercial Enterprises Pte Ltd, 95 Kallang Avenue #04-00, AIS Industrial Building, 339420. Tel: (65) 629 27238 Fax: (65) 629 27235 Email: marketing@alby.com.sg

SOUTH AFRICA: Struik Christian Books, 80 MacKenzie Street, PO Box 1144, Cape Town 8000. Tel: (021) 462 4360 Fax: (021) 461 3612 Email: info@struikchristianmedia.co.za

SRI LANKA: Christombu Publications (Pvt) Ltd, Bartleet House, 65 Braybrooke Place, Colombo 2. Tel: (9411) 2421073/2447665 Email: dhanad@bartleet.com

USA: David C Cook Distribution Canada, PO Box 98, 55 Woodslee Avenue, Paris, Ontario N3L 3E5, Canada. Tel: 1800 263 2664 Email: swansons@cook.ca

CWR is a Registered Charity - Number 294387
CWR is a Limited Company registered in England - Registration Number 1990308

The original Bit Part Players

Learn much that is relevant to your life from over 100 lesser-known Old Testament characters including Lot, Caleb, Deborah, Boaz and Eli.

You will be better equipped to play your own part in God's never-ending story and discover how you might be impacting the lives of others.

by Ray Markham

270-page paperback, 129x197mm
ISBN: 978-1-85345-445-5

£8.99*

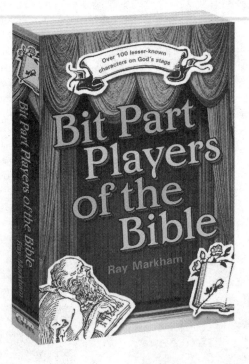

Cover to Cover Complete

Reference Book of the Year 2008 (UK Christian booksellers)

Take an exciting, year-long journey through the Bible, following events as they happened, and see God's purposes unfold across the centuries. You will be amazed at the genius of God's promise-plan, and you will come to know your heavenly Father in a deeper way as you read through His Word chronologically.

The full text of the Holman Christian Standard translation in a daily reading structure provides a highly motivating reading experience making it easy to complete the entire Bible in one year. Key Scripture verses and devotional thoughts make each day's reading more meaningful.

1,632-page hardback
ISBN: 978-1-85345-433-2

£19.99*

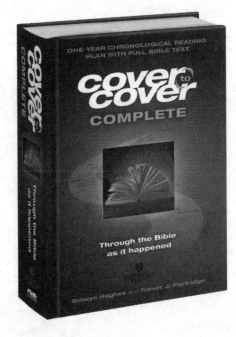